And it shall come to pass in the last days that the mountain of the Lord's house shall be established as the highest of the mountains... and all the nations shall flow to it, and many peoples shall come, and say: "Come, let us go up to the mountain of the Lord, to the house of the God of Jacob; that he may teach us his ways and that we may walk in his paths. (Isaiah 2:2-3)

SPIRITUAL JOURNEY
THE BAHÁ'Í FAITH

I. Walter Tunick, Ed.D.

Order this book online at www.trafford.com/06-1891
or email orders@trafford.com

Most Trafford titles are also available at major online book retailers.

© Copyright 2007 I. Walter Tunick Ed.D.

All rights reserved. No part of this publication may be reproduced, stored in a retrieval system, or transmitted, in any form or by any means, electronic, mechanical, photocopying, recording, or otherwise, without the written prior permission of the author.

Note for Librarians: A cataloguing record for this book is available from Library and Archives Canada at www.collectionscanada.ca/amicus/index-e.html

Printed in Victoria, BC, Canada.

ISBN: 978-1-4251-0134-3

COVER PHOTO: Shrine of The Bab, Bahá'í World Center, Haifa, Israel
BOOK PHOTOS: Reprinted with permission as noted. © Bahá'í International Community
http://media.bahai.org

ABOUT THE AUTHOR: After years of search culminating in what was for him a definitive spiritual experience, the author embraced the Bahá'í Faith in 1989. His work experience includes a 30-year career as teacher, counselor and administrator in public education, both in the United States and with the Dependents Schools of the U.S. military forces in Europe. He holds a Master's Degree in Counseling from San Francisco State University and a Doctorate in Education from the University of Southern California. The author has been a member of six different Local Spiritual Assemblies, two of them first-time Bahá'í communities. He and his wife served three years as pioneers in Costa Rica. He helped establish a Bahá'í School in Belmont, California, and served as its director for one year. He resides with his wife in Florence, Oregon.

We at Trafford believe that it is the responsibility of us all, as both individuals and corporations, to make choices that are environmentally and socially sound. You, in turn, are supporting this responsible conduct each time you purchase a Trafford book, or make use of our publishing services. To find out how you are helping, please visit www.trafford.com/responsiblepublishing.html

Our mission is to efficiently provide the world's finest, most comprehensive book publishing service, enabling every author to experience success. To find out how to publish your book, your way, and have it available worldwide, visit us online at www.trafford.com/10510

www.trafford.com

North America & international
toll-free: 1 888 232 4444 (USA & Canada)
phone: 250 383 6864 ♦ fax: 250 383 6804
email: info@trafford.com

The United Kingdom & Europe
phone: +44 (0)1865 722 113 ♦ local rate: 0845 230 9601
facsimile: +44 (0)1865 722 868 ♦ email: info.uk@trafford.com

10 9 8 7 6 5 4

TABLE OF CONTENTS

FOREWORD 7
   TABLE OF CONTENTS—DETAILS 8
   SUGGESTIONS FOR READING THIS BOOK 12
PROLOGUE 14
   FOR THOSE NOT SURE THERE IS A GOD 20
CHAPTER ONE — KEY TERMS 25
   MANIFESTATION OF GOD 25
   DIVINE ATTRIBUTES 28
   DIVINE LAWS 29
   DISPENSATION 29
   REVELATION (OR DIVINE REVELATION) 30
   PROGRESSIVE REVELATION 31
CHAPTER TWO — EARLIER RELIGIONS 35
   JUDAISM 37
      ABRAHAM 38
      MOSES 39
      LEGACY OF JUDAISM 42
      THE PROMISE OF BAHÁ'U'LLÁH 43
   CHRISTIANITY 46
      THE PRE-CHRISTIAN WORLD 48
      JESUS 49
      THE PROMISE OF BAHÁ'U'LLÁH 51
   ZOROASTRIANISM 55
   ISLAM 57
      MUHAMMAD 57
      ISLAMIC EMPIRE 60
      BASIC TEACHINGS 62
      THE PROMISE OF BAHÁ'U'LLÁH 64
CHAPTER THREE—THE BAB 69
   THE ADVENT MOVEMENT 69
      THE SHAYKHIS 71
   THE BAB 72
      MULLA HUSAYN 72
      LETTERS OF THE LIVING 74
      PUBLIC PROCLAMATION 75

VAHID 76
CONFINEMENT AT MAH-KU 77
IMPRISONMENT AT CHIRIQ 78
BADASHT CONFERENCE 80
MASSACRE AT FORT SHAYKH TABARSI 80
MARTYRDOM OF TAHIRIH 84
MARTYRDOM OF THE BAB 85
MESSAGE OF THE BAB 88

CHAPTER FOUR—BAHÁ'U'LLÁH 93

IMPRISONMENT IN THE SIYAH-CHAL 94
BAGDAD—THE FIRST EXILE 96
ISTANBUL—THE SECOND EXILE 100
ADRIANOPLE—THE THIRD EXILE 101
  LETTERS TO THE KINGS OF THE EARTH 102
AKKA—THE LAST EXILE 105
  CALL FOR WORLD UNITY 107
THE PERSON OF BAHÁ'U'LLÁH 109
THE POWER OF BAHÁ'U'LLÁH 111
FINAL YEARS 112

CHAPTER FIVE—'ABDU'L-BAHA 115

COVENANT OF BAHÁ'U'LLÁH 116
  CENTER OF THE COVENANT 116
  THE MASTER 117
END OF IMPRISONMENT 119
  EARLY NORTH AMERICAN BAHÁ'ÍS 119
  VISIT TO THE WEST 121
WAR YEARS 125
FINAL YEARS 127

CHAPTER SIX—SHOGHI EFFENDI 133

EDUCATION AND TRAINING 133
EARLY YEARS 134
GUARDIAN'S LITERARY OUTPUT 137
BUILDING THE ADMINISTRATIVE ORDER 142
  HANDS OF THE CAUSE OF GOD 145

CHAPTER SEVEN—FUNDAMENTALS 148

ONENESS 148
  ONENESS OF GOD 148
    GENDER 149
    RECOGNIZING GOD 149
  ONENESS OF MANKIND 151

ONENESS OF RELIGION 153
MATERIAL EXISTENCE.................................... 156
   DUAL NATURE OF MAN 158
      HUMAN EVOLUTION 159
      SOUL..161
      DEVELOPING SPIRITUALITY 163
SPIRITUAL EXISTENCE..................................... 164
   GOD'S CREATION 167

CHAPTER EIGHT—BASIC TEACHINGS 172

INDEPENDENT INVESTIGATION OF TRUTH 172
   ONENESS OF MANIFESTATIONS OF GOD..... 176
   WAS JESUS REALLY GOD? 178
   DID JESUS DIE FOR OUR SINS?.................... 180
   RESURRECTION OF JESUS 182
RELIGION AND SCIENCE AGREE...................... 183
   SCIENTIFIC METHOD 184
   TESTIMONY OF LEADING SCIENTISTS.......... 185
   TRUE RELIGION AND SCIENCE ARE TRUE ... 187
   THE DIFFERENCES ARE NOT SCIENTIFIC 189
   THE COMPLEX COMPUTER ANALOGY 191
EQUALITY OF MEN AND WOMEN 192
ELIMINATION OF PREJUDICE 194
UNIVERSAL LANGUAGE 195
UNIVERSAL EDUCATION 196
   DIVINE EDUCATOR.. 197
   AGREEMENT AMONG DIVINE EDUCATORS .. 198
   JUSTICE AND MERCY................................... 199
   METAPHORICAL PROCESS 201
   TEACHING THE FAITH TO OTHERS 204
WORLD GOVERNMENT—WORLD PEACE........... 205
   GLOBAL ECONOMY 205
   UNIFIED WORLD.. 207
   THE UNITED NATIONS.................................. 211
   DEVELOPMENTAL PROCESS 214
      THE LESSER PEACE 215

CHAPTER NINE—ADMINISTRATION 220

SYSTEM OF COVENANTS 220
BASIS OF THE ADMINISTRATIVE ORDER 221
THREE-TIERED GOVERNMENT 223
   INSTITUTION OF THE LEARNED 227
   CONSULTATION.. 228

CHAPTER TEN—BAHÁ'Í TOPICS....................... 233

BAHÁ'Í CALENDAR 233
   BAHÁ'Í MONTHS 234
   BAHÁ'Í DAYS... 235
BAHÁ'Í HOLY DAYS... 235
NINETEEN-DAY FEAST 236
CYCLES AND UNIVERSAL CYCLES 236
BAHÁ'Í WORLD CENTER..................................... 239
   BAHJI 241
BAHÁ'Í TEMPLES 241
BAHÁ'Í FIRESIDES... 246
AGES OF THE BAHÁ'Í FAITH............................... 247
SYMBOLS IN RELIGION 248
   COMMON BAHÁ'Í SYMBOLS........................ 248
      NUMBER NINE 248
      NINE-POINTED STAR.................................248
      GREATEST NAME......................................249
      SYMBOL OF THE GREATEST NAME   250
INVESTIGATING THE BAHÁ'Í FAITH 250
   BECOMING A BAHÁ'Í 252
BAHÁ'Í FUNDS.. 253

CHAPTER ELEVEN—GENERAL TOPICS 257

MAN AND THE ENVIRONMENT 257
HEALTH AND HEALING 258
DRUGS, ALCOHOL AND TOBACCO 259
NUTRITION 260
SELF DEFENSE 261
EUTHANASIA (MERCY KILLING) 261
CREMATION 261
PARTY POLITICS 261
MUSIC AND ART 262
REINCARNATION 262
HOMOSEXUALITY... 264

CHAPTER TWELVE—PLAN OF GOD 267

PERSPECTIVES ON UNITY 267
   EVERYTHING IS RELATED 268
   SYSTEM THEORY... 271
THE PLAN OF GOD 272
   OLD ORDER/NEW ORDER............................ 274
   NEW ORDER—NEW DAY.............................. 277

SPIRITUAL JOURNEY
THE BAHÁ'Í FAITH

FOREWORD

This book is an introduction to the Bahá'í Faith. It would be suitable for individual and small-group study, for use with classes on the Bahá'í Faith, and as a text in classes studying comparative world religions.

The book is intended for serious and thoughtful people in their late teens and older. This implies anyone who seeks to know more about the ultimate questions many have asked throughout history.

One can find books on religion in many libraries. Books introducing the Bahá'í Faith were found in some libraries, but a limited few were written as a classroom text appropriate for senior high school, college and adult levels.

Religion has long been a touchy subject for the American public education system. Discussion had to be addressed with trepidation and distant objectivity, or by-passed and avoided entirely because of the restrictions imposed by 'separation of church and state' codes.

Despite the constant barrage of criticism besieging the American education establishment, and the problems of student social unrest, which tend to mirror conditions in the larger society, some good things are happening in education. An evolving curriculum designed to provide relevant education for younger students reflects a growing emphasis on the teaching of moral and religious values. This is seen by the inclusion of 'values education' in the elementary program of many of the traditional subjects. At the secondary and college levels can be found courses entitled **"Bible as Literature," "Bible as History,"** or other comparative religion electives. It is possible to teach about religion without proselytizing.

The deteriorating moral conditions that are spreading globally have caused devastating gaps in social behavior that endanger the well-being of all societies and nations. The growth of interest in moral and religious values has been stirring calls to action among the established religions. The Bahá'í Faith, claiming hereditary connections with its older sister religions, offers relevant explanations for current world problems that do not conflict with the earlier teachings.

The growth of the Bahá'í Faith in recent years has brought it an expanded visibility. It has grown fifteen-fold in the last forty years. Its scriptures have been translated into more than 800 languages. It vies with Christianity as the most widespread religion in the world.

The Bahá'í Faith is a distinct religion based upon the teachings of Bahá'u'lláh, and not a collection of teachings from other religions, as some critics have portrayed it. Arnold Toynbee calls the Bahá'í Faith **"an independent religion on a par with Islam, Christianity, and the other recognized world religions... [It is] not a sect of some other religion; it is a separate religion, and it has the same status as the other recognized religions."** (British Bahá'í Journal, No. 141, p. 4, November 1959).

The Bahá'í Faith serves as a major participant in numerous conferences, studies and development projects around the world. The United Nations has officially recognized the Bahá'í Faith as an international NGO (non-governmental organization) member and consultant.

This book is organized into twelve chapters. The first six chapters deal mainly with introductory background information and biographical history. The last six chapters are concerned mainly with Bahá'í concepts and teachings. Suggestions for discussion and exercises to challenge and stimulate further thought and reflection can be found at the end of each chapter.

TABLE OF CONTENTS—DETAILS

CHAPTER ONE—Key Terms

Certain terms and concepts are fundamental to an understanding of the Bahá'í Faith, and are used in

explaining other concepts. These include:
Manifestation of God—God's choice of the person to carry His message.
Divine Attributes—the only way man can know God.
Dispensation—historically the period of authority for a Manifestation of God.
Divine Laws—some laws are eternal and others are conditional, or temporary.
Revelation—God's message revealed through every Manifestation of God.
Progressive Revelation—God's continuing message to humanity renewed periodically according to the level of humanity's spiritual maturity and capacity.

CHAPTER TWO—Earlier Religions

The Holy Land is closely associated with the Semitic religions, specifically Judaism, Christianity, and Islam. The histories of these religions are explored to identify similarities in the lives of their founders and in their basic teachings. A brief mention of Zoroastrianism is included in this section because it arose in Persia, birthplace of the Bahá'í Faith.

CHAPTER THREE THROUGH CHAPTER SIX—History of the Bahá'í Faith

Unlike the other religions whose historical roots are encrusted with myth, legend and tradition, the history of the Bahá'í Faith is told in the context of recent world history. References to events, dates and people are liberally documented. Bahá'í history begins with the movement known as the Advent Awakening, a period of religious search, particularly by religious scholars. Four individuals played a key role in the first century of the Bahá'í Faith:

CHAPTER THREE—The Bab

Founder of the Babi Faith and Herald of Bahá'u'lláh.

CHAPTER FOUR—Bahá'u'lláh

Founder of the Bahá'í Faith.

CHAPTER FIVE—'Abdu'l-Baha

Son of Bahá'u'lláh and his designated successor as the head of the Bahá'í community.

CHAPTER SIX—Shoghi Effendi

Grandson of 'Abdu'l-Baha, and his appointed successor to the leadership of the Bahá'í community as the Guardian of the Bahá'í Faith.

After the death of Shoghi Effendi, in 1957, a group of dedicated followers, called *Hands of the Cause of God*, led the worldwide Bahá'í community until the election, in 1963, of the world governing body of the Bahá'í Faith, the first Universal House of Justice.

CHAPTER SEVEN—Fundamental Concepts

Several fundamental concepts underlie the teachings of the Bahá'í Faith, including:

Unity—the oneness of God, of mankind, and religion.

Material Existence—one part of God's creation.

Dual Nature of Man—his special endowments that enable him to understand God's message.

Spiritual Existence—the world of the spirit, inhabited by every human soul after the body dies.

CHAPTER EIGHT—Basic Teachings

Basic principles of the Bahá'í Faith contribute to an integrated belief system that is relevant to mankind's current spiritual maturity level. These include:

Independent Investigation of Truth—the obligation of each individual to search out truth for himself.

Harmony of Science and Religion—there can be only one truth, regardless of its source.

Equality of Women and Men—all human beings are equal in the sight of God.

Elimination of Racial Prejudice—the human race is one family.

Universal Language—communication is a powerful tool for uniting all peoples.

Universal Education—extremely important for developing each person's distinctive human powers.

World Government and World Peace—the next stage in mankind's social development.

CHAPTER NINE—Administrative Order

The structure and certain processes of the Bahá'í Administrative Order are a key feature of the plan Bahá'u'lláh conceived to establish and preserve the unity, peace and security of a world community.

CHAPTER TEN—Bahá'í Topics

Some Bahá'í topics include the *Bahá'í Calendar*, *Bahá'í Holy Days*, the *Nineteen-Day Feast*, *Firesides*, *Bahá'í Temples*, *Universal Cycles*, *Ages of the Bahá'í Faith*, *Religious Symbols*, *Bahá'í Funds*, and *Learning More About the Bahá'í Faith*.

CHAPTER ELEVEN—Various Topics
The Bahá'í view on some general topics have relevance for today. These include: *Man and the Environment, Health and Healing, Nutrition, Drugs, Alcohol and Tobacco, Self Defense, Music and Art, Euthanasia, Cremation, Reincarnation,* and *Homosexuality.*

CHAPTER TWELVE—Plan of God
Humanity's destiny can be understood in the light of Bahá'u'lláh's Revelation.

All general references to man and mankind are intended as the generic definition and refer equally to women. Endnotes are used to clarify terms, names or expressions that have special significance in a Bahá'í context.

To Bahá'ís, the Bab and Bahá'u'lláh are infallible instruments of the Divine Will (God). Their writings, together with those of 'Abdu'l-Baha, constitute the Bahá'í sacred scriptures. 'Abdu'l-Baha, although not considered a Manifestation of God, is recognized as divinely inspired in all of his writings. His writings are equal in authority, but not in rank, to the writings of the Bab and Bahá'u'lláh.

In the various scriptures and writings, reference to the persons of the founders of all religions are often (but not always) capitalized. The Christian Bible frequently, but not always, capitalizes or emphasizes references to Jesus. This practice is also customary among Bahá'ís, who in their writings extend this same courtesy equally to all of the major religions. Following this practice, references to the founders of all the major religions are capitalized.

Because of His special rank and station, 'Abdu'l-Baha, Bahá'u'lláh's designated successor, holds a special place in the hearts of all Bahá'ís. Bahá'í authors generally capitalize all references to 'Abdu'l-Baha, although He is not ranked as a Manifestation of God.

The extensive writings of Bahá'u'lláh, 'Abdu'l-Baha and Shoghi Effendi are excerpted liberally in the later chapters. Texts in bold print are quotations, even though they are not enclosed by quotation marks. Quotation marks are used with quotations contained within text paragraphs. Bible references throughout the book use translations from the Revised Standard Version except as noted.

Persian and Arabic words and names are generally expressed in their simplest form instead of using the standard protocols. Because this book is an introduction to the Bahá'í Faith, the use of exotic punctuation and spelling constructions is minimized.

The text is pitched to better-than-average readers. For those readers who find the vocabulary level somewhat challenging, don't give up—just selecting this book indicates that the reader is intellectually curious and open to ideas and concepts of great substance.

For a determined reader with a good dictionary nearby, exploring great thoughts can bring exciting new insights as well as a larger vocabulary. Reading books that explore significant ideas sometimes change the course of a person's life.

A primary goal in writing this book is to motivate readers to investigate further the deeper meanings underlying key ideas and concepts which are explored at little more than a rudimentary level.

I acknowledge with deep gratitude and appreciation the support, patience, love and encouragement of my wife, Joy Asturias Tunick, in writing this book. The invaluable comments and suggestions by the Literature Review Office at the Bahá'í National Center in Wilmette, Illinois, were of great help in maintaining accuracy and clarity regarding the presentation of Bahá'í concepts, teachings and historical details. I am also indebted to the following for their assistance in proofreading and editing the manuscript: Milton Goldman, Bill Skuce, Natalie Bowen, Robert Travell, Richard Elfving and Kitty Schmitz. What is written about the Bahá'í Faith in this book reflects my own understanding of its principles and teachings. I assume sole responsibility for any errors contained herein and the manner in which it is presented.

SUGGESTIONS FOR READING THIS BOOK

This book is appropriate for two types of readers: (1) those who are familiar with the Bahá'í teachings, and (2) those who are not.

After a preliminary perusal of the table of contents and a cursory browse of any eye-catching topics, the interested reader is ready. Each chapter is important in understanding the Bahá'í Faith. Some key concepts, particularly in the latter half of the book, are fairly deep and must be digested slowly for maximum benefit.

For readers unfamiliar with the Bahá'í teachings, this book should be read from the beginning, as some names, key ideas and concepts discussed in later chapters are introduced in earlier chapters. For small, informal study groups, read aloud the selected portion, noting any questions arising from the reading. Follow-up should include flexible, open-ended discussion; if possible, a deepened Bahá'í should be part of the discussion group.

The reviews at the end of each chapter also offer discussion questions to help stimulate further exploration. Some questions call for specific answers; many others present open-ended ideas touched upon in the book that open up new directions for deeper reflection.

For readers deepened in the Bahá'í teachings, the book serves as a review of key concepts. But most of all, it is a vehicle for teaching Bahá'í principles. Open discussion should not attack anyone's ideas or beliefs. Each member should feel comfortable about examining her or his own beliefs in the light of the discussion without threat or pressure. Supplement these discussions with photos and multimedia materials readily available through the Internet and numerous Bahá'í sources. Try to end each discussion on a positive, uplifting note.

PROLOGUE

It is not easy to be a true follower of any religion. Sincere followers of any religion share basic beliefs, those which are reflected in their conduct and which shape their life goals. When conduct and life goals appear to conflict with beliefs, it indicates weak commitment to those beliefs. Based on these criteria, many of those who claim to be following any of the major religions reveal insincerity (and in some cases, hypocrisy), regardless of their denials. World events, news reports, and numerous personal observations support this conclusion.

The Bahá'í Faith accepts the teachings of the founders of Judaism, Christianity and Islam, as it does those of the founders of the other great world faiths (such as Hinduism and Buddhism). For example, Moses, Jesus and Muhammad are all considered true Prophets, or Messengers of God. The teachings each Prophet brought to His followers form the core of the respective Holy Scriptures.

One of the major sources of the teachings of each religion is its Holy Scriptures. Whatever these Holy Scriptures say form the basis for the teachings of that religion. Bahá'ís believe that the Holy Scriptures of each religion recognizes the Prophets who will come later, and calls for its followers to acknowledge Them, too. Because these Holy Scriptures do not clearly identify the later Prophets by name, the claim of the new Prophet is rejected when He appears. Later in this book you will find quotations from the earlier scriptures in support of the later Prophets, and particularly of Bahá'u'lláh, the Founder-Prophet of the Bahá'í Faith.

The aim of this book is to acquaint readers with the message of the Bahá'í Faith, its history and its principles. It is directed toward those who wish to explore the fundamental truths in religion and religious values, and who are willing to recognize truth wherever they find it.

New ideas have lasting worth if they are true. And truth can be recognized when it is examined without bias or prejudice—with an open mind. Great scientific discoveries were made by minds that started from a completely unbiased point of view, minds that examined and analyzed data with scrupulous honesty, and did not flinch from deductions or conclusions that may have run contrary to cherished and long accepted beliefs or traditions. Rejecting a position solely because it opposes a revered and time-honored custom or practice does not permit a fair intellectual evaluation. It takes courage to risk an exploration that may prove damaging to long-held views. Unless you examine new ideas with a new eye, "**...ye shall see, and not perceive**" (Acts 28:26). The Bahá'í teachings are best evaluated when examined without preconceived notions.

Historically, all religions have been concerned essentially with the development of the individual. The Bahá'í Faith teaches that the individual's personal development and his social development are interrelated. The process of perfecting and developing both the individual and human society must be pursued at the same time.

Unity is a fundamental theme taught by the Bahá'í Faith. Its importance in human affairs is illustrated by the example of an evolving social and political unity discussed in the next few pages. The international tensions and the plunder of our planet cannot be stopped until mankind has attained such unity on a global level.

Just as a child grows to maturity and develops the characteristics of mature thinking, so has mankind grown, from childhood to adolescence. The Bahá'í teachings proclaim that mankind is now ready to enter the stage of its maturity. This is reflected in the growth of the social institutions of our day.

From love for and loyalty to the basic social unit, the family, mankind's thinking has developed to encompass, in turn, love and loyalty for clan, tribe, city-state and nation. Each larger social institution united its smaller units in a more effective and smoothly functioning larger society.

For example, the independent and individually weak city-states of ancient Greece overcame their relatively minor differences and formed a larger and more powerful group (a temporary alliance) to withstand successfully the threat from the larger society (nation) of the Persian Empire.

Another example is the formation of the kingdom of Italy in the nineteenth century. After several hundred years of petty squabbling, warfare and invasions from larger neighboring nations, the fiercely proud and independent Italian city-states finally chose to unite as a single and more powerful independent nation.

The Bahá'í teachings call for mankind to now recognize its own readiness for the next stage of its development—global unity and a world state. This is a truth that many Bahá'ís and non-Bahá'ís can acknowledge as a natural course of events.

From the time these teachings were first proclaimed more than one hundred years ago, history can record the **"trend toward ever-increasing interdependence and integration... the fusion of world financial markets... [reflecting a] reliance on diverse and interdependent sources of energy, food, raw materials, technology and knowledge."**[1]

Mankind's initial faltering steps toward a world state could be seen in the political turmoil associated with the creation of the League of Nations at the end of World War I. American President Woodrow Wilson was its chief architect and enthusiastic promoter. After generating support from the world's most powerful nations, Wilson was embarrassed and bitterly disappointed by his own country's reluctance to join. The refusal of the U.S. Congress to ratify America's membership in the League of Nations crippled the League's effectiveness in preserving world peace.

A second effort came at the end of World War II with the formation of the United Nations. An international forum of last resort, the United Nations **"stands as a noble symbol for the collective interests of humanity as a whole"**[2]. Although it cannot be considered a world state in its present organization, the UN today does serve a number of global functions (see Chapter Eight, World Government—World Peace).

It is generally considered a sign of maturity to look at things objectively, to take the long view. A child finds it difficult to postpone immediate satisfaction and gratification, even if it means a greater satisfaction later. The immature person is attentive only to the needs of **me** and **now**. And what is true of the individual is also true of groups of people, societies, and ultimately of all mankind.

Let us look objectively at, i.e. take a mature view of, world conditions that are moving mankind toward its ultimate destiny. In every social group, and even in the more advanced societies, there are signs of social breakdown, a loss of moral and ethical values. Man cannot seem to overcome the evils that are undermining the social systems that worked so well in the past.

Crime, drugs, disease, war, pollution—all are increasing despite the valiant efforts of many selfless people and humanitarian organizations. Family groups, village and city communities, individual nations, even groups of nations, cannot muster sufficient means to deal effectively with the ills that are, for the most part, afflicting all societies and social levels in all parts of the world. Only a united world community can organize the resources needed to resolve the current problems besetting all societies, both large and small.

The need for a world state is a practical idea not generally recognized as a concern of religion. It is, however, an integral part of the Bahá'í teachings; a world state, peace, and global unity are inseparably linked.

The earlier religions hinted at global unity, but it was not stated specifically because mankind was not ready for such an idea. The Christian concept of love your fellow man, which is also taught by all the other religions, implies love for all of humanity, and this is needed to teach the concept of global unity. The Bahá'í Faith is the most recent of the many religions that have developed during mankind's long painful struggle to understand the meaning of its existence.

Religions traditionally have been concerned with such questions as: "What is the purpose of our existence?" "How did it all start?" "What happens after we die?" "What is the nature of God?" "Is there really a heaven; hell; soul?" With the world-threatening social crises emerging in today's multi-societies, religions now must also respond to the more practical questions raised by these mundane problems.

Today, a religion may be classified as a world religion or major religion if it:
(1) has believers in large numbers,
(2) has believers in many lands,
(3) was founded by a prophet or messenger, and
(4) is based upon a written Holy Book or scriptures covering a set of special beliefs, rules and regulations.

Examples of a major or world religion are Hinduism, Buddhism, Judaism, Christianity, Islam, and the Bahá'í Faith. In its more than 150-year history, the Bahá'í Faith has gained a following approaching seven million believers. It is almost equal to Christianity in its geographical spread. Its prophet-founder was Bahá'u'lláh (pronounced Ba-HA-o-LA). Its scriptures include a large collection of Bahá'u'lláh's writings, written over a forty-year period, and enough to fill more than one hundred volumes.

Christian scriptures are based upon the teachings of Jesus over a three-year period, and Islamic scriptures are based on Muhammad's teachings over a twenty-year period.

It is understandable that Bahá'u'lláh's accumulated writings, recorded by scribes (and some by His own hand) over a period of forty years, embody an amount much larger than the scriptures of all previous religions. The enormous amount of Bahá'í scriptures, some of which has not yet been translated, covers a wealth of knowledge. It discusses numerous topics personally written or dictated by Bahá'u'lláh in greater detail than was possible in the time allotted to the founders of the earlier religions.

New religions often develop from the background of an earlier religion. At first the new religion is viewed by outsiders as a sect or branch of the parent religion. From a Hindu background in India, Buddhism was recognized as an independent religion when it began attracting followers in China, Japan and Southeast Asia. Christianity won its independence from Judaism when it began attracting followers all over the Roman

Empire.

In the same manner, the Bahá'í Faith was seen as separate from Islam when it attracted followers in the western hemisphere, in Europe and in America.

FOR THOSE NOT SURE THERE IS A GOD

The age-old 'God/no God' debate between believers and nonbelievers, whether or not He exists, cannot be resolved. It is useless for one side to demand, "Prove that God Exists!" because the response, "Prove that he doesn't!" creates a stalemate, not a resolution.

"Does God exist?" requires a rationale or reason for even raising the question. If we assume that a creation by an intelligent creator (God) must have a logical purpose, then the true question should be **"whether or not we have a universe that works more efficiently with an intelligent originating principle (that)... can illuminate or explain other phenomena."**[3] More simply put, the universe is operating according to a reasoned plan, or it is operating in a random way, purely by chance; the latter would suggest that the universe may have come into being by accident.

Whatever we know about God comes from religious teachings, but because we can't be sure on logical grounds alone, it becomes advisable that we at least explore what the religions have to say. However they may appear to differ, the teachings of all the major religions begin with one common assumption—that there is a God. Although by definition God is unknowable and indefinable, all of these religions are universally agreed that He exists.

We first learn about God from others—usually from parents, teachers, or friends, and their information ultimately comes from the teachings of religion. Later we may decide to accept or reject the fact of His existence. If we accept, we are believers (deists or theists), if we reject we are nonbelievers (atheists), and if we doubt or are unsure, then depending on the degree of our uncertainty, we are lukewarm believers or lukewarm nonbelievers (agnostics).

While both deists and theists believe in the existence of God, deists reject the revelations of God found in the teachings of the major religions. Their belief in God is based solely on reason. Deists believe that the natural world itself is sufficient proof of His existence, and that reports of supernatural events are highly doubtful. They believe that God created the world but has since remained indifferent to His creation. Deistic views were held by such well-known figures as the 17th and 18th century rationalists, Voltaire and Rousseau, and by the early American statesmen, Benjamin Franklin, George Washington, and Thomas Jefferson. Many of those who today call themselves agnostics are deists.

Theists, on the other hand, believe in God as the creator and ruler of the universe. They generally accept the structure of formal religious creeds and the existence of spiritual powers. The existence of both a material and a spiritual reality are a theistic concept common to all of the major religions. Sincere theists follow the teachings of their own religion with great humility. Confirmed atheists, on the other hand, assert with pride their infallible reason and logic in rejecting these same teachings, and also the one God whose source they are.

All three categories (believers, nonbelievers, and those in-between) are part of a belief continuum. Everyone can be placed somewhere along this line. Few people would be found at either extreme end, as even confirmed believers and nonbelievers may have an occasional doubt.

All three categories can profit from a study of religions and religious teachings. Most agnostics would like to be more sure they know which way they should lean, and the atheists and theists (and deists) may wish to confirm what they already profess they believe.

Atheists	**Agnostics**	**Deists or Theists**
	_____	_____	

Belief in God Continuum

The tendency to believe or not believe varies with individuals. The very thing that attracts and convinces one person fills another with skepticism and reservation. Some spiritually receptive souls easily recognize the evidence of God's existence, while many others need years of search and thought before they can tear away the veils of their own preconceived notions and look at certain ideas without prejudice.

Volumes have been written to prove the existence of

God. As this is not the purpose of this book, the author presents some brief arguments for a belief in God's existence, primarily to help the reader establish a basic mindset for a sincere investigation of the ideas presented.

Our world of existence is often proposed as an example of creation to show that there must be a God. René Descartes, the 17th century French philosopher, wrote, in Latin, "Cogito, ergo sum" (I think, therefore I am), referring to man's awareness of his own thoughts as proof that he exists.

Man's thoughts in terms of his environment lead to the awareness of an existing creation. The Creator of this creation, as He cannot create Himself, must exist as an entity separate from His creation and is thus not bound by the *'laws'* governing His creation.

A painter creates a painting, an inventor creates an invention, and a thinker creates a thought. The painter, inventor and thinker are the creators of their creations. They understand their creations whereas the creations cannot understand their creators. The creators, therefore, possess greater capacities than their creations.

The world of creation, i.e. our world of existence (the universe and everything it contains), must have a creator. How can an existent creation come into being from a non-existent creator? If the creation exists, then its creator must also exist because the creator is greater than his creation. Conversely, if God does not exist, then His creation does not exist, because a creation cannot exceed the capacities and qualities of its creator.

The creator of the human brain, which has the capacity for self-awareness and generation of complex thoughts, must Himself possess even greater capacities than His creation. By definition, those capacities that exceed our own finite human capacities cannot even be imagined; the capacity of human powers of imagination is also thus limited. The powers we attribute to God must therefore be less than those He actually possesses. It must also be thus clear that God's capacities exceed our capacity to understand fully the true nature of God.

Even for nonbelievers, this is, at the very least, a possibility. The common atheist hedge, that man has not yet discovered all there is to know, is less satisfying to a logical mind.

CHAPTER ONE — Key Terms

A clear understanding of key terms and concepts is necessary for an accurate picture of the Bahá'í Faith. Other religions may use these terms and concepts in a different sense, but it is essential that they be understood as Bahá'ís use them.

MANIFESTATION OF GOD

Bahá'u'lláh called the great Prophets of God—His chosen divine messengers who appear in every age (usually 500 to 1000 years apart)—Manifestations of God. The Bahá'í writings identify the founders of other religions as Manifestations of God. Examples are Krishna, Abraham, Moses, Zoroaster, Buddha, Jesus, Muhammad, the Bab and Bahá'u'lláh. The Minor Prophets, such as the Old Testament prophets, Elijah, Samuel, Isaiah and Jeremiah, are not Manifestations of God.

Some followers of other religions claim that the founder of their own religion is a true Messenger of God and that the other religious founders are either false prophets or at least inferior to their own prophet. Many Jews, for example, believe that Moses was a true Prophet of God, but that Jesus was not. Christians believe Moses was a Prophet, but inferior to Jesus, and the Revelation of Jesus was the fulfillment of Moses' Revelation. Christians reject Muhammad as a false prophet. Muslims accept both Moses and Jesus, but consider Muhammad's teachings as the ultimate authority.

In all of the major religions, it was the Prophet Himself who acknowledged and honored the earlier Prophet. It was also true that in His own time the Prophet was ridiculed, scorned and rejected by the followers of the earlier Prophet.

Manifestations of God, as termed by Bahá'ís, are not just *great or super-charismatic* men who happened to be in the right place at the right time. Neither are They God in His Essence and totality. Bahá'ís consider all of these Prophets spiritual beings, unlike ordinary human beings, specifically chosen and endowed by

God with special powers to carry out a specific mission. Their dedication to His service is total—to an extent that is beyond the capacity of an ordinary human being.

The Bahá'í writings assert that the Manifestations of God are special human beings who reflect perfectly God's attributes, just as a mirror reflects the sun but is not the sun itself. All the Manifestations have the same spirit, although their outward forms (bodies) are different. Speaking with the authority of God, Bahá'u'lláh said, **"There is no distinction whatsoever among the Bearers of My Message. They all have but one purpose..."**[4]

```
SUN = GOD
RAYS = HOLY SPIRIT
MIRROR = Moses or Christ or Baha'u'llah
HUMANITY

JOHN 14
He who has seen me has seen the Father.
...the Father is in me.
...the Father who dwells in me does His works.
```

Sometimes the Manifestation speaks as the voice of God; at other times He speaks as a messenger of God. But at all times He is the servant of God. All the Manifestations of God, Bahá'u'lláh explained, **"have been made manifest in the uttermost state of servitude, a servitude the like of which no man can possibly attain."**[5] **I have no will but Thy will, O my Lord, and cherish no desire but Thy desire. From my pen floweth only the summons which Thine own exalted pen hath voiced...**[6]

The *"Voice of God"* and the *"Messenger of God"* reflect the two key stations of the Manifestation of God. As the "Voice of God," each Manifestation is a spiritual being identical to the other Manifestations of God. In this station, each may refer to God in the first person, such as "I, thy Lord...." The Manifestation reflects perfectly the spiritual light of God's teachings to humanity. **"It is the sun shining within the mirror that is responsible for the light. It is not the mirror itself."**[7]

As the "Messenger of God," each Manifestation has a distinct human individual identity, separate from all the others. In this station, He can refer to God in the third person, such as, "And the Lord said..." In His unique human identity, each Manifestation will **"walk in the greatest lowliness and simplicity, choosing a life of poverty... and... behave personally as the meekest of the meek, the gentlest of the gentle... Each is like a teacher, suiting the lesson to the capacity of the pupils."**[8]

In His human identity, the Manifestation of God is a man of little human learning. Compared with the great and powerful earthly leaders, He appears as the weakest of the weak. Like any other man, He can suffer hunger, thirst, weariness and sickness. He is an easy victim for His enemies.[9]

Bahá'u'lláh Himself identifies the key characteristics of every Manifestation of God:

And since there can be no tie of direct intercourse to bind the one true God with His creation, and no resemblance whatever can exist between the transient and the Eternal, the contingent and the Absolute, He hath ordained that in every age and dispensation a pure and stainless Soul be made manifest in the kingdoms of earth and heaven. Unto this subtle, this mysterious and ethereal Being He hath assigned a twofold nature; the physical, pertaining to the world of matter, and the spiritual, which is born of the substance of God Himself. He hath, moreover, conferred upon Him a double station. The first station, which is related to His innermost reality, representeth Him as One Whose voice is the voice of God Himself. To this testifieth the tradition: "Manifold and mysterious is My relationship with God. I am He, Himself, and He is I, Myself, except that I am that I am, and He is that He is." ...He similarly saith: "There is no distinction whatsoever

between Thee and Them, except that They are Thy Servants." The second station is the human station... These Essences of Detachment, these resplendent Realities are the channels of God's all-pervasive grace. Led by the light of unfailing guidance, and invested with supreme sovereignty, They are commissioned to use the inspiration of Their words, the effusions of Their infallible grace and the sanctifying breeze of Their Revelation for the cleansing of every longing heart and receptive spirit from the dross and dust of earthly cares and limitations.**[10]**

Because they have innate knowledge, the Manifestations provide perfect (infallible) guidance to humanity through Their words while They live, and through Their writings (scriptures) after They die. The teachings of these Manifestations are thus considered Revelations from God.

DIVINE ATTRIBUTES

Also known as *spiritual attributes*, or the *names of God*, these are the virtues or qualities by which we can recognize God. We can only allude to the spiritual qualities of God through language that is designed for material qualities. As God, by definition, is infinite and indefinable, He cannot be known in His true reality (the essence of God). He can reveal Himself only through His attributes, such as love, mercy, beauty and trustworthiness.

Every created thing has some of these attributes, but only man has, potentially, all of them; this is why man is said to be made in the *image* of God. A wild animal, for example, does not possess the quality of mercy, and so it cannot understand the spiritual attribute of mercy.

The essence of every created thing has been granted the **"light of one of His names... Upon the reality of man, however, He hath focused the radiance of all of His names and attributes, and made it a mirror of His own Self. Alone of all created things man hath been singled out for so great a favor... These energies... lie, however, latent within him..."[11]**

One of man's purposes in life is to develop the divine

attributes that already exist potentially within him. He learns how to do this from the Manifestation of God, who possesses, exemplifies and teaches all of these virtues. Man's effort to perfect his own virtues is a lifelong process. No matter how well he displays these qualities, there is always room for improvement, and only God knows how successful his (man's) efforts have been.

DIVINE LAWS

If God's teachings are all basically the same, why are there differences among the religions? If the Manifestations of God all speak the truth, how can their words be different? Bahá'u'lláh explained that each Manifestation brings God's message for mankind according to mankind's capacity and needs. They have **"proceeded from one Source and are the rays of one Light."**[12]

There are two degrees of God's laws. One is the spiritual laws that never change, such as the law requiring each person to acknowledge and worship God, or to love his fellow man. Second are the social laws that vary according to the needs and conditions of society at that time, such as the prohibition on eating certain foods, or laws of inheritance.

Unlike spiritual laws, which constitute the unchanging code of morality taught by all the Manifestations of God, the social laws are conditional. They are changed by each new Manifestation of God according to the practical needs and requirements of the people at that particular time.

These practical needs deal **"with exterior forms and ceremonies... and guides the customs and manners of the people."**[13] As examples of changing needs, 'Abdu'l-Baha noted that cutting off the right hand as punishment for theft is no longer appropriate for today's society. **"In this age... a man who curses his father is allowed to live, when formerly he would have been put to death."**[14]

DISPENSATION

In a religious sense, a Dispensation is the period of time during which the authority of a Manifestation of

God's social or temporary teachings stay fresh; spiritual (permanent) laws are affirmed by each Manifestation.[15] The Dispensation begins with the declaration of His mission and ends with the declaration of the next Manifestation of God. The laws of the new Dispensation supersede those of the previous one.

The length of a Dispensation is usually hundreds of years but it can vary greatly. In the course of a dispensation, the influence of its Founder follows a process of growth and decay that is similar to the life cycle of a tree.

The cause of each Prophet springing from the minutest beginnings by slow degrees matures, striking its roots deep, and in its increasing strength spreading in all directions upwards and about; till when it has reached the limit of its power it slowly decays and at last, giving no shade nor fruit, it dies and falls.[16]

Every Dispensation experiences a cyclic pattern of growth and decay. In the beginning the Prophet's appearance infuses His followers with the power of spiritual teachings that kindle a spiritual fire and energy that is unstoppable. At the end, His followers tend to lose touch with the Spirit of the ascended Prophet; the old forms remain, but without the enthusiasm and quickening vigor of the original teachings. Love grows cold and faith weakens. A spiritual void appears in the ranks of the believers. This is why a new Dispensation must arise to rekindle and reinvigorate the older teachings with new hope and new faith.

REVELATION (OR DIVINE REVELATION)

During His lifetime, teachings revealed by the Manifestation of God are part of His revelation. After He has passed on, His recorded teachings (the Manifestation's words, which become the scriptures or sacred writings) are considered the revelation (revealed words) of that religion.

Prior to the revelations of the Bab and of Bahá'u'lláh, earlier revelations were not always written by the Manifestations Themselves. In the case of the Bab and of Bahá'u'lláh, however, all of Their writings were written by Their own hands or dictated to scribes or secretaries, after which they were personally authenticated.

In Judaism, for example, the Torah (holiest of the Hebrew Scriptures) consists of the first five books of the Old Testament, a collection of thirty-nine sacred books. These were recorded by a number of writers over several hundred years, and are based upon traditions of holy teachings.

The Gospels, holiest of the Christian scriptures, are the first four books of the New Testament, which totals twenty-seven books. The Gospels were written by four different writers between thirty and one hundred years after the death of Jesus.

PROGRESSIVE REVELATION

Progressive revelation is the premise that Divine Revelation is not final, but continuing. All the great prophets of the past were Manifestations of God who appeared in different ages with their messages from the same Source but tailored to the needs of the time, according to humanity's spiritual capacity.

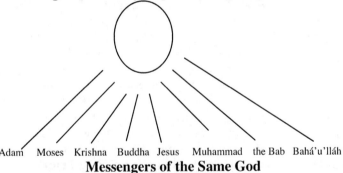

Adam Moses Krishna Buddha Jesus Muhammad the Bab Bahá'u'lláh
Messengers of the Same God

The appearance of a new Messenger of God has never been represented in any of the major religions as a one-time event. He has always been identified with the fulfillment of an ancient authoritative promise. Moses foretold a successor. Jesus equated Himself with Moses. Muhammad testified of Moses and Jesus.

It was not the person of Jesus that was important, but the Holy Spirit of Christ which shone within Him. The same principle was true of Moses. It is true of every Messenger of God. They are all Mirrors that reflect the light of the Sun of God's truth. If the light does not shine within Them, they are merely frames and glass, nothing more.[17]

Regarding His own revelation, Bahá'u'lláh wrote, **"Whatever I manifest is nothing more or less than ... [that] which God has bidden me reveal."**[18]

The message of each Manifestation of God affirmed the earlier Manifestation and proclaimed the coming of the next one. Whether He spoke as the "voice of God" saying **"I will come again,"** or as the "Messenger of God" saying, **"Another like me will come,"** the meaning and purpose was the same—an affirmation of the continuity of revelation from the one God.

From the people of His own time, He experienced rejection and vigorous opposition. **"Why is it that the advent of every true Manifestation of God hath been accompanied by such strife and tumult, by such tyranny and upheaval? This notwithstanding the fact that all the Prophets of God, whenever made manifest unto the peoples of the world, have invariably foretold the coming of yet another Prophet after them, and have established such signs as would herald the advent of the future Dispensation..."**[19]

Bahá'u'lláh describes each Manifestation as an All-Knowing Physician who **"perceiveth the disease, and describeth, in His unerring wisdom, the remedy. Every age hath its own problem... The remedy the world needeth in its present-day afflictions can never be the same as that which a subsequent age may require. Be anxiously concerned with the needs of the age ye live in, and center your deliberations on its exigencies and requirements."**[20]

With each succeeding Dispensation, human society has advanced as man's group loyalty widened—from family to clan, tribe, city-state, nation, and now moving toward recognition of world unity, according to the needs of our present globally aware society.

The history of humanity, therefore, appears to be goal oriented. It is not just an endless circle, a continual appearance of a succession of Manifestations repeating God's message. Neither is it a linear progression "...**as Christianity often sees it, moving from a point at the beginning to a point at the end. The recurrence of the same events always takes place on a higher plane; the course of world history resembles a spiral.**"[21]

"**The true religion of the future,**" according to the renowned theologian, F. Max Müller, "**will be the fulfillment of all the religions of the past... There never was a false god, nor was there ever really a false religion, unless you call a child a false man. All religions... were links in a chain which connects heaven and earth, and which is held, and always was held, by one and the same hand.**"[22]

Shoghi Effendi, Guardian of the Bahá'í Faith, said that Bahá'ís view the great religions of the past as different stages in the eternal history and constant evolution of one religion. The Bahá'í teachings assert that "**religious truth is not absolute but relative, that Divine Revelation is progressive, not final... it proclaims all established religions to be divine in origin, identical in their aims, complementary in their functions, continuous in their purpose, indispensable in their value to mankind.**"[23]

Differences in mankind's spiritual capacity at various appearances of the Manifestations of God account for differences in Their messages (revelations). Each Manifestation of God taught all of the divine virtues, and emphasized a main or principal theme of His own Dispensation.

Date	Religion	Manifest'n	Theme	Book
Unknown	Hinduism	Krishna	Introspection	Gita
1900 BCE	Hebrew	Abraham	Monotheism	Torah
1300 BCE	Judaism	Moses	Law (Justice)	Torah
9-600 BCE	Zoroastrianism	Zoroaster	Purity	Gathas
560 BCE	Buddhism	Buddha	Detachment	Tripitaka
1 CE (AD)	Christianity	Jesus	Love	Gospels
622 CE	Islam	Muhammad	Submission	Qur'an
1844 CE	Babi Faith	Bab	the Gate[24]	Bayan
1863 CE	Bahá'í Faith	Bahá'u'lláh	Unity	Aqdas

CHAPTER REVIEW—Key Terms

Summary
▶The founders of all the major religions, called Manifestations of God, are chosen as God's special messengers.
▶The Manifestations of God are the same spiritually though different physically.
▶Divine attributes are spiritual qualities that exist potentially in all human beings.
▶Spiritual laws are permanent; social laws may be changed by each Manifestation of God.
▶A Dispensation is the period of authority for the teachings of each Manifestation of God.
▶Revelation refers to the recorded words of each Manifestation of God.
▶Progressive revelation is the continuous message of God brought by the succession of His Manifestations.

Discussion
1. Distinguish between the major and the minor Prophets. List three examples of each.
2. Name five divine attributes.
3. Why are only human beings said to be made in the image of God?
4. What is meant by the essence of God?
5. What is a spiritual law? Give examples.
6. Distinguish between conditional and permanent laws of God.
7. Is 'revelation' the words the Manifestation of God speaks, or words he has written?
8. Which are the holiest books of the Old Testament? The New Testament?
9. How can the concept of 'progressive revelation' be explained in terms of social development?
10. From a 'progressive revelation' perspective, can one religion be superior to another? If so, how?

Activities
A. Using the table at the end of the chapter, make a blank table and complete from one given clue for each row.
B. Using the table at the end of the chapter, make a timeline including major milestones in human history.

CHAPTER TWO — Earlier Religions

Although Bahá'ís view all true religions as coming from the same one Source, Bahá'í philosophical roots are traced back through Zoroastrianism, Judaism, Islam, Christianity, and the Far Eastern religions, Hinduism and Buddhism. Each developed their own traditions within their own cultural contexts and, while their teachings do not conflict (because of their same Source), their geographical separation in those times provided very little opportunity for contact.

After a time, all of the earlier religions encountered new trends, ideas that resulted in splits into groups or sects. In the Western religions, the groups were categorized as modern, reform or liberal, and orthodox, conservative or fundamental, and various stages in between.

A thumbnail sketch of the major Holy Land religions is presented to show some of the similarities in their histories and the lives of their Founders, the Manifestations of God, which would uncover the threads of their connection. From the scriptures of each religion, and from other available information, we can discern certain common characteristics.

Each Manifestation:
- proclaimed Himself a Messenger of God. At times He would deliver the message as a messenger; at other times He would speak as if God were speaking through His mouth.
- preceded a new civilization.
- was rejected and opposed by the people of His own time.
- honored and affirmed earlier Manifestations.
- announced the coming of future Manifestations.

Christians call the Holy Scriptures of Judaism and Christianity the Old Testament and the New Testament, respectively. The Christian Bible commonly includes both. The Bible of Judaism does not recognize nor contain the New Testament writings. Christianity recognizes both but considers the New Testament the greater of the two.

The Bahá'í Faith recognizes both as equally authoritative chapters in the eternal revelation of God. A discussion of several basic Christian beliefs and how they are viewed from a Bahá'í perspective is presented in Chapter Eight.

While the earliest of the major Holy Land religions is Judaism, there are some faint and not clearly substantiated traces of still earlier religions in the greater Holy Land region.

Adam and Noah are mentioned in the Bahá'í writings as if they were Manifestations of God, but it is not clear whether they were actual historical figures, where and when they lived, or what they taught.

The *Sabaean Faith* refers to Saba, or Sheba (mentioned in the Qur'an), a country believed to be located at the southern part of the Arabian Peninsula or in the vicinity of Ethiopia on the continent of Africa.

Shoghi Effendi, the Guardian of the Bahá'í Faith, asserted that very little is known about the origins of Sabaeanism, although Bahá'ís recognize the Founder of this religion as a divinely-sent Messenger. The country where Sabaeanism became widespread and flourished was Chaldea, and Abraham is considered to have been a follower of that Faith.[25]

The Bahá'í and Islamic writings mention *Hud* and *Salih*, who appear to be earlier Arab Manifestations, but little is known about them or their missions.

JUDAISM

In Judaism's four thousand year history its two founder prophets, Abraham and Moses, tower above all others.

Among the earliest of the Western religions of which we have significant knowledge, Judaism traces its earliest beginnings in 19th century BCE, to Abraham, a native of the ancient Sumerian city of Ur. He was the first of the Hebrew Patriarchs and is recognized by Bahá'ís as a Manifestation of God.

Abraham is the first man known to enter into a covenant with God. In return for His obedience to God's commands, Abraham was promised by God that **"...I will make of you a great nation."** (Genesis 12:2) **"...you shall be the father of a multitude of nations."** (Genesis 17:4) **"...and I will make nations of thee, and kings shall come out of thee. And I will establish My covenant between me and you and your descendants after you throughout their generations for an everlasting covenant, to be God to you and to your descendants after you."** (Genesis 17:7)

Such an agreement implied for the first time in history the existence of an ethical God who acts as a kind of benign constitutional monarch bound by his own righteous agreements.[26]

Moses, Jesus and Muhammad all affirmed the fatherhood of Abraham and claimed Him as Their ancestor. Each of the Western religions identify themselves, through Abraham's three wives, as descendants of Abraham and the inheritors of His covenant with God.

The Jews trace their descent through Abraham's first wife, Sarah, and her son, Isaac, to Moses. Christians continue this descent in a direct line to Jesus. Muslims trace their descent through Hagar, Abraham's second wife, and her son, Ishmael, to Muhammad.

Bahá'ís follow this line directly from Muhammad to the Bab. Zoroastrians and Bahá'ís trace their descent through Abraham's third wife, Keturah, and her son, Jokshan, to Zoroaster, and continuing in a direct line through the last of the Zoroastrian kings, Yazdegird III, to Bahá'u'lláh.

The *Torah*, also called the *Five Books of Moses* (or the *Pentateuch*), is the holiest and most authoritative of the thirty-nine books of the Old Testament. The Torah includes the *Ten Commandments*, called *the moral bedrock of Western civilization.*

Genesis, the first of these five books, describes man's earliest history. It begins with the creation of the world and the appearance of man in the symbolic story of Adam and Eve and their descendants, to the time of the three Patriarchs (Abraham, Isaac and Jacob). It ends with the move of Jacob, his family and followers, to Egypt.

The remaining four books of the Torah tell the story of the Jews as a people, called Hebrews, or Israelites. These books include laws, teachings and prophecies, as well as the dramatic narrative of Moses, their deliverer from slavery in Egypt. Moses is generally considered their greatest leader, and the one many consider the true founder of Judaism.

The Torah ends with the death of Moses and the arrival of the Israelites in their Promised Land. The remainder of the Old Testament includes books of sacred writings and books of the prophets, representing several hundred years of Jewish history.

In addition to the sacred books of the Old Testament, there is the *Talmud*, a large body of scholarly and authoritative supplemental writings compiled over hundreds of years to enhance, clarify, and interpret the books of the Old Testament. The Talmud also reinterpreted ancient laws that would otherwise be obsolete and outdated, to make them more relevant for newer times and circumstances.

ABRAHAM

Abraham left His native Ur, in what is now southern Iraq, as a member of His father's household, and moved to Haran, an ancient city in the Kingdom of Mari[27], in what is now southern Turkey. With His wife, Sarah, He left His father's household and established Himself as the master of His own household in Haran.

According to the Bible, Abraham left Haran on God's instructions, and moved His household, servants and all His possessions, on a six-hundred-mile trek to the land of Canaan (presently part of Israel and Jordan), at that time an Egyptian colony.

The first of the major figures in the history of the Jews, Abraham is recognized as the One who fearlessly proclaimed the concept of *monotheism* and one universal God in a polytheistic world of disparate regional gods. Abraham thus legitimized the messages brought by the Founders of the subsequent Western religions. Their own messages from the same one God established Their spiritual connection.

According to the Torah, the fulfillment of God's covenant with Abraham began after Abraham had reached an advanced age. Abraham sired His first son, Ishmael, by His second wife, Hagar (Sarah's Egyptian slave, whom she gave to Abraham when He was more than eighty years of age because Sarah had already passed her seventieth year and had not yet borne Him a child).

To Sarah's surprise she herself, at the age of ninety, bore their first son, Isaac, when Abraham was one hundred. After Sarah died, Abraham, who was now past the age of one hundred thirty, took another wife, Keturah, who bore Him six sons. Abraham died at the age of one hundred seventy five.

MOSES

The story of Moses is narrated in the last four of the Five Books of Moses. The Biblical account notes that Jacob, Isaac's son and the third of the three Hebrew Patriarchs, was an old man. Joseph, the favorite of Jacob's twelve sons, had become a high-ranking minister to the Egyptian pharaoh.

During a famine, Joseph arranged for Jacob and his sons and all their households, seventy people in all, to live in Egypt as honored guests, in the beautiful province known as *the land of Goshen*. Life in their new homeland was pleasant and the Hebrews prospered and multiplied.

In the course of 400 years, the Hebrews evidently

overstayed their welcome because the new government officials forgot Joseph and his past services to Egypt. Egyptian hospitality wore thin, and the formerly honored guests were reclassified as slaves in the army of forced laborers now needed by the pharaoh for the building of pyramids.

This move was politically expedient because it served to control the prosperous Hebrew foreigners whose growing numbers were perceived as a threat to the Egyptian power structure. It also helped to keep down the escalating labor costs of the pyramid projects.

But the pharaoh's cautious royal advisers were still fearful that these foreigners might realize their potential power to organize an effective opposition to the increasingly oppressive work requirements imposed upon them. The advisers persuaded the pharaoh to reduce the perceived threat by a simple precautionary measure—a decree calling for killing all Hebrew first-born male infants. The birth of Moses, eldest son of two Hebrew slaves, occurred during the time of this decree.

In an effort to circumvent the pharaoh's decree His mother placed the infant Moses in a basket and set it adrift in the Nile River. As the basket drifted by the royal palace, it was stopped by one of the royal princesses, who retrieved the infant and adopted Him as her own. Thus, Moses spent His early years as a prince of Egypt.

Details of Bible accounts are sketchy regarding Moses' early life. The one account that stands out is that He killed an Egyptian, and consequently Moses had to flee Egypt. He wandered across the desert to Midian (near Mount Sinai), where for forty years He lived as a shepherd, married and raised a family.

It was here that Moses had His first encounter with God on Mount Sinai, at *the burning bush.* God instructed Moses to return to Egypt. He was to persuade the pharaoh to release the suffering Hebrews from their captivity and lead them back to Canaan, the land of their forefathers.

With His brother, Aaron, at His side, Moses began His celebrated encounters with the pharaoh, who was reluctant to release his slave army of pyramid-builders just for the asking. According to the Bible, Moses then began, on God's instructions, a series of persuasive power plays, a sequence of plagues, to be inflicted only on the Egyptians.

The first was a plague of blood, in which all drinking water in rivers, canals and reservoirs turned red and became undrinkable. God then brought, in succession, plagues of frogs, gnats, flies, livestock disease, boils, hail, locusts, and darkness to convince the pharaoh that keeping the Israelite slaves was not in Egypt's best interests.

Each plague brought the pharaoh's reluctant capitulation to Moses' demands, but a quick retraction after the plague was removed. In a dramatic finale, God brought the dreaded *plague on first-born males*, similar to but more effective than the Egyptian decree that the infant Moses barely escaped. When the plague struck down his own son, the pharaoh's resistance collapsed.

Until this time, the Israelites had doubted Moses and His claims to be God's chosen Messenger, their Deliverer from Egyptian slavery. But now, with the proof of an invincible leader who had crushed the dreaded pharaoh himself, they followed Moses, some reluctantly, but all without question. A long procession of thousands, with carts, donkeys, cattle, and all their possessions, fell in behind Moses, on their way to the Promised Land.

The Biblical account of the Israelites and their march to freedom continued, using a series of miracles to overcome major obstacles. After several weeks, the Egyptians started to forget the plagues they had suffered, and the pharaoh noticed how the progress of the pyramid projects had slowed, now that a large part of his slave work force was gone.

Reports on the slow-moving marchers convinced the pharaoh that their attempts to cross the Red Sea would prove insurmountable; it would cause great confusion and long delays, and thus give him the opportunity he needed to catch them by surprise and recover his lost slave workers. He quickly assembled a strike force and set out for the Red Sea.

The first major obstacle for the Israelite caravan did

indeed appear at the Red Sea—how to cross with animals, loaded wagons and carts, and all their belongings. It would take a miracle to get everyone across safely. They looked to their leader, Moses. He prayed to God, stretched His staff out over the waters, and complied—the needed miracle took place!

The waters parted to provide a dry path for the marchers to cross. The pursuing Egyptians arrived just as the last Israelite stragglers emerged at the opposite side of the dry sea bed. The dry path remained in place until all of the Egyptian chariots racing toward their prey were in the way of the water walls that were now released to wash over and spread havoc among the pursuers. The survivors gave up the pursuit and the Israelites proceeded according to plan.

When they reached Mount Sinai, Moses ascended the mountain to perform the most important task of His Dispensation, a significant event in the history of human civilization—Moses brought the Tablets of the Ten Commandments (representing God's law) to His people, the Israelites (representing mankind).

For the next forty years, Moses led His people through the desert wilderness until another generation of wanderers grew up, instilled with the message of God. The wanderers were now prepared for the next stage of their spiritual journey, the return to Canaan and the conquest of the Promised Land.

The Bible's account of Moses' mission ends at the entrance to Canaan. Moses was one hundred twenty years of age when He ascended Mt. Nebo, a peak outside Canaan, near Jericho, for one look at the Promised Land before He returned to His Lord.

LEGACY OF JUDAISM

The Torah, the Holy Scriptures Moses revealed to the Jews, is the foundation of Judaism, and thus ranks Moses above all other prophets.[28] The importance of Moses' role in the spiritual development of human civilization is difficult to overstate.

Fundamental to the message of Judaism is **the law**. The concept of justice and the unifying effect of one law for everyone has made respect for law, love of learning, education, and intellectual achievement supreme virtues among the Jewish people. In pursuit of these supreme virtues, the dedication of the Jews to God's law is inextricably entwined with Jewish history.

For the past thirty centuries the Jews have survived as an identifiable people. Surprisingly, they were exiled from their own land for twenty of those centuries. And despite the odds, they managed to maintain their cultural identity, and fight their way back to recover their native land (now the nation of Israel), a feat unparalleled in human history.

Although many consider this historical event simply a rare combination of coincidence and incredible good fortune, both the exile and return of the Jews were prophesied in several Biblical passages.

Moses warned the Israelites that their failure to heed God's laws would lead to their exile. **"And the LORD will scatter you among all peoples, from one end of the earth to the other.** (Deuteronomy 28:64) **When their thoughts turned again to God, Moses continued, "And when all these things come upon you, the blessing and the curse, ...where the LORD your God has driven you, And return to the LORD your God, and obey his voice..., you and your children, ...then the LORD your God will restore your fortunes, and have compassion upon you, and he will gather you again from all the peoples, where the LORD your God has scattered you."** (Deuteronomy 30:1-3)

The prophet Isaiah also referred to the exile and return when he proclaimed that God will **"assemble the outcasts of Israel, and gather the dispersed of Judah from the four corners of the earth."** (Isaiah 11:12)

THE PROMISE OF BAHÁ'U'LLÁH

Moses connected His message from God with other Messengers to come. In the fifth book of the Torah, Moses foretold another prophet, a descendant from a neighboring people, whom God would send. *Neighboring people* refers to a more distant bloodline than His own people, the Israelites.

The LORD your God will raise up for you a Prophet like me from among you, from your brethren—him you shall heed... And the LORD said to me, ...I will raise up for them a Prophet like you from among their brethren, and I will put my words in his mouth; and he shall speak to them all that I command him. (Deuteronomy 18:15-19)

Bahá'ís say that the use of the term, *brethren*, is more logically a reference to the distant bloodline, to Muhammad, and later to Bahá'u'lláh, than it is to Jesus, as Christians claim. If He had meant Jesus, the term seed would have been used.[29]

Before He died, Moses described the line of Prophets who would follow Him. **"The LORD came from Sinai,** (referring to Himself) **and dawned from Seir** (referring to Jesus) **upon us; he shone forth from Mount Paran,** (referring to Muhammad) **he came from the ten thousands of Holy Ones"** (referring to Bahá'u'lláh). (Deuteronomy 33:2) *Seir* is a mountain in Galilee and *Paran* is a mountain in Arabia. References to Bahá'u'lláh in the Bahá'í Writings call Him *the Lord of Hosts*.

The Minor Prophets preached about the *Latter Days*, the *Glory of God*, and the *Mountain of God* (a reference to Mount Carmel, present site of the Bahá'í World Center). In that future time, they said, the Lord (God's representative) would be known by a new name. He would judge among people and nations. War would be abolished and all of humanity would live in universal peace.

In that day they will come to you, from Assyria (Persia) **to Egypt, and from Egypt to the River, from sea to sea, and from mountain to mountain.** (Micah 7:11-12)

...the majesty of Carmel and Sharon, they shall see the glory of the Lord, (Bahá'u'lláh in Arabic means 'Glory of God') **the majesty of our God.** (Isaiah 35:2)

It shall come to pass in the latter days that the mountain of the house of the Lord shall be established as the highest of the mountains, and shall be raised above the hills; and all the nations shall flow to it, and many peoples shall come and

say: "Come, let us go up to the mountain of the Lord, to the house of the God of Jacob; that he may teach us his ways and that we may walk in his paths." For out of Zion shall go forth the law, and the word of the Lord from Jerusalem. He shall judge between the nations. He shall decide for many peoples; and they shall beat their swords into plowshares, and their spears into pruning hooks; nation shall not lift up sword against nation, neither shall they learn war any more.
(Isaiah 2:2-4)

As I live, says the King, whose name is the Lord of hosts, like Tabor among the mountains, and like Carmel by the sea, shall one come.
(Jeremiah 46:18)

And I will set my throne in Elam, (Persia) and destroy their king and princes, says the Lord.
(Jeremiah 49:38)

The nations shall see your vindication and all the kings your glory: and you shall be called by a new name, which the mouth of the Lord will give.
(Isaiah 62:2)

CHRISTIANITY

Christianity was born in the heart of Judaism. Jesus was a Jew descended in a direct line from Jewish ancestors. All of the early Christians were Jews. The term Christ is the Greek word for *messiah*, a Jewish concept meaning "*anointed one.*"[30] Christians claim that Jesus is the spiritually anointed one who was promised in the Jewish scriptures. Jews reject this claim; Baháʼís accept it. Many (but not all) Christians claim that Jesus is God; this claim is rejected by the Baháʼí Faith and by all the other religions.

Jesus was a Jew who preached to Jews in the Holy Land about God and His message for that time. He is considered the founder of what later became a religion of statistical superlatives. Christianity claims more followers than any other religion. Geographically it is the most widespread. Its scriptures have been translated into the most languages. It is the primary religion of the world's most powerful nations. It controls more of the world's wealth than any other religion.

Jesus is the subject of more books, articles, studies and writings than any other single topic. And finally, but on the negative side, Christianity is also subdivided into more sects and splinter groups than any other religion.

However its detractors might criticize it, the preeminence of Christianity as the world's most recognized religion is unquestioned. Based on its present prominence, one could say **"that Jesus' teachings let loose upon the soul and heart of man a spiritual power such as never had been known in the world before. Historians have said that Jesus' teachings have done more to elevate human nature and civilization than all the laws of legislators and the disquisitions of philosophers combined."**[31]

The intense probing and analysis of all this writing about Jesus inevitably raised questions about the accuracy of any statement about Him. The Baháʼí view of Jesus accepts what is written about Him in the Bible. The Guardian of the Baháʼí Faith, Shoghi Effendi, affirmed Jesus as a Manifestation of God, equal in all respects to the other Manifestations of God. Bahá'ís recognize **"the divine origin of all the Prophets of God—including Jesus Christ and the Apostle of God** (Muhammad)**... [T]he continuity of their Revelations is affirmed..."**[32]

As a religion separate from Judaism, Christianity was inspired by Jesus, but it was established by two of His followers, Saint Peter and Saint Paul. It was their unstinting efforts to spread the teachings of Jesus that resulted in the organization of the most prestigious institution in all of religious history, the Christian Church.

In the course of its two thousand-year history, the Christian religion has experienced many divisions. There are more than twenty five thousand divisions of Christianity, from the oldest and largest branch, the Roman Catholic Church, to independent small congregations, all affirming the Lordship of Jesus.

They differ on grounds that are both major and minor, from doctrinal views, or emphasis on special teachings, to small variations in rites and ceremonial practices. Despite these attacks on Christianity, its foundational structure, the stature of Jesus and the truths of His teachings, remained unassailable.

The two oldest branches of Christianity, the Roman Catholic and the Eastern (or Greek) Orthodox branches, separated after the Roman emperor, Constantine, established the eastern Roman capital at Byzantium, later called Constantinople. Each later broke off into numerous other branches and divisions.

The Western (Roman Catholic) branch, after centuries of corruption, lost a large portion of its followers in western and northern Europe to Protestantism. Soon Protestantism also broke down into its own separate sects. Such division in the interpretations of religious teachings weakened Christianity.

The connecting thread among all of these Christian branches and splinter groups is their common devotion to the teachings of Jesus as written in the holiest Christian scriptures, the Gospels. Sadly and perversely, the principal teaching of Jesus, love for God and fellow men, was not sufficient to prevent the religious wars, hostility and wholesale slaughter of hundreds of thousands in the name of Jesus. This characterized the relations among these various sects during most of Christianity's history.

THE PRE-CHRISTIAN WORLD

Moses left the Israelite wanderers at the borders of the Promised Land more than one thousand years earlier. They evolved socially during the space of two hundred years from a loose confederation of tribes led by elders and judges to the glory days of a feared and respected Jewish nation united by their warrior-hero, King David, and his son, the widely celebrated King Solomon.

From that high point in their political history, the Jews experienced a long period of growing disunity and gradual political decay. Internal tensions split the kingdom into two nations, Israel and Judah. The Assyrian Empire assimilated Israel, the northern nation; the Babylonian Empire then conquered Assyria and also Judah. The Persian Empire in turn conquered Babylonia and restored the Jews of Judah from their exile back to the Holy Land.

In subsequent wars against numerous stronger foes, including the undefeated conqueror, Alexander the Great, Judah was permitted to maintain its identity as a subject state. But the Roman conquest of Judah, then called *Judea*, ended with the expulsion of the Jews and the loss of their homeland.

Of all the subjugated peoples making up the Roman Empire, the Judeans were among the most rebellious. **"One rebellion after another was sweeping the turbulent land of Judea as political zealots and warrior messiahs stirred the population into successive uprisings against Rome."**[33]

Rome could not afford to allow this tiny subject people to flout its authority, and serve as a model for other colonies chafing under the Roman yoke. A large and costly Roman garrison maintained in Judea could barely contain an uneasy peace. An almost constant political tension made the country seem like a powder keg with a lit fuse. This was the kind of world in which Jesus appeared.

JESUS

Most of what we know of the life of Jesus is based upon the Gospels, the first four books of the New Testament. Each tells the story of His life as seen by the Evangelists, Saints Matthew, Mark, Luke and John.

Jesus was born in Bethlehem, during the reign of King Herod, who ruled the country under the protection (and control) of the Roman Empire. As a child, Jesus displayed remarkable wisdom and great interest in matters related to God. On one occasion when He was twelve, Jesus was found in the temple courts in Jerusalem, in deep discussion with the learned, **"and all who heard Him were amazed at his understanding and his answers."** (Luke 2:47)

Jesus was almost thirty years of age when John (the Baptist) began preaching about the coming of the Messiah, the Great One who would bring the people back to God. John attracted many followers whom he baptized in the River Jordan as a symbol of their repentance for their sins. John baptized Jesus, after which, according to the Bible, the spirit of God in the form of a dove descended upon Jesus.

He then went into the wilderness to prepare Himself spiritually for His teaching mission, and when He returned after forty days, He undertook His duties as God's chosen Messenger.

Jesus spent a good deal of time among humble artisans and fishermen in the area around the Sea of Galilee, today called Lake Tiberias. He preached in synagogues and in open areas, anywhere He could gather an audience. It was in the Galilee that He began selecting disciples to travel with Him, to teach them His message. He appointed twelve disciples, or apostles, to carry on His teaching work after Him.

The spiritual message that Jesus brought provided a sharp contrast to the short-term plots and rebellions against the Roman oppressors, which were the themes of the other messiah claimants at that time. For the great majority of the people who heard Him, His words of comfort kindled in their hearts a spark of love and hope they had never before known.

His audiences were mainly the poor, the

downtrodden and the uneducated. Jesus taught them the word of God through simple homilies that reached their hearts. He made extensive use of parables—short allegorical stories that illustrated spiritual truths.

There were numerous reports about His miraculous cures and healing of the diseased and crippled. He electrified the masses with His words. Wherever He went, crowds gathered to sit at the feet of this gentle soul whose love seemed to reach out and embrace them in a protective aura.

For three years Jesus spread the word of God among these people, and they responded by flocking to Him in great numbers. As His fame spread, the Jewish clergy became suspicious and wary of the claims imputed to Jesus as the promised Messiah.

He was summoned by the highest court in the land, the *Sanhedrin*, for a hearing to test these claims. The gathered judges failed to understand the spiritual nature of His replies to their questions, and thus He was found guilty of violating religious law. Jesus was sent to the Roman procurator, or governor, Pontius Pilate, for Roman judgment and subsequent punishment.

According to the Bible, Pontius Pilate did not consider the charges against Jesus worthy of a death penalty, but the clergy demanded it. Pilate was unwilling to strain further the already tense relations between Rome and the Jews.

For Pilate, political expediency took precedence over justice. It was easier to sacrifice an innocent and powerless Jew than to challenge the powerful clergy. So he agreed to Jesus' execution as an easy way out and '*washed his own hands*' of the matter.

Pilate's cowardly surrender to expediency coincides with findings of later scholars, who said existing records reported the Roman procurator to be violent, immoral, unjust and corrupt. Pilate's ruling in this case also revealed his own weakness and cowardice at confronting the Jewish clergy by taking the path of least resistance at the expense of his own better judgment. But then, the Roman attitude toward Jews was complete contempt; Jews were considered no better than animals.

During his tenure as procurator, Pontius Pilate made several decisions that resulted in armed opposition, and one that was quelled in a bloody massacre extending throughout the province of Samaria. In the year 37 CE, Pontius Pilate was recalled to Rome on account of his brutality.[34]

The Jews condemned Jesus for His heretical claims and the Romans killed Him to forestall a political uprising. Jesus was sentenced to death by crucifixion, the most common punishment of that day. Three days after His death, He was reported to have risen to heaven. His body, which had been entombed securely in a cave, was never found.

THE PROMISE OF BAHÁ'U'LLÁH

Bahá'ís believe that Christian scriptures, even more than the Torah, contain numerous references to Bahá'u'lláh through the spiritual return of Jesus, not His physical return. Bahá'ís believe that Moses referred to Bahá'u'lláh when He said God "would raise up a Prophet from the brethren of the Jews." Jesus also indicated Bahá'u'lláh in several Bible quotations:

And I will pray the Father, and he shall give you another Counselor, to be with you for ever; even the Spirit of truth; whom the world cannot receive, because it neither sees him nor knows him... (John 14:16-7)

I have yet many things to say to you, but you cannot bear them now. When the Spirit of truth comes, he will guide you into all the truth; for he will not speak on his own authority, but whatever he hears he will speak, and he will declare to you the things that are to come. He will glorify me, for he will take what is mine and declare it to you. (John 16:12-14)

But the Counselor ...whom the Father will send in my name, he will teach you all things, and bring to your remembrance all that I have said to you. (John 14:26)

But when the Counselor comes, whom I shall send to you from the Father, even the Spirit of truth, who proceeds from the Father, he will bear witness to me... (John 15:26)

Nevertheless I tell you the truth: it is to your advantage that I go away: for if I do not go away, the Counselor will not come to you; but if I go, I will send him to you. (John 16:7)

The signs of the end times were clearly described as a time of great turmoil:

And when you hear of wars and rumors of wars, do not be alarmed; this must take place, but the end is not yet. For nation will rise against nation, and kingdom against kingdom; there will be earthquakes in various places, there will be famines; this is but the beginning of the sufferings... But take heed to yourselves; for they will deliver you up to councils; and you will be beaten in synagogues... (Mark 13:7-9)

And there will be signs... and upon the earth distress of nations... Men fainting with fear and with foreboding of what is coming on the world; for the powers of the heavens will be shaken.
(Luke 21:25-6)

For then there will be great tribulation, such as has not been from the beginning of the world until now, no, nor ever shall be. (Matthew 24:21)

For men will be lovers of self, lovers of money, proud, arrogant, disobedient to their parents, ungrateful, unholy... haters of good... lovers of pleasures rather than lovers of God, holding the form of religion, but denying the power of it. Avoid such people. (2 Timothy 3:1-5)

All the religions (including Hinduism and Buddhism) spoke of a *return* and a *new day*. Despite the good intentions, the praying, and the studying of their religious writings, most people were unprepared when the time came.

The Jewish elders who examined the claims of Jesus did not recognize their spiritual nature. Jesus reiterated Moses' prophecy about a coming prophet from their 'brethren', and warned that His own promised return (the Bahá'í view of the spiritual return in the person of Bahá'u'lláh) would go largely unnoticed, and that He would have a *new name*.

Being asked by the Pharisees when the kingdom of God was coming, he answered them, **"He who** conquers, I will make him a pillar in the temple of my God, never shall he go out of it, and I will write on him the name of my God, and the name of the city of my God, the New Jerusalem, which comes down from my God out of heaven, and my own new name." (Revelation 3:12)

The kingdom of God is not coming with signs to be observed; nor will they say, 'Lo here it is!' or 'There!' for behold, the kingdom of God is in the midst of you. (Luke 17:20-21)

Watch therefore, for you do not know on what day your Lord is coming. (2 Matthew 24:42)

Take heed, watch; for you do not know when the time will come. (Mark 13:33)

If you will not awake, I will come like a thief, and you will not know at what hour I will come upon you. (Revelation 3:3)

...you must understand this, that scoffers will come in the last days with scoffing... saying, "Where is the promise of his coming?"
(2 Peter 3:10)

Moses said, 'The Lord God will raise up for you a prophet from your brethren, as he raised me up. You shall listen to him in whatever he tells you. (Acts 3:22)

George Townshend, a canon at St. Patrick's Cathedral, Dublin, Ireland, wrote of a common Christian misconception that Christ was the Lord of Hosts described in the Old Testament. He referred to the Jewish prophecy that the Jews would have been scattered among the nations and living in misery and degradation when the Lord of Hosts came. However, the Romans expelled the Jews from their homeland in 70 CE, many years after the death of Jesus.

It was common practice to read in all churches on Christmas morning the passage from Isaiah (9:6-7) about the Lord of Hosts, which Christians mistakenly believe is a reference to Christ:

For to us a child is born, to us a son is given; and the government shall be upon his shoulder, and his name shall be called "Wonderful, Counselor, Mighty God, Everlasting Father, Prince of Peace." Of the increase of his government and of peace there shall be no end, upon the throne of David, and over his kingdom, to establish it, and to uphold it with justice and with righteousness from this time forth and for ever-more. The zeal of the LORD of hosts will do this.

Townshend noted that Jesus specifically repudiated some of the titles given by Isaiah:

Isaiah: Everlasting Father
Jesus: "my Father is greater than I" (John 14:28)
Isaiah: Prince of Peace
Jesus: "I came not to send peace, but a sword" (Matthew 10:34)
Isaiah: with justice and with righteousness from this time forth and for ever-more
Jesus: "My kingdom is not of this world" (John 18:36)

Townshend went on to say:

"Probably few churchgoers realize today that the Gospel of Christ as known to the few in the pulpit is wholly different from the Gospel which Christ preached in Galilee as recorded in the Bible. In spite of Christ's promise of further revelation of Truth, through the Comforter, through His own return, through the Spirit of Truth, the Christian Church regards His revelation as final, and itself the sole trustee of true religion."[35]

ZOROASTRIANISM

Zoroaster (also Zarathushtra) was a Manifestation of God who brought God's message to ancient Persia. His influence coincided with the period of the great Zoroastrian kings beginning with Cyrus the Great, and extending through the Achaemenian and Sassanian dynasties.

The teachings of Zoroaster emphasized pure thoughts, pure words, and pure deeds. Zoroaster's message of one God was advanced far beyond the old nature worship that existed in Persia at that time. He also spoke of a succession of messengers who appear from age to age for the enlightenment of mankind.

Zoroaster prophesied a time of the end, a great, final battle for the minds and souls of mankind between the forces of light, represented by the good spirit, Spenta Mainyu, and the forces of darkness, led by the evil spirit, Angra Mainyu. From this battle, God, called *Ahura Mazda*, would emerge triumphant, and mankind would then reside in a golden age of peace.

The sacred scriptures of the Zoroastrians are known as the Avesta[36], which includes hymns (*the Gathas*), among the oldest and most important of the Zoroastrian Holy writings. The Gathas mention a time when the present cycle of the world will be completed and the consummation of the ages will have arrived. At that time, the last of the world's saviors, the *Shah-Bahram*, will arise to initiate a new cycle.

Persia in Zoroaster's time was a lawless, immoral, wild, nomadic tribal society. Witchcraft and demon-worship were a common practice. It was Zoroaster's mission to develop an agricultural society that was ethical and spiritual.

After He received the call from God at age thirty, Zoroaster encountered great difficulty in spreading God's word. It was ten years before Zoroaster won His first believer—His own cousin. He managed to take His teachings to the royal court, where after much opposition (including Zoroaster's imprisonment and starvation) the king was won over, and Zoroaster began attracting more believers.

It is said He was murdered while at prayer. After His

death, Zoroaster's teachings were corrupted and changed to a dualistic concept in which the good God of light, Ahura Mazda, was engaged in an endless struggle with the dark, evil spirit, Ahriman, for control of man's soul.

The *Magi*, a priestly class, later ritualized Zoroaster's teachings, and kept a holy flame burning in the temple. The purity theme emphasized ritual over ethics. After they became the state religion, Zoroaster's teachings were further corrupted, moving from a dualism to polytheism.

When the Persian Empire collapsed, the state religion was still further infected with a cult called *Mithraism*, which was devoted to the worship of the god, Mithras, who in earlier times had been one of the guardian spirits, a lesser deity in the Zoroastrian cosmology.

The religion became international, and spread rapidly all over the Roman Empire, and as far north as Britain. When Christianity became the state religion of Rome under Constantine the Great, all other religions were mercilessly suppressed.

Of those who did not convert to Christianity, many sought a new and suddenly popular cult called *Manichaeism*, proclaimed in the year 215 CE by Mani, a Persian who claimed to be the return of Jesus. When Mani was captured and executed in the year 276 CE, his cause died soon after.

Zoroastrianism survived the ravages of its many corruptions, but it never regained its lost popularity. It is reported that no more than 130,000 Parsees in India and 25,000 Gabars in Iran still practice Zoroastrianism.[37]

ISLAM

The roots of the Bahá'í Faith are found in the history of Islam, much as the roots of Christianity are found in the history of Judaism.

The founder-prophet of the Islamic Faith, Muhammad, was an Arabian[38] caravan merchant who, in the year 622 CE, proclaimed to His pagan Arab neighbors that He had been given the message of Allah, the one true God, in fulfillment of the teachings of Moses and Jesus. Allah is the Arabic word for God, the same God of the Jews and the Christians.

Muhammad said that Moses and Jesus were earlier Messengers of God and that He was next in the series of God's messengers sent to update the earlier messages. Islam was the new message brought by Muhammad as a continuation and renewal of the Word of God as revealed by Moses, and later by Jesus.

MUHAMMAD

Muhammad was born about the year 570 CE in Mecca, a trading post serving as the commercial and religious center for the many tribes of the Arabian Peninsula. Europe at this time was starting its descent into the Dark Ages.

A number of Jewish and Christian tribes were living on the peninsula in what is now Saudi Arabia and Yemen, but the majority of the Arabian tribes were a wild nomadic society engaged in fighting and thieving, and practicing a pagan worship of idols and numerous tribal gods. One of their most odious practices was female infanticide, the killing of unwanted female infants.

In Mecca a special structure enshrined the idols and images of the most popular deities. This was the *Kaaba*, a pantheon attracting pagan pilgrim worshippers from all parts of the peninsula.

Muhammad's family was of the Hashem clan, part of the powerful and wealthy Quraish tribe, which controlled the commercial activity among the crowds of pilgrims in Mecca visiting the shrines and the idols in the Kaaba. Muhammad's father, Abdullah, died before He was born and His mother died when He was six.

His grandfather assumed the guardianship of Muhammad, and when he died two years later, Muhammad was passed on again, this time to an uncle, Abu Talib.

Like the earlier Prophets, little is known of Muhammad's early life. As a young man, He worked for a wealthy widow, Khadija, who, impressed by His business judgment and honesty, later married Him. Their twenty-six year marriage was happy and fruitful, producing five boys and one girl. Only His daughter, *Fatima*, survived her Father.

Muhammad was a member of a group of seekers of truth who rejected the existing pagan practices. From time to time Muhammad used to go alone for meditation to a cave on Mt. Hira, outside of Mecca.

According to Muslim tradition, it was there that one night, at the age of forty, He received His call to Prophethood through an appearance by the angel Gabriel. After several such visitations, the fearful and reluctant Muhammad, with encouragement from Khadija, accepted His mission. His message to His fellow Meccans focused on repentance before the one true God, abandonment of pagan idols and corrupt practices, and social reforms such as honest trading, better treatment for women, care of orphans, and an end to the practice of infanticide.

As might be expected, Muhammad's proclamation of His prophethood (and His program of reforms) was rejected. At first this rejection was passive—He was ignored. In three years Muhammad had won but thirty converts, including Khadija, Ali (His cousin and son-in-law), and a wealthy merchant named Abu-Bakr (who, after Muhammad's death, was chosen to be His successor and the first caliph). As His preaching continued, so grew the hostility of His audience. He was mocked, ridiculed, and then ostracized.

When He denounced the Kaaba's idol exhibit and its attraction for pagan pilgrims, the powerful Quraish tribal leaders took this as an attack on their major source of wealth. Muhammad was first threatened, then attacked, and later hounded unmercifully until finally He and His few followers had to flee for their lives, from Mecca to Yathrib.

Yathrib was the second chief town of the Arabian Peninsula, about 300 miles north of Mecca. It was the home of several Arab and Jewish tribes, all struggling for political power. The people saw this incessant power struggle as a deterrent to their economic well-being (they admired the profitable and well-organized operations of the rich Quraish tribe in Mecca).

They were impressed with the honesty and integrity of Muhammad and His teachings. They saw Him as the reformer and unifier they needed to change the corruption and economic bankruptcy of their internal tribal struggles.

A group of Yathrib elders offered Muhammad and his band of followers an opportunity to establish the reforms He preached, and promised to follow His leadership. This also gave Him a respite and a haven from the intensifying persecution of His Meccan tormentors. Muhammad and His dwindling band of Muslim followers had been under constant threat of death from their unrelenting foes. After the death of His wife, Khadija, and soon after that, of His beloved uncle, Abu Talib, Muhammad agreed to the offer.

The migration (known as the *hegira, or hijra*) of Muhammad and His beleaguered Muslim followers to Yathrib in the year 622 CE was the highlight of His mission and the turning point in His fortunes. It also marks the beginning of the Muslim calendar.

For Muslims, the hegira is comparable to Moses presenting the Ten Commandments to the Israelites. The move to Yathrib was carefully planned in stages to avoid the Meccan authorities who might try to prevent their escape. But Muhammad's determination to win the hearts of the Meccans never wavered. For practical reasons, He agreed to move to Yathrib with His followers and establish a community of God, from which He could resume His efforts to win Mecca.

With Muhammad in charge, Yathrib soon became a united city. Its name was changed to *Medina* (Arabic for city), from which now emanated a spiritual power of dedication, optimism and brotherhood. The brotherhood of the love of God took precedence over family and tribal loyalties. All rallied to a defense of Islam, and it was this feeling of unity that strengthened the power of the Muslims against the overwhelming numbers of their enemies.

Muhammad's persistent efforts ultimately won over the people of Mecca in 630, and then spread to all of Arabia, and when He died two years later, in 632, the foundation had been set for a whirlwind expansion of the *Message of Islam* by military force.

ISLAMIC EMPIRE

For the first time Arabs were united by an Arab faith preached by an Arab prophet. Arab armies, inspired and united by the fire of Muhammad's message, formed a victorious tide that pushed outward in all directions, carrying the banner of Islam throughout the Middle East, in an eastern direction as far as India, and west to North Africa and Europe.

The Persian and the Byzantine Empires controlled the territories surrounding the Arabian Peninsula. Both had become exhausted from years of constant warfare with each other, and from incessant guerrilla skirmishes with disaffected groups within their own borders.

From their Medina headquarters in the heartland of Arabia, the Islamic forces spread outward and crushed both the Persians and the Byzantines, and suddenly they found themselves almost unopposed. Thus encouraged, they moved on into Syria and Palestine. The lightning campaigns of the Islamic armies swept forth over the Syrian capital, Damascus, in 635, then Palestine in 638, and Egypt in 655. By 705, all of North Africa had come under Islamic control.

From North Africa, they continued their drive into Spain in 711 and crossed the Pyrenees Mountains into France, where they were finally defeated in 732 at the Battle of Tours by the forces of Charles Martel, a Frankish chieftain who later became the grandfather of Charlemagne.

Europe thus remained Christian and the Muslims had to retreat back to Spain, behind the Pyrenees, where they proceeded to consolidate the new Islamic Empire, larger than the Roman Empire had been at the height of its glory. This Islamic civilization became the wonder of the known world.

The Christian villages and cities of Europe were suffering from cold, disease, poverty, unsanitary conditions, and the ignorance and superstition of a society chained by the restrictions of feudalism. At the same time, the Islamic civilization was enjoying the benefits of universal education, lighted streets and paved roads.

In the arts, music, literature and architecture, and in the sciences, medicine, astronomy and mathematics, the Islamic achievements made significant contributions to human knowledge. Arabic became the official language of a unified empire in which Arabs were but a small, yet powerful, minority.

The first major disagreement among Muslims was about succession to the Prophet's leadership. This occurred almost at the moment Muhammad breathed His last, and it split Islam into its first two major groups. The smaller group, the *Shiah*[39] sect of Islam, claimed that Muhammad intended the leadership of the faithful to be inherited by His blood descendants. These chosen ones, called *Imams*[40], or leaders, were deemed infallible in their leadership functions.

An opposing view is the one held by the great majority of Muslims, the *Sunni*[41]. The Sunni claimed that the way of the Prophet—His teachings, should govern the selection of His successors. It was the Sunni who, less than thirty years after Muhammad's death, succeeded in establishing the first of two successive ruling dynasties of the Islamic Empire, the Umayyad and the Abbasid families. In Muhammad's time these families were numbered among His most relentless enemies. Because the Bahá'í Faith was born in Persia, within the Shiah branch of Islam, it is the Shiah perspective that is examined more closely in this book.

The political intrigue and power struggle for leadership of the Muslim community immediately after the death of Muhammad went unnoticed in the meteoric rise of the most brilliant civilization the world had known up to that time. The Islamic civilization reached its peak about the tenth century. Its decline became evident first when the Islamic empire became the prime target of the dreaded Mongol armies of

Genghis Khan in the twelfth and thirteenth centuries. The second piece of evidence was the growth of a number of offshoot Islamic sects, and the third was a steadily shrinking empire. Probably the greatest decline occurred in Persia, where the Shiah sect was most prevalent.

Political maneuvering among Muhammad's closest followers after His passing resulted in the selection of the Sunni candidate, Muhammad's father-in-law, Abu-Bakr. He was selected as *caliph*[42] over the Shiah choice of Ali, Muhammad's cousin and son-in-law; Ali's wife was Fatima, Muhammad's only surviving child.

After the passing of Abu-Bakr, the second and third caliphs, Omar and Othman served in turn, until their murder, by assassination. Ali was finally selected as the next caliph.

The Shiahs believed Ali to be Muhammad's own choice to succeed Him. Although he was the fourth caliph appointed by the power elite of the Muslims to be their official leader, Ali is considered by the Shiahs to be the first Imam in direct hereditary line from Muhammad; the first three caliphs are considered usurpers.

To the [Shiahs], Ali was not the fourth in a long line of caliphs but the first in a line of divinely guided imams. The Imamate is a fundamental precept of Shiism and the one that most distinguishes it from Sunni Islam... the Imam is a divinely inspired, infallible spiritual leader.[43]

BASIC TEACHINGS

Like the Torah, the holy book of the Jews, and the Gospels, holy book of the Christians, the Muslims have their own holy book, the *Qur'an*[44], their basic source of divine authority. This is the word of God as given by Muhammad.

The Qur'an prohibits gambling, usury, drinking, and all forms of vice. It is the first of the Holy Books to restrict the practice of polygamy; it teaches belief in all the Prophets of God. Muhammad specifically directed His followers to protect Christians and Jews, and allow them to practice their faiths freely.

Although there is universal agreement among the

Muslims regarding the prime authority of the Qur'an, there are, like Judaism and Christianity, numerous groups within each faith who cling to their own variations of belief in the holy book and their own interpretations of its teachings.

While the Qur'an consists of God's words proclaimed by Muhammad, a secondary authority called the *sunna*, the path, or the Way of the Prophet, are the utterances of Muhammad (also called *hadith*) on religious practice, social affairs and interpretations of the Qur'an. A third authority is the *sharia*, a code of man-made law based upon the Prophet's teachings.

Muslims view Muhammad as mortal, but infallible. There is no priesthood, but there is an informal group of religious positions, such as *qadis* (judges), *ulama* (legal experts), *mujtahids* (doctors of law) and, among the Shiah sect of Islam, a broad category of theologians called mullas. All of these are sometimes identified as Muslim clergy, but they are less formal than the lines of authority in the Christian hierarchies.

The objective of life, Muhammad said, is to fulfill the commands of God (as written in the Qur'an) in the hope of admission to Paradise. This is accomplished by following the five pillars of Islam[45]:

Shahada—the profession of faith—"There is no god but God, and Muhammad is the messenger of God."

Ritual Prayer—five times daily, at dawn, midday, afternoon, evening and night.

Zakat—alms-tax, a mandatory donation to charity.

Fasting—during Ramadan, one of the twelve lunar months of the Islamic calendar, from dawn to dusk.

Hajj—pilgrimage to Mecca at least once in a lifetime, if possible.

Starting with Ali in 655, there were twelve Imams in direct line up to the year 873, when the twelfth appointed Imam, Muhammad al-Muntazar,[46] only a child at the time, withdrew into *concealment* to escape the fate of his predecessors, most of whom had been executed by enemies and assassins. Shiahs believe that this Imam will return from his concealment at the time of the end as the *Mahdi*[47] and the Qa'im.

It wasn't until the nineteenth century that the appearance of the twelfth Imam, the long-awaited

Mahdi and Qa'im, brought forth an unprecedented messianic fervor throughout the Muslim world. A gentle, charismatic young man, known to history as the Bab,[48] proclaimed Himself the return of the twelfth Imam, and the Herald of *He Whom God Will Make Manifest.*

THE PROMISE OF BAHÁ'U'LLÁH

In both Christian and Islamic scriptures, there are numerous references (but in veiled language) to the coming of the Kingdom. Both Jesus and Muhammad testified to the Bahá'í Era in reference to the 1260 Days. **"And I will grant my two witnesses power to prophesy for one thousand two hundred and sixty days, clothed in sackcloth."** (Revelation 11:3).

Religious scholars recognize prophetic days to be actual years. The year 1260 of the Islamic calendar corresponds to 1844, considered the beginning of the Bahá'í Era.

Both Jesus and Muhammad heralded the coming of Bahá'u'lláh and the Kingdom of God:

I (Jesus) **must preach the good news of the kingdom of God ... for I was sent for this purpose.** (Luke 4:43)

Surely we (God) **have sent thee** (Muhammad) **as a witness, good tidings** (of the coming of the Kingdom) **to bear...**[49] (Qur'an 48:8)

Bahá'u'lláh proclaimed His mission as the establishment of that Kingdom of God (Chapter 7) which all of His Predecessors referred to as a promise to be fulfilled at a later time.

Like Christians, Muslims are also alerted in their Scriptures to be watchful for the day when the *'voice of truth'* will summon the people to rise up from their graves of ignorance and heedlessness.

And listen for the day when the caller will call out from a place quite near—the day when they will hear the cry of truth. That will be the day of coming forth. (Qur'an 50:41-42)

And the earth will shine with the glory of its Lord, and the book will be set up, and the prophets and the witnesses will be brought forward and a just decision pronounced between them... (Qur'an

39:69)

Scriptures of the Islamic *Hadith*, also known as '*traditions of the Prophet*', include a number of references to Akka, the prison city just north of the seaport city of Haifa, Israel, wherein Bahá'u'lláh was incarcerated.

Enshrined in Akka is the tomb of Bahá'u'lláh, a major site for Bahá'í pilgrimage. Muslims generally do not reflect on the significance of these writings as do Bahá'ís.

I announce unto you a city, on the shores of the sea, white, whose whiteness is pleasing unto God – exalted be He! He that hath been bitten by one of its fleas is better, in the estimation of God, than he who hath received a grievous blow in the path of God. And he that raiseth therein the call to prayer, his voice will be lifted up unto Paradise.

There are kings and princes in Paradise. The poor of Akka are the kings of Paradise and the princes thereof.

A month in Akka is better than a thousand years elsewhere.

Blessed the man that hath visited Akka, and blessed he that hath visited the visitor of Akka.[50]

CHAPTER REVIEW—Earlier Religions

Summary
▶Abraham is recognized as the common ancestor of Judaism, Christianity, Zoroastrianism and Islam.
▶Moses was the major prophet of the Jewish people, their lawgiver, and their deliverer.
▶For 3,000 years and two exiles from their own land, the Jews managed to retain their own identity.
▶Despite their later corruptions, Zoroaster's teachings were faithful to the same One God taught by the other religions.
▶The Jews rejected Christianity's claim that it fulfills the prophecies of Judaism.
▶Jesus denounced the corruptions of the Jewish teachings as practiced by the Jews.
▶The Christians rejected Muhammad's claim to be a Messenger of God.
▶Muslims accept the Christian claim that Jesus was the Son of God.
▶Muhammad's teaching about the brotherhood of man influenced the establishment of the nation as a social institution.

Discussion
1. Identify some similarities among the founders of the earlier Holy Land religions.
2. What was God's covenant with Abraham?
3. How do the four western religions in the Holy Land trace their connections to Abraham?
4. Describe the major incidents in the life of Moses after His first encounter with the Divine on Mount Sinai.
5. What evidence from the Old Testament can be offered to show that Moses foretold the coming of Bahá'u'lláh?
6. How were Zoroaster's teachings corrupted after His death?
7. Identify the most prominent figures in the spread of Christianity.
9. Christianity professes a set of beliefs, or doctrines, that are part of the belief system of almost every true Christian. Name and describe at least two of these

doctrines.

10. Compare the 'five pillars' of the Islamic Faith with the teachings of the other Holy Land faiths.

Fill in the Blanks

A. Abraham, a native of the ancient Sumerian city of __.
B. Abraham's eldest son was named_____.
C. The first book of the Torah is called _____.
D. Through Moses, God inflicted the Egyptians with __ plagues. Name five of these.
E. The Roman attitude toward Jews was _____.
F. The four books of the Gospels are: _____, _____, _____ and _____.
G. The Zoroastrian Holy Scriptures are called _____.
H. Name two of the 'five pillars' of the Islamic Faith.
I. The leaders of the Shiah sect of Islam are called ____.

Check if this statement is generally accepted by:
Judaism Christianity Islam Bahá'í

Judaism	Christianity	Islam	Bahá'í	
☐	☐	☐	☐	- Physical resurrection of Jesus
☐	☐	☐	☐	- Physical resurrection of Moses
☐	☐	☐	☐	- Jesus is God incarnate
☐	☐	☐	☐	- God's covenant with Abraham

GOD'S MESSENGER

Judaism	Christianity	Islam	Bahá'í	
☐	☐	☐	☐	- Moses
☐	☐	☐	☐	-Muhammad
☐	☐	☐	☐	- Jesus
☐	☐	☐	☐	-Bahá'u'lláh

CHAPTER THREE—The Bab

THE ADVENT MOVEMENT

In the early nineteenth century, something strange occurred in both Christian and Muslim societies. Based upon prophecies contained in the holy books of all the great religions, expectation of the return of a Great Redeemer began to sweep across the world. In Europe and America, Christian groups such as the *Millerites*[51] had concluded from their study of the Bible that the promised return of Jesus Christ was imminent. More than one thousand clergymen in England and America preached the momentary return of Jesus.

Devout believers dressed in *ascension robes*[52] in preparation for Christ's arrival. This *advent*, or great arrival, became known as the "Advent Awakening" or the "Great Awakening." William Miller, and several hundred other Christian scholars, preached and wrote about Christ's expected return, according to their Biblical calculations and interpretations, in the period 1843 to 1845.

The chief reason for the widespread expectation was the sudden unfolding of the time prophecies in the scriptures of several of the great religions. In the Christian world many seekers of truth came to the same or similar conclusions. They found the mid-19th century to be the appointed time of Christ's return... Many prominent figures of that period discovered or proclaimed the exact or approximate *"time of the end,"* when God would *"cleanse His sanctuary"* and inaugurate a new era in human history.[53]

In the Muslim world, a comparable awakening was also underway. The Sunni sect, comprising the large majority of Muslims, also expected the return of Christ according to their reading of the Qur'an.[54] Some Muslims expected, independently of the Christians, the return of Christ in the year 1844.

Persia in the eighteenth century was in a pitiable

condition when compared with its glory days of empire twenty centuries earlier. The ancient Persian Empire in the days of Cyrus and Darius was influenced by the teachings of an earlier Manifestation of God, the Persian prophet, Zoroaster. But His teachings were corrupted, and in time, the empire lost its greatness and splendor.

Ten centuries later, in neighboring Arabia, the spiritual power of the Islamic revelation reached out to envelop and inspire all the people of the Middle East, and Persia once again had the opportunity to shine, in the glory and brilliance of the Islamic Empire. But the social decline that accompanied the corruption of God's message through Zoroaster was repeated, and Persia once again lost touch, this time with the truths contained in the teachings of Muhammad. Of all the countries in the world, Persia had once again become one of the most decadent.

John E. Esslemont, an Englishman who visited 'Abdu'l-Baha in the Holy Land after World War I, wrote of Persia's cultural abasement in the early twentieth century:

Her ancient glory seemed irretrievably lost. Her government was corrupt and in desperate financial straits; some of her rulers were feeble, and others monsters of cruelty. Her priests were bigoted and intolerant, her people ignorant and superstitious. Most of them belonged to the Shiah sect... but there were also considerable numbers of Zoroastrians, Jews and Christians, of diverse, and antagonistic sects.

All professed to follow sublime teachers who exhorted them to worship the one God and to live in love and unity, yet they shunned, detested and despised each other, each sect regarding the others as unclean, as dogs or heathens. Cursing... was indulged in to a fearful extent. It was dangerous for a Jew or a Zoroastrian to walk in the street on a rainy day, for if his wet garment should touch a Muhammadan, the Muslim was defiled, and the other might have to atone for the offense with his life. If a Muhammadan took money from a Jew, Zoroastrian or Christian he had to wash it before

he could put it in his pocket. If a Jew found his child giving a glass of water to a Muhammadan beggar he would dash the glass from the child's hand, for curses rather than kindness should be the portion of infidels! The Muslims themselves were divided into numerous sects, among whom strife was often bitter and fierce.

Social as well as religious affairs were in a state of hopeless decadence. Education was neglected. Western science and art were looked upon as unclean and contrary to religion. Justice was travestied. Pillage and robbery were of common occurrence. Roads were bad and unsafe for travel. Sanitary arrangements were shockingly defective.[55]

THE SHAYKHIS

Memories of former empire greatness contrasted sharply with Persia's present pretense to greatness, as a puppet state of the Turkish Empire[56]. The clergy had strayed far from the spirit of Islam, and maintained a firm hold on the beliefs and conduct of the people. But among one group of Shiah scholars, known as Shaykhis[57], the memories of closeness to God during Muhammad's time carried a note of expectation. According to the teachings of the Qur'an, a return of the twelfth Imam, the Mahdi and Qa'im, was to be expected soon.

In Persia, the founder of the Shaykhi sect, Shaykh Ahmad-i-Asai, and his successor, Siyyid[58] Kazim-i-Rashti, gradually aroused excitement and anticipation regarding the return of the Imam Mahdi, the twelfth Imam who had gone into concealment centuries ago. This matched the growing interest that contemporary Christian groups like the Millerites were raising in the western world about the imminent return of Jesus. And both groups focused on the year 1844 as '*the time.*'

Shaykh Ahmad, a devout Persian Muslim, was troubled by the corruption, ignorance and fanaticism displayed by the many Islamic sects whose squabbling had been diluting the teachings of Islam. After much prayer and soul-searching, he concluded that nothing could restore the early strength and purity of Islam except the power and authority of a new Messenger of God. He was also convinced that the time promised by Muhammad for the new Messenger was getting close. In 1770 he began to teach this doctrine.

His forceful arguments and extensive writing earned him great honors and many disciples. When he met the young Siyyid Kazim in 1815, the aging Shaykh was delighted that he had at last found the brilliant scholar who recognized his vision and who could carry on his mission. The two worked together until the Shaykh's death in 1826, after which the Siyyid carried on alone.

Siyyid Kazim continued to proclaim the imminent arrival of the Promised One until his death in 1843. He urged his disciples to persevere in their search. He promised the faithful ones that they would see the coming Messenger of God face to face, and some would even see His Successor, for twin Revelations were promised in all the holy books.

THE BAB

In Judaism, Christianity, and also in Islam, the stories we have about their Founders are often sketchy and lacking in detail because they lived thousands of years ago. Frequently the stories are mixed with legendary half-truths. There are some people who even question whether Moses and Jesus actually lived, saying that very little hard evidence can be found to prove Their existence. Because Muhammad lived more recently, there is more evidence to support proofs of His existence.

The Bahá'í Faith dates its beginnings to 1844, the year in which the Bab proclaimed His message. Numerous records provide detailed accounts of people and events, including written reports by official and professional observers and eyewitnesses, plus books, documents and newspaper accounts that confirm beyond doubt the basic facts of its major figures and events.

MULLA HUSAYN

One of the leading disciples of Siyyid Kazim was a young Shaykhi from the city of Bushihr. Mulla Husayn, as he was called, was following the urgings of his recently departed master, on the quest for the Promised One.

He arrived in the late afternoon at the outskirts of the city of Shiraz, Persia, on May 22, 1844. As he breathed a silent prayer for help in his search, he saw a young man hurrying toward him. The young man wore a green turban—a sign that he was a Siyyid, a descendant of the Prophet Muhammad.

The Siyyid, Ali-Muhammad, approached Mulla Husayn and greeted him like a long-lost brother. He invited him home to refresh himself after his long journey. After some cooling refreshments, Mulla Husayn told his host about his quest. Siyyid Kazim had described the Promised One as **"of illustrious descent ...more than twenty and less than thirty ...and endowed with innate knowledge." The Siyyid looked at him and said, "Behold, all these signs are manifest in me."**[59]

As Mulla Husayn sat in wonder and listened enraptured, the Siyyid proceeded to write and explain some religious teachings that Mulla Husayn earlier had found difficult to understand, but which he had not mentioned in their discussion. Mulla Husayn later wrote about that night of 22 May 1844:

I sat spellbound by his utterance, oblivious of time and of those who awaited me... Sleep had departed from me that night. I was enthralled by the music of that voice which rose and fell as he chanted... All the delights, all the ineffable glories, which the Almighty has recounted in His Book as the priceless possessions of the people of Paradise, these I seemed to be experiencing that night...

He then addressed me in these words: "O thou who art the first to believe in me! Verily, I say, I am the Bab, the Gate of God, and thou art the Babu'l-Bab, the gate of that Gate. Eighteen souls must, in the beginning, spontaneously and of their own accord, accept me and recognize the truth of my revelation. Unwarned and uninvited each of these must seek independently to find me."[60]

Jesus first proclaimed His mission to simple fishermen. Now the Promised One of this age had given the first declaration of His mission to this humble

Persian student, Mulla Husayn. Never before in the history of a religion has an eyewitness preserved the exact words of such an unforgettable meeting.

Siyyid Ali-Muhammad, the Bab, was born in Shiraz, Persia, on October 20, 1819. Both His father and mother were descended in a direct line from the Prophet Muhammad. While He was still a child, His father died. The Bab was raised by a maternal uncle, Haji Mirza Siyyid Ali, who later became one of His most devoted followers.

The Bab's formal schooling consisted of no more than elementary training in reading and writing, though He displayed both an unusually spiritual nature and surprising wisdom. His teacher at the school quickly recognized his new pupil's surprising insight and academic brilliance, and confessed his own inadequacy to further His education.

When He was fifteen, the Bab joined His uncle in the family business and soon won a reputation for ability and honesty in His business dealings.

He later married a distant cousin, Khadijih, the daughter of another merchant family. Two years later He held His momentous meeting with Mulla Husayn.

LETTERS OF THE LIVING

Within a few weeks after that meeting, seventeen seekers succeeded in reaching Him, and they accepted the Bab's claim to be the promised messenger. The Bab appointed these first eighteen believers as Letters of the Living.

One of these Letters was Tahirih, a talented poetess, brilliant, beautiful and utterly fearless in expressing her own views. She never actually met the Bab; she recognized Him as the Promised One in a dream. Tahirih had become a student of the Shaykhi leader, Siyyid Kazim, despite strong opposition from her husband and family. Her brother-in-law, also a student of Siyyid Kazim, was appointed a Letter of the Living. He carried with him a letter from her to the Bab, in which she declared her belief in Him, and He accepted her also as a Letter of the Living.

The Bab's final instructions to the Letters of the Living inspired them to go forth fearlessly and proclaim this *new day.*

O My beloved friends! You are the bearers of the name of God in this Day... The very members of your body must bear witness to the loftiness of your purpose, the integrity of your life, the reality of your faith, and the exalted character of your devotion... Such must be the purity of your character and the degree of your renunciation... You are the witnesses of the Dawn of the Promised Day of God...[61]

The Bab once again drew His disciples' attention to the One who was soon to come after Him, and for whom He was but the Herald.

I am preparing you for the advent of a mighty Day... Scatter throughout the length and breadth of this land, and with steadfast feet and sanctified hearts, prepare the way for His coming. Heed not your weaknesses and frailty, fix your gaze upon the invincible power of the Lord, your God, the Almighty...[62]

With such words as these the Bab launched His disciples upon their mission. On fire with these inspiring words, each of the Letters hastened to his own homeland to convey the message of his Lord

PUBLIC PROCLAMATION

The Bab now prepared Himself to publicly proclaim the new faith. He journeyed to the center of pilgrimage, the heart of Sunni Islam, to the twin cities of Mecca and Medina in December 1844.

In Mecca, at the holiest Muslim shrine, the Kaaba, the Bab called out to the pilgrim crowd three times, **"I am that Qa'im whose advent you have been awaiting!"**[63] He also wrote a tablet, or letter, to the Sherif of Mecca, the guardian of the shrines, proclaiming His mission. Having made public His declaration, the Bab returned to Persia, where a storm of excitement was brewing among both clergy and the public as a result of the teaching activities of the Letters of the Living.

The Bab's declaration was a serious challenge to the Muslim clergy, particularly the Shiahs. To the

Muslims, Muhammad was the *Seal of the Prophets*, the last prophet of God until Judgment Day. For Muslims, this meant that Muhammad's words, recorded in the Qur'an, contained all that humanity would need, and that there would be no further Revelations from God until that time.

In Persia, the Shiah clergy taught that the Hidden Imam (the last Imam, who had gone into concealment) had unlimited authority over all human affairs, and that the shah[64] and the clergy (who interpreted the Word of God) represented that authority.

The Muslim clergy violently opposed the Bab, and when it became clear that the Bab viewed the clergy as the main obstacle to the progress of Persia's spiritual development, their opposition knew no bounds.

The Shiah clergy in those days held power and authority almost equal to the shah himself. Islamic law was the law of the land, so the interpreters of that law could challenge the state, if necessary. Because the clergy addressed a captive audience from their pulpits, they could arouse mobs of fanatical townsfolk to defend what they said was the one true faith.

From 1845 to 1847 the *Babis*, or followers of the Bab, greatly increased in number. The Bab and His Letters of the Living, undaunted by the fierce opposition of the clergy, continued to spread the message of the New Day to everyone who would listen.

Among these new followers were a surprising number of the clergy themselves who, well versed in the teachings of the Qur'an, were astounded by the profound explanations of the uneducated Bab. The Bab was placed temporarily under house arrest while the furor His message had aroused raged throughout Persia, but He continued His teaching among the many visitors who were curious about His unprecedented claim.

VAHID

One of these visitors was Siyyid Yahyay-i-Darabi, one of the most respected and brilliant theologians in Persia, sent by Muhammad Shah, the ruler of Persia, as a special envoy to investigate the Bab. After three meetings with the Bab, this Siyyid was completely won over. He wrote a report of his meetings with the Bab and summed up his report to the king: **"Such was the state of certitude to which I had attained that...** [nothing could] **shake my confidence in the greatness of His Cause."**[65] The Bab named him Vahid (Peerless, or Unique).

Vahid did not return to the capital, but instead chose to serve his Lord. He journeyed to all parts of Persia, teaching the message of the Bab, and later, when the persecutions of the Babis escalated to mobs, violence and wholesale slaughter, Vahid ultimately suffered martyrdom fighting for his adopted cause. Vahid's story was one of many illustrious people who were won over to the cause of the Bab.

Muhammad Shah, the king, was impressed by Vahid's report of his conversion. He, too, wanted to meet the Bab. The Prime Minister, Haji Mirza Aqasi, who was also the shah's childhood tutor and closest advisor, feared losing his influence over the ailing king. He prevailed upon the king to postpone any meeting with the Bab, to avoid incurring the active opposition of the powerful clergy, and thereby aggravating the increasing political unrest created by the Bab's growing popularity.

CONFINEMENT AT MAH-KU

The Bab's temporary house arrest was changed to temporary seclusion, to keep Him from influencing the people. Under the guise of protecting Him from possible harm, the Prime Minister ordered the Bab removed to the fortress of Mah-Ku, in the northern province of Azerbaijan. It was hoped that the Bab could not sway the wild Kurdish tribes who lived there. The new faith, however, had already spread to Azerbaijan.

The modesty and gentle manners of their young captive soon subdued the governor and his staff at the fortress. Many placed themselves where they could catch a glimpse of Him each morning. Hundreds of curious visitors flocked to Mah-Ku hoping for an audience with the Bab.

During His nine-month stay at Mah-Ku, the Bab wrote the Persian Bayan, the holy book of the Babi Faith. In this book, He defined His mission as two-fold: to call the people back to God, and to announce the advent of the Promised One of all ages and all religions. He repeatedly emphasized that He was but the Herald of the One whom the scriptures of all religions had promised—the One the Bab called 'Him Whom God Shall Make Manifest.'

IMPRISONMENT AT CHIRIQ

The people of Persia were aware of the Bab's mistreatment by the clergy and the government. This persecution resulted in a growing sympathy for the Bab and His cause. The Prime Minister, frustrated by this setback to his plans, had the Bab transferred from Mah-Ku to the more remote castle prison of Chiriq, with strict orders that no one was to see Him.

But the word got out and the crowds who flocked to see the Bab exceeded those at Mah-Ku. Yahya Khan, the Kurdish leader in charge of the castle, was so fascinated by the Bab that he could not refuse anything He requested. Word of His growing popularity was carried back to reinforce the efforts of His followers in the larger population centers. The numbers of Babis multiplied.

The now desperate Prime Minister, fearful that the ailing shah might die and leave him to face the growing public tempest without royal support, entered into a plot with the powerful Muslim clergy to formally condemn the Bab's cause. In 1848, the Bab was ordered to Tabriz to stand trial before an ecclesiastical court. The purpose of the trial was not to examine the Bab's claims but to humiliate Him publicly.

A large crowd of curious people packed the courtroom. When the presiding officer asked, "Who do you claim to be," it was like the story of Christ retold. When Jesus was taken before the priests, He was asked, "Art thou the Christ?" He did not deny it, and that was all they needed to condemn Him. "I am," the Bab replied three times to the court waiting to condemn Him, "I am, I am the Promised One! I am the One whose name you have

for a thousand years invoked... whose advent you have longed to witness, and the hour of whose Revelation you prayed God to hasten."⁶⁶

Now that they had their evidence to condemn Him, the court had only insults and flippant inquiries to hurl at Him, which gave the Bab no opportunity to talk about His message. The official court report condemning the Bab was a mockery of justice. Dr. T.K. Cheyne, a Christian clergyman and a student of that period, wrote:

As for the Muslim accounts (of that trial), **those which we have before us do not bear the stamp of truth... Knowing what we do of the Bab, it is probable that he had the best of the argument, and that the leaders and functionaries attending that meeting were unwilling to put on record their own fiasco.**⁶⁷

After the trial, the Bab was taken to the home of the head of the court, where He was humiliated by the bastinado⁶⁸, personally applied by the infuriated head of the court. One of the blows struck the Bab across the face, causing an open wound. Dr. William Cormick, an English physician residing in Tabriz at that time, was called to treat the Bab. Dr. Cormick later wrote his impressions of the Bab:

He was a very mild and delicate-looking man, rather small in stature and very fair for a Persian, with a melodious soft voice... his whole look and deportment went far to dispose one in his favour.⁶⁹

After His punishment, the Bab was sent back, under heavy guard, to the prison of Chiriq. In Tabriz, the memory of the farcical trial became a victory for the Bab. Many who were present at the trial were outraged at the Bab's cruel and unfair treatment by the religious leaders. Many who had opposed Him now became followers. Some recalled the well-known prophecy about the Promised One: **"In that day most of his enemies shall be the** [religious authorities]."⁷⁰

The Bab's victory was evident in other parts of the country where His followers were finding many more sympathetic ears for their teaching efforts. Such was the impact of the Babi movement and the intense teaching fervor of His disciples that, in approximately three years from the time of His first meeting with Mulla Husayn, the Bab's followers now numbered in the tens of thousands.

BADASHT CONFERENCE

At the same time that the Bab was on trial in Tabriz, an important conference of Babi leaders was underway in the village of Badasht. There were two main reasons for this conference. One was to decide on the steps to be taken to liberate the Bab from His imprisonment in Chiriq, an effort that proved unsuccessful. The other, which was successful, was to clarify some of the implications of the Bab's message.

The rapid growth of the faith under such stormy political unrest had gained followers because of the Bab's personal appeal rather than their spiritual commitment. Many Babis, including some of the leaders, had not had much instruction about the significance of the Bab's teachings.

One of the most prominent leaders at this conference was Tahirih, the only female 'Letter of the Living'. She stressed some major elements of the Bab's message:

▶The Bab was not just another religious reformer, He was the long-awaited Mahdi.
▶He was a Messenger of God, the Founder of a new religious dispensation.
▶The Babis must free themselves from Islamic laws that conflicted with the Bab's teachings.
▶New social teachings, such as the equality of men and women, superseded Islamic restrictions.

Tahirih dramatized this last point by appearing with her face unveiled, a very daring and shocking[71] violation of Muslim tradition in 1848.

MASSACRE AT FORT SHAYKH TABARSI

The death of the king, Muhammad Shah, in September of 1848, spelled even more political tension throughout the country. The Prime Minister, Mirza Aqasi, was overthrown, and the usual intrigue for succession to the throne got underway.

The Muslim clergy, released from the mild restraints of the government, took further steps to completely eradicate what they termed the Babi heresy. This proved to be a disastrous turning point for the fortunes of the Babi movement.

Sixteen-year-old Nasiri'd-Din Shah succeeded his father as king. Both he and his new prime minister, Mirza Taqi Khan, were violently opposed to the Bab. They wholeheartedly supported the new harsher measures proposed by the clergy.

Now began a murderous campaign of wholesale slaughter that resulted in the extermination of more than 20,000 Babis, including the Bab, all the Letters of the Living, and almost the entire Babi leadership. The Babi groups who were scattered around the country spreading the Bab's message now found themselves the targets of mobs trying to kill them without provocation, encouraged by the combined authority of the religious and civil leaders. Mirza Taqi Khan, the Prime Minister, with firm clerical support, issued orders to punish the Babis, declaring that the properties of all of these *apostates* were forfeit.

Nabil-i-Azam[72], writing an eyewitness account of this eventful period, relates the dramatic episode at Fort Shaykh Tabarsi. Mulla Husayn and Quddus, the Bab's foremost Letter of the Living, were part of a group of Babis who had been spreading the Bab's message in the province of Mazindaran.

At the shrine of a Muslim saint, Shaykh Tabarsi, they suddenly found themselves besieged by a mob incited by clergy from several local villages. The young band of Babis were outnumbered many times over, but put up a defensive position from which they could defend themselves. Mulla Husayn held back his group and sent messages to the mob leaders that he did not want a battle. But when they attacked, the Babis, led by Quddus and Mulla Husayn, counterattacked and sent the foe running.

This first battle, which the Babis reluctantly entered into in self-defense, is described in several accounts, including one by the French historian and consular official, A.L.M. Nicolas, and another by one of the enemy.

Mulla Husayn, the frail student untrained in military matters, distinguished himself as an incredible warrior. After seeing several beloved companions killed beside him, he spurred his horse and led the counterattack with such strength, heroism and fury that the enemy recoiled in terror.

One of the killers took refuge behind a small tree. He held his musket in front of his body to shield himself as Mulla Husayn swept down upon him... and, with a single slash of his sword, he cut through the trunk of the tree, through the musket, and severed the body of his enemy in two.[73]

The mob leaders later rallied their men enough to return and surround the Babis while a request for government troops was dispatched. Army units responded rapidly, and the battle that followed turned into a siege that resulted in a great humiliation for the government.

Despite the government's overwhelming numbers and superior firepower, the Babis at Fort Shaykh Tabarsi defeated in numerous battles all attempts to dislodge them from their positions. This went on for almost nine months, but not without cost. At the end the defenders had lost most of their numbers, including the brave scholar, Mulla Husayn.

The defenders, exhausted and wounded, and fighting without food, supplies or ammunition, finally accepted the enemy's sworn offer of their lives in return for surrender. As soon as the defenders left the fort, the treacherous enemy set upon them. Many were killed, others tortured to death, and the remainder were chained and released to the fury of mobs who paraded them through the streets before they were mutilated and finally killed. The saintly young Quddus was one of the torture victims torn apart by the merciless mobs.

The massacre of Fort Tabarsi, including nine of the eighteen Letters of the Living, was just one of many similar scenes of violence in other parts of the country. Encouraged by royal orders, maddened mobs incited by unrelenting clergy inflicted unbelievable atrocities on the survivors of hopeless last-stand battles. Men, women, children, infants as well as the aged and infirm, Babis were unmercifully hunted and exterminated in a genocidal bloodbath that has few parallels in all of religious history.

The tortures accompanying this mass murder chill the imagination. Victims **"had their eyes gouged out, were sawn asunder, strangled, blown from the mouths of cannons, chopped in pieces, hewn apart with hatchets and maces, shod with horse shoes, bayoneted and stoned. Torture-mongers vied with each other in running the gamut of brutality, while the populace, into whose hands the bodies of the hapless victims were delivered, would close in upon their prey, and would so mutilate them as to leave no trace of their original form. The executioners, though accustomed to their own gruesome task, would themselves be amazed at the fiendish cruelty of the populace. Women and children could be seen led down the streets by their executioners, their flesh in ribbons, with candles burning in their wounds..."**[74]

For Western readers, the horrors perpetrated during this reign of terror numb the mind. European journalists and observers recorded eyewitness accounts of these events.

An Austrian officer, Captain Von Goumoens, in the employ of the Shah at that time, was so horrified at the cruelties he was compelled to witness that he tendered his resignation. **"Follow me, my friend,"** is the Captain's own testimony... **"you who lay claim to a heart and European ethics, follow me to the unhappy ones who, with gouged-out eyes, must eat, on the scene of the deed, without any sauce, their own amputated ears; or whose teeth are torn out with inhuman violence by the hand of the executioner; or whose bare skulls are simply crushed by blows from a hammer; or where the bazaar is illuminated with unhappy victims, because on right and left the people dig deep holes in their breasts and shoulders, and insert burning wicks in the wounds.**

I saw some dragged in chains through the bazaar, preceded by a military band, in whom these wicks had burned so deep that now the fat flickered convulsively in the wound like a newly extinguished lamp. Not seldom it happens that the unwearying ingenuity of the Oriental leads to fresh

tortures. They will skin the soles of the Babi's feet, soak the wounds in boiling oil, shoe the foot like the hoof of a horse, and compel the victim to run... Give him the coup de grace! Put him out of his pain! No! The executioner swings the whip, and—I myself have had to witness it—the unhappy victim of hundredfold tortures runs... As for the end itself, they hang the scorched and perforated bodies by their hands and feet to a tree head downwards, and now every Persian may try his marksmanship to his heart's content... I saw corpses torn by nearly one hundred and fifty bullets." "When I read over again," he continues, "what I have written, I am overcome by the thought that those who are with you in our dearly beloved Austria may doubt the full truth of the picture, and accuse me of exaggeration. Would to God that I had not lived to see it!"[75]

About Fort Shaykh Tabarsi, the French historian, A.L.M. Nicolas, noted ly the futility of the government's attempts to cover up the whole episode by razing the fortifications and leveling the ground: **"They imagined that this would silence history."**[76]

MARTYRDOM OF TAHIRIH

Tahirih, the only female Letter of the Living, was also martyred for her Faith. She was the daughter of a well-known religious leader in Persia, and was renowned for both her intelligence and her beauty.

In his report, A.L.M. Nicolas wrote that **"her reputation became universal throughout Persia, and** (prominent scholars respected and even adopted) **some of her hypotheses and opinions."**[77] She lived in Tihran, the capital, where she had been creating a storm of excitement spreading the Bab's message with fiery eloquence.

One of her major themes from the Bab's teachings was the equality of men and women. Tahirih openly denounced the Muslim traditions of polygamy, the veil to be worn by women, and all the other restraints that were required on pain of death.

The Muslim clergy, unable to defeat her in debate, eventually condemned her to death. On her way home after the Babi conference in Badasht, Tahirih was taken prisoner. Despite the efforts of prominent friends to avert her death sentence, she was taken to a garden outside the gates of Tihran where she was strangled and thrown down a dry well that was then filled with earth and stones.

Thus ended the life of Tahirih. One of the foremost disciples of the Bab, Tahirih was also the first woman-suffrage martyr. Numerous reports of her remarkable career, in a country as socially backward as Persia, and finally ending in her tragic death, fired the imagination of readers all over Europe. **"This noble woman,"** wrote Dr. T.K. Cheyne, the English clergyman, **"has the credit of opening the catalogue of social reforms in Persia."**[78] Professor E.G. Browne, a prominent British orientalist and student of Persian culture, noted that the appearance of such a woman as Tahirih is a rare phenomenon in any country, but in such a backward country as Persia it is almost a miracle.

The famous Turkish poet, Sulayman Nazim Bey, wrote: **"O Tahirih! You are worth a thousand Nasiri'd-Din Shahs."** Lord Curzon, the British statesman, said, **"The heroism of the lovely but ill-fated poetess is one of the affecting episodes in modern history."**

Sarah Bernhardt, the world-renowned French actress, commissioned a play to be written for her to perform, based on the life of Tahirih, whom the playwright described as *the Persian Joan of Arc.* [79]

MARTYRDOM OF THE BAB

In the midst of the continuing raging pogrom against His followers, the Bab, with most of His ablest disciples now gone, suffered untold agonies at reports of unbelievable horrors inflicted on His loved ones while He was helplessly confined in prison. He Himself was now called upon to make the last and ultimate confrontation with His persecutors.

Mirza Taqi Khan, the Prime Minister, as a final blow to the Babi movement, ordered the Bab removed to Tabriz for execution. He was charged with heresy, a religious rather than a civil crime, so His judges were the clergy, and thus His death warrant was inevitable.

The final event, the details of which comprise one of the most dramatic episodes in recent history, is excerpted from *The Bahá'í Faith: The Emerging Global Religion:*

On July 9, 1850, in the presence of a crowd of thousands who thronged rooftops and windows of a public square, arrangements were made to carry out the sentence. What followed was a most extraordinary event.

The Bab and one of his disciples were suspended by ropes against the wall of a military barracks and a regiment of 750 Armenian Christian troops were drawn up to form a firing squad. The colonel of the regiment, a certain Sam Khan, was reluctant to carry out the order of execution, which he feared would bring down the wrath of God on his head. The Bab is reported to have given him the following assurance: "Follow your instructions, and if your intentions be sincere, the Almighty is surely able to relieve you of your perplexity."

Many eyewitnesses testified to what followed. The regiment was drawn up and 750 rifles were discharged. The smoke from these muzzle-loading rifles shrouded the square in darkness. When the smoke cleared, incredulous onlookers saw the Bab's companion standing unscathed beside the wall; the Bab had vanished from sight! The ropes by which the pair had hung had been severed by the bullets. A frenzied search ensued, and the Bab was found unhurt in the room he had occupied the night before. He was calmly engaged in completing his final instructions to his secretary.

The crowd was in a state of near pandemonium and the Armenian regiment refused to take any further part in the proceedings. Mirza Hasan Khan[80] was faced with the real possibility that the fickle mob, which had first hailed the Bab and then denounced him, might view his deliverance as a sign from God and rise up in his support. A Muslim regiment was thus hastily assembled, the Bab and his companion were once again suspended from the wall, and a second volley was discharged. This time the bodies of the two prisoners were riddled with bullets, though their faces were untouched. The last words of the Bab to the crowd were:

"O wayward generation! Had you believed in Me every one of you would have followed the example of this youth, who stood in rank above most of you, and would have willingly sacrificed himself in My path. The day will come when you will have recognized Me; that day I shall have ceased to be with you."[81]

The extraordinary circumstances of the Bab's death provided a focal point for a new wave of interest in His message. The story spread like wildfire, not only among the Persians, but also among the diplomats, merchants, military advisers, and journalists who made up the substantial European community in Persia at the time. The words of the French consular official, A.L.M. Nicolas, suggest the impact which the drama in Persia made on educated Westerners:

This is one of the most magnificent examples of courage which mankind has ever been able to witness, and it is also an admirable proof of the love which [the Bab] had for his fellow countrymen. He sacrificed himself for mankind; he gave for it his body and his soul, he suffered for it hardships, insults, indignities, torture and martyrdom. He sealed with his blood the pact of universal brotherhood, and like Jesus he gave his life in order to herald the reign of concord, justice and love for one's fellow men.[82]

The famous Cambridge scholar, E.G. Browne, wrote: "Who can fail to be attracted by the gentle spirit of [the Bab]? His sorrowful and persecuted life, his purity of conduct and youth; his courage and uncomplaining patience under misfortune... but most of all his tragic death, all serve to enlist our sympathies on behalf of the young Prophet of Shiraz." The English clergyman, Dr. T.K. Cheyne, stated, "That Jesus of the age... a prophet and more than a prophet. His combination of mildness and power is so rare that we have to place him in a line with super-normal men."[83]

MESSAGE OF THE BAB

After losing most of its leaders and thousands of its members, the death of the Bab was a devastating blow for the remainder of the Babi community. Besides, it was still experiencing unrelenting persecution. In practical terms, it seemed that every possible misfortune that could have happened to the Babi movement did, in fact, happen. By worldly standards, the Bab's life had been one of the saddest and most fruitless in history. His mission seemed to have been a colossal disaster.

By the same worldly standards, the life of Jesus, too, had been a catastrophic failure. Of His chosen disciples, one had betrayed Him, another had denied Him, and only a few were at the foot of the cross. Centuries passed before the world ever heard of His name.

In terms of the Bab's message, however, what happened was, like the story of Jesus, successful by divine standards. At the height of the Bab's popularity, as thousands were rallying to His cause, the entire country was undergoing major social upheaval. Had He wished to do so, the Bab could have seized power during the political vacuum created by the old shah's death. That He did not so choose, even at the cost of His own life, is clear evidence of the peaceful character of His mission and His total reliance on the power of God.

The central theme of the Bab's message, we will recall, was two-fold: to call the people back to God, and to announce the advent of the Promised One of all ages and all religions. Calling the people back to God is the mark of a prophet—in this case, not just a prophet, but a Prophet, a Manifestation of God.

The Bab was the Founder of the Babi Faith, an independent religion. The Old Testament identifies numerous minor prophets[84] who called the people back to God; these were Jewish prophets calling the people back to the original teachings of their major Prophet, Moses, from which they had strayed.

The Bab called the people back to God through new

teachings and a new holy book, the Bayan, which superseded the Islamic scriptures, the Qur'an. Christianity, too, offered new teachings and new scriptures, the Gospels, which superseded the older scriptures, the Torah of Judaism. As they are all from the same source, it should be noted that in each case the older scriptures were not being rejected, they were being fulfilled.

The second part of the Bab's central theme was the announcement that the Promised One of all ages was about to appear. The Bab proclaimed His role of the Gate, or the Forerunner of the Promised One as the central theme of His own mission. Every chapter of His holy book, the Bayan, carried this message. In it, He said that the world must prepare for the coming of the Promised One, the one He called Him Whom God Shall Make Manifest. His purpose, then, was the spiritual and social transformation of the people to be ready for this momentous event, the event that was awaited and promised by all religions.

In the earlier religions, a herald had proclaimed the coming of the Manifestation of God for that day. John the Baptist, though not a Manifestation of God himself, is generally recognized as the herald of the Manifestation of God, Jesus Christ. The Bab, who served as the Herald of Bahá'u'lláh, was also a Manifestation of God in His own right.

The Bab promised that before the end of the ninth year after His proclamation to Mulla Husayn, the Promised One of all religions would appear. Some of His followers, the Bab declared, would see the Promised One with their own eyes. There was never a moment of doubt in His teaching. The seed had been planted in the meadows of human hearts. The Bab was the Dawn; the Sun was yet to come.

CHAPTER REVIEW—The Bab

Summary
▶In the mid-nineteenth century the expectation of the return of a Great Redeemer began to sweep across the world.
▶The Bahá'í Faith dates its beginnings to 1844, the year in which the Bab proclaimed His message.
▶The Bab appointed his first eighteen believers as Letters of the Living.
▶The Bab was the founder of a new religious dispensation.
▶The Bab's declaration was a serious challenge to the Muslim clergy.
▶The central theme of the Bab's message was to call the people back to God, and to announce the advent of the Promised One of all ages and all religions.

Matching
Match the names in Column 1 with the letter of the correct statement in Column 2.

 Column 1
Letters of the Living
 Nasiri'd-Din Shah
 Him Whom God Shall Make Manifest
 Mulla Husayn
 Mah-Ku
 Vahid
 Bayan
 Shiraz
 Tahirih
 Siyyid Kazim
 Fort Shaykh Tabarsi
 Millerites
 Qa'im
 Tabriz
 Badasht
 E.G. Browne

Column 2
A. North American group expecting Christ's return
B. Leader of the Shaykhi sect
C. A castle prison in Persia
D. Where Babis withstood the Persian army
E. The Bab's Holy Book
F. The first Babi martyr
G. Where the Bab first declared who He was
H. Site of Babi conference
I. A western scholar in Persia
J. The scholar sent by the Shah to investigate the Bab
K. Where the Bab was executed
L. The first Babi
M. The one promised by the Bab
N. The Bab's appointees
O. Ruler of Persia
P. The only female Letter of the Living
Q. Title claimed by the Bab

Discussion
1. How do the standards of justice and forms of punishment in western and eastern countries (such as Persia) differ? Cite examples experienced by the persecuted Babis.
2. What was the almost miraculous event that took place during the execution of the Bab that almost transformed the crowd of spectators into believers?
3. Why was there such an interest in the return of Jesus in the mid-nineteenth century?
4. What was the principal message of the Shaykhi sect?
5. Describe European reaction to reports about the Babi persecutions.
6. Discuss the role of Tahirih in the growth of the Babi Faith.
7. How could the death of the Bab be compared with the death of Jesus?
8. What was the central theme of the Bab's mission?
9. How could the Bab's mission be compared with that of Jesus Christ?
10. How are the roles of the Bab and John the Baptist comparable?

CHAPTER FOUR—Bahá'u'lláh

Mirza Husayn-Ali was one of the few Babi leaders who survived the massacres of 1848-1853. Husayn-Ali, later known as Bahá'u'lláh, accepted the Faith of the Bab at the age of twenty-seven, when Mulla Husayn delivered a personal message to Him from the Bab, in 1844.

Four brothers of Bahá'u'lláh also accepted the Bab, including a younger half-brother, Mirza Yahya. Bahá'u'lláh soon became an active follower of the new faith. For the first few years, because of His social position, He was shielded from the physical attacks His fellow Babis increasingly had to endure.

Bahá'u'lláh was born in the capital city of Tihran, the son of a prominent Persian nobleman whose family held extensive estates in the province of Mazindaran, north of Tihran. When He was twenty-two years of age, His father, the chief minister of the province, died. Bahá'u'lláh, who had already established a reputation for honesty and integrity, was offered this same post. He declined the offer, choosing instead the task of managing the family estates, and the training of the younger family members. He was also a generous supporter of numerous charities, which earned Him the title *Father of the Poor*.

After that first momentous meeting with the Bab, Mulla Husayn was instructed to find a special person in Tihran and deliver a letter to him. The Bab did not name this person; His instructions to Mulla Husayn were that if his faith was strong and pure, he would find the one he sought. His unerring search led him to Bahá'u'lláh.

Though they never met in person, Bahá'u'lláh and the Bab maintained their correspondence until the Bab's execution in 1850. The moment He read that first letter carried by Mulla Husayn, Bahá'u'lláh proclaimed His acceptance of the Bab as a true *Messenger of God*.

Bahá'u'lláh tried to convince friends and relatives in positions of authority that the Babis were peaceful and law-abiding. He warned them that the government's persecutions and the enmity of the clergy could only bring disorder and public unrest to Persia.

IMPRISONMENT IN THE SIYAH-CHAL

After the Bab's execution, the Babi community, deprived of most of its leadership and unsure of the deeper meanings of the Bab's spiritual message, felt lost and depressed. Morale was very low and many felt their cause was hopeless. Until now, the Babis had never used force except in defense of their own lives, in accordance with the teachings of the Bab.

Two young Babis, in a moment of desperation, decided to avenge their Master and made a frantic and futile attempt to assassinate the shah. Both youths were immediately seized and one was killed on the spot.

The Babi community was now subjected to a renewed tide of persecution. Its enemies now felt they had clear proof that the Babis were a deadly menace.

Bahá'u'lláh and the remaining Babi leaders were arrested and taken to the notorious prison in Tihran, the Siyah-Chal (Black Pit). This was a subterranean dungeon that once had served as a water reservoir for the city. As the prisoners were approaching the prison, a large crowd gathered to jeer at Bahá'u'lláh. He who had been called Father of the Poor was now the victim of their hatred.

In later years, Bahá'u'lláh wrote of this experience:

We were consigned for four months to a place foul beyond comparison... Upon our arrival we were first conducted along a pitch-black corridor, from whence we descended three steep flights of stairs to the place of confinement assigned to us. The dungeon was wrapped in thick darkness, and our fellow prisoners numbered nearly a hundred and fifty souls: thieves, assassins and highwaymen... No pen can depict that place, nor any tongue describe its loathsome smell. Most of these men had neither clothes nor bedding to lie on.[85]

Nabil, the first historian of the Bahá'í Faith, recorded Bahá'u'lláh's words:

We were all huddled together in one cell, our feet in stocks, and around our necks fastened the most

galling of chains. The air we breathed was laden with the foulest of impurities, while the floor on which we sat was covered with filth and vermin. No ray of light was allowed to penetrate that pestilential dungeon or to warm its icy coldness.[86]

The cruelties perpetrated by the Persians far exceeded Western styles of punishment. Day by day an official would come to the prison cell and call out the names of those who were to be executed. Out they would walk, the Babis with beaming smiles and firm steps, eager to sacrifice themselves for God.

These executions were not simply a merciful hanging or shooting; they often followed excruciating torture. Sometimes the condemned would be murdered on the spot. In some cases, a hammer and peg were used to drive a heavy wooden gag down the throat of the victim, whose body might be left lying for hours or even days chained to those still alive. Such were the prison conditions Bahá'u'lláh endured for four agonizing months.

During this time in prison, however, a rare event took place—Bahá'u'lláh received the first intimation of His great Mission. Later, He explained this experience.

Not of Mine own volition have I manifested Myself, but God, of His own choosing, hath manifested Me... I was but a man like others, asleep upon My couch, when lo, the breezes of the All-Glorious were wafted over Me...[87] **One night in a dream, these exalted words were heard on every side: 'Verily, We shall render Thee victorious by Thyself and by Thy pen. Grieve Thou not for that which hath befallen Thee, neither be Thou afraid, for Thou art in safety.**[88]

The prophecy of the Bab was thus fulfilled. The time, however, had not yet come for a public declaration. Ten more years were to elapse before Bahá'u'lláh announced Himself.

His captors were reluctant to release Him because of His importance to the Babi community. But, as the other Babi youth had confessed to the attempted assassination, no charges could be placed against Bahá'u'lláh. Due to His family's social position and the personal intervention of the Russian ambassador,

Prince Dolgorukov, the government reluctantly freed Bahá'u'lláh after confiscating all of His properties and inherited wealth.

He was sentenced to permanent banishment. Bahá'u'lláh was invited to go to Russia where He would be safe. But He declined the invitation; instead He chose exile in neighboring Iraq—in the city of Baghdad. Iraq at that time was part of the Ottoman Turkish Empire.

In January 1853, Bahá'u'lláh left with His wife, three small children and a few attendants. Under extremely adverse conditions, in the midst of a severe winter, the little party painstakingly crossed the snow-covered mountains separating Persia and Iraq.

BAGDAD—THE FIRST EXILE

Two months later, the small party of exiles arrived in Baghdad. His harsh imprisonment, followed by a long and difficult journey, was a drain on Bahá'u'lláh's physical strength. His enemies and persecutors in Persia had hoped this would shorten His life and minimize His power to reinvigorate the dying Babi community.

Bahá'u'lláh, however, recovered His strength and began efforts to revitalize the spirits of His Babi compatriots. During the next three years, a group of Babis gathered around Bahá'u'lláh, attracted by His magnetic personality. Among these was Bahá'u'lláh's half-brother, Mirza Yahya, who later turned out to be the center of one of the first major internal threats to Bahá'u'lláh's mission.

Bahá'u'lláh had raised and protected His young brother, thirteen years His junior. Mirza Yahya was timid, fearful, impressionable, and easily swayed by stronger personalities. For a while Mirza Yahya served as his Brother's secretary. The Bab, while in prison, consulted with Bahá'u'lláh by letter, and They agreed that the Bab would appoint Mirza Yahya as head of the Babi community in the event of the Bab's death.[89]

The purpose of this *in name only* appointment was to leave Bahá'u'lláh free to guide the affairs of the new faith through His influence on Mirza Yahya, and still avoid the prominence and notoriety the title would automatically confer. Mirza Yahya, at the time of his appointment, was in little personal danger, as he spent most of his time on family estates in the north, and was the first to flee when trouble appeared.

But Mirza Yahya fell under the influence of an unscrupulous Muslim theological student named Siyyid Muhammad. Siyyid Muhammad was an opportunist seeking to become a power in the Babi community during the time when the true Babi leaders were fully involved with the community's survival.

Siyyid Muhammad and some of his self-seeking friends persuaded Mirza Yahya to reject Bahá'u'lláh's guidance and, as the Bab's designated successor, assume the actual leadership of the community. Siyyid Muhammad would then serve as Yahya's chief advisor. Bahá'u'lláh had not yet proclaimed Himself as the Promised One and He had no designated standing among the Babis.

Rather than contribute to the community's disunity by provoking a leadership confrontation with Yahya, Bahá'u'lláh removed Himself from any dispute. Without telling a soul, He left home to seek seclusion in the mountains near Sulaymaniyyih, in neighboring Kurdistan.

Under Yahya's leadership and assisted by his new mentor, Siyyid Muhammad, the Babi community quickly degenerated to a condition bordering on anarchy. Yahya, unable to handle the pressures of leadership, withdrew and left Siyyid Muhammad to demonstrate his inability to function as leader. When Bahá'u'lláh was finally located, even Yahya joined with the family and other Babis in an appeal for Him to return, which He did in March 1856.

The two years of Bahá'u'lláh's self-imposed seclusion in Kurdistan was a period of reflection, meditation and creativity during which His mission began to take definite form. He composed many poems, prayers and meditations. It was a time in His life that was comparable to periods of seclusion in the lives of the Founders of the world's other great faiths. Consider the wanderings of Buddha, Moses in the desert of Sinai, the forty days and nights of Jesus in the wilderness, and Muhammad's retreat in the cave on

Mt. Hira.

With Bahá'u'lláh's return, the fortunes of the Babi community, which no longer questioned the position of Bahá'u'lláh's leadership, were gradually restored to the health it had enjoyed when the Bab was alive. Mirza Yahya remained in seclusion under Bahá'u'lláh's protection. Despite His efforts to shield Mirza Yahya from the plotters and agitators who had sought to replace Bahá'u'lláh's leadership of the Babi community, Bahá'u'lláh sadly noted His gullible brother's inability to resist falling in once again with their nefarious scheming.

Many visitors from all walks of life came to see Bahá'u'lláh. His reputation as a spiritual teacher spread throughout all the neighboring regions. The Babi community was reinvigorated under Bahá'u'lláh's spiritual guidance. The Babis began to mirror in their conduct the noble teachings of their charismatic leader. Although the community was still nominally followers of the Bab, it was Bahá'u'lláh's spiritual guidance that gradually began to assert itself, and the Bab's teachings slowly evolved into Bahá'u'lláh's teachings.

Though Bahá'u'lláh had not yet declared Himself publicly, the transformation of the Babi community into the Bahá'í[90] community was gradually taking place. The Bab's mission to prepare the people for the coming of the Promised One (Bahá'u'lláh) was achieved despite the overwhelming opposition of ruthless and powerful enemies.

It was during His stay in Baghdad that Bahá'u'lláh began a period of creativity, producing a body of literature, including tablets (letters), books, prayers, teachings, discourses and other evidence of His message from God that is known as the Revelation of Bahá'u'lláh. His best-known writings completed in Baghdad are the *Hidden Words*, the *Seven Valleys*, and the *Kitab-i-Iqan*, (Book of Certitude).

The Hidden Words are a collection of brief gemlike utterances, eternal truths 'that stand at the core of every revealed religion'. Bahá'u'lláh introduced the Hidden Words:

This is that which hath descended from the

realm of glory, uttered by the tongue of power and might, and revealed unto the Prophets of old. We have taken the inner essence thereof and clothed it in the garment of brevity...

Examples of the Hidden Words:

O Son of Man! Veiled in My immemorial being and in the ancient eternity of My essence, I knew My love for thee; therefore I created thee, have engraved on thee Mine image and revealed to thee My beauty.   (Arabic 3)

O Son of Being! Love Me, that I may love thee. If thou lovest Me not, My love can in no wise reach thee. Know this, O servant.   (Arabic 5)

O My Servant! Free thyself from the fetters of this world, and loose thy soul from the prison of self. Seize thy chance, for it will come to thee no more.   (Persian 40)

O Son of Spirit! Noble have I created thee, yet thou hast abased thyself. Rise then unto that for which thou wast created.   (Arabic 22)

The Seven Valleys is a small book composed in answer to a learned Sufi[91]. It describes in mystical language the stages a seeker must travel in his search to know God. The seven valleys or stages are the Valleys of Search, Love, Knowledge, Unity, Contentment, Wonderment, True Poverty and Absolute Nothingness. The first is the Valley of Search.

The steed of this Valley is patience; without patience the wayfarer on this journey will reach nowhere and attain no goal. Nor should he ever be downhearted; if he strive for a hundred thousand years and yet fail to behold the beauty of the Friend (the Manifestation of God), **he should not falter.**[92]

The Kitab-i-Iqan, or Book of Certitude, was written in answer to questions posed by an uncle of the Bab. Sometimes called the key to the study of comparative religion, the Book of Certitude offers a logical explanation of the symbolism found in the Scriptures of past religions, the nature of God and the spiritual evolution of mankind. It clarifies the concept of progressive revelation, and presents proofs of the Bab's mission as well as that of Bahá'u'lláh.

Bahá'u'lláh was highly respected by the Iraqi officials in Baghdad. As His growing influence and reputation spread, Bahá'u'lláh's enemies in Persia became suspicious and alarmed that He would rekindle the Babi movement in Persia and once again endanger the country's stability.

The shah's government petitioned their overlord, the Ottoman government in Istanbul, for help. In April of 1863, Bahá'u'lláh was advised that He and His family had to leave Baghdad and move further away from Persia, this time to Istanbul.

Again Bahá'u'lláh and His family made plans, this time for their second exile. Bahá'u'lláh moved to a temporary residence for twelve days, to a garden on an island in the Tigris River, while preparations were made for the caravan journey on the road to Istanbul.

It was in this garden, now known to Bahá'ís as the *Garden of Ridvan* (Paradise), that Bahá'u'lláh confided to some of His closest followers that He was He Whom God Will Make Manifest, the One promised by the Bab, as well as by the scriptures of earlier religions.

ISTANBUL—THE SECOND EXILE

Istanbul, since 1453 the capital city of the Turkish Empire, was as well or better known by its two earlier names, Constantinople, and before that, Byzantium. Built and renamed by the Roman Emperor Constantine in the year 330, Constantinople served as the eastern capital of the Roman Empire. After the fall of Rome in 476, the eastern part of the Roman Empire became known as the Byzantine Empire, after the city's earlier name. The city fell to the Seljuk Turks a thousand years later, and became known as the Turkish Empire.

Now long past its prime and destined to be overthrown in less than 50 years, the Turkish Empire during Bahá'u'lláh's exile was ruled by an incompetent sultan served by ministers who, for the most part, were guided by greed and self-interest. Intrigue and bribery were the standard protocols for the conduct of government affairs. It was in the midst of this corrupt society that Bahá'u'lláh and His party arrived in August, at the end of a three-month journey.

Impervious to the approaches of malcontents and plotters who called on Him to make deals or to join their circles, Bahá'u'lláh likewise refused to approach officials and ministers to request assistance or buy influence.

The shah's government, fearful that Bahá'u'lláh, now so close to people of great influence and power, would somehow once again gain support for His views and stage a return to Persia. The Persian ambassador began a campaign to convince the Turkish authorities to move Bahá'u'lláh once again, to a more remote part of the Empire. The campaign was successful, and four months after His arrival, in December of 1863, Bahá'u'lláh was once again forced to leave, this time to Adrianople (Edirne), in European Turkey.

ADRIANOPLE—THE THIRD EXILE

Despite His continued persecution by the Persian government authorities and, by their instigation, the Turkish authorities, Bahá'u'lláh maintained and increased the scope of His leadership activities. His ever-wider-ranging correspondence and His influence among the Babis in Persia, plus the constant stream of visitors who came to Him from all walks of life, proved His *de facto* leadership of the Babi community. Bahá'u'lláh decided that the time had come to declare His mission openly.

Mirza Yahya, Bahá'u'lláh's half-brother, was by now fully committed once again to the plotting and scheming of Siyyid Muhammad and his cronies. The plotters began a campaign to restore their former leadership positions in the community. They tried everything, including two attempts at assassination, one by murder and the other by poisoning. The poisoning attempt, by Yahya himself, almost succeeded; Bahá'u'lláh survived, but He suffered the effects of the poison for the rest of His life.

Proclaiming His mission through a tablet addressed to the Bab's appointed temporary successor, Bahá'u'lláh called upon Yahya to recognize and support Him as the Bab had instructed. Yahya, however, claimed that he, and not Bahá'u'lláh, was the One promised by the Bab. Most of the Babis accepted

Bahá'u'lláh's proclamation and from that time they styled themselves Bahá'ís. Only a handful of Babis remained loyal to Yahya, and these became known as Azalis[93].

LETTERS TO THE KINGS OF THE EARTH

In September 1867, Bahá'u'lláh composed a series of tablets, initiating His public proclamation. In these tablets, letters addressed to the major world powers whom He called *the Kings of the earth*, Bahá'u'lláh declared Himself to be the One promised in the Torah, the Gospels, and the Qur'an.

O Kings of the earth! He Who is the sovereign Lord of all is come. The Kingdom is God's, the omnipotent Protector, the Self-Subsisting. Worship none but God, and, with radiant hearts, lift up your faces unto your Lord, the Lord of all names... Ye are but vassals, O Kings of the earth! He Who is the King of Kings hath appeared, arrayed in His most wondrous glory... Take heed lest pride deter you from recognizing the Source of Revelation, lest the things of this world shut you out as by a veil from Him Who is the Creator of heaven... It is not Our wish to lay hands on your kingdoms. Our mission is to seize and possess the hearts of men.[94]

He warned that a new world civilization would be born out of the devastation which the present world civilization was bringing upon itself. The underlying theme of the new age was unity, the oneness of the human race. He stressed the importance of the world's leaders to work toward the goal of world unity. Those who resisted the process of unifying mankind, He warned, invited ultimate frustration of their efforts and disaster for themselves.

Bahá'u'lláh hinted at the coming establishment of international organizations such as the League of Nations and later the United Nations. He called for a conclave of all the world's leaders to discuss ways and means for establishing a world peace. It was imperative, He said, that **"the Great Powers should resolve, for the sake of the tranquillity of the peoples of the earth, to be fully reconciled among themselves... It is not for him to pride himself who loveth his own country, but rather for him who loveth the whole world. The earth is but one country, and mankind its citizens.[95]

Similar words were addressed to other world leaders, including the presidents of the American republics.

Major Rulers Receiving Letters From Bahá'u'lláh

Emperor Napoleon III	France
Sultan Abdu'l-Aziz	Turkey
Kaiser Wilhelm I	Prussia
Nasiri'd-Din-Shah	Persia
Queen Victoria	Britain
Tsar Alexander II	Russia
Emperor Franz Joseph	Austria-Hungary

To Pope Pius IX, Bahá'u'lláh wrote: **O Pope! Rend the veils asunder. He Who is the Lord of Lords is come overshadowed with clouds, and the decree hath been fulfilled by God... He, verily, hath again come down from Heaven even as He came down from it the first time.**[96]

Bahá'u'lláh sent numerous messages to the clergy of other faiths informing them of the new day that had dawned.

At one time We address the people of the Torah and summon them unto Him Who is the Revealer of verses, Who hath come from Him Who layeth low the necks of men... At another, We address the people of the Evangel and say: 'The All-Glorious is come in this Name whereby the Breeze of God hath wafted over all regions.'... At still another, We address the people of the Qur'an saying: 'Fear the All-Merciful, and cavil not at Him through Whom all religions were founded... Know thou, moreover, that We have addressed to the Magians (Zoroastrians) **Our Tablets, and adorned them with Our Law...**[97]

The Ottoman Turkish Empire had already begun to collapse. The numerous minorities in the European part of the Empire were breaking away to form independent states, such as Greece, Bulgaria and Serbia.

Yahya's open rejection of Bahá'u'lláh's proclamation

103

effectively ended his influence among most of the Babis, but it did not end the opposition and the hopes of the Azali schemers. They now turned to the Turkish authorities, whose minds had already been poisoned against Bahá'u'lláh by the Persians and other enemies. Yahya and his co-conspirators again tried to undermine Bahá'u'lláh's influence by claiming that the letters Bahá'u'lláh addressed to the European powers were proof of His plots to overthrow the Empire; they pointed to the constant stream of visitors Bahá'u'lláh was receiving from all parts of the Empire. The Turkish officials already knew of earlier offers of protection for Bahá'u'lláh by the British and Russian governments. The jittery Turkish authorities took fright at this new evidence of possible treachery and decided to remove all of these troublesome Babi exiles from Adrianople.

Yahya and his little band of plotters were included in this expulsion. Bahá'u'lláh and most of the exiles were sent to Akka, in Palestine, while Yahya and a few others were banished to the island of Cyprus. Both Bahá'u'lláh and Yahya remained in their respective exiles for the rest of their lives. Yahya spent the last forty-four years of his life in Cyprus, embittered and forgotten, the victim of his own selfish ambition.

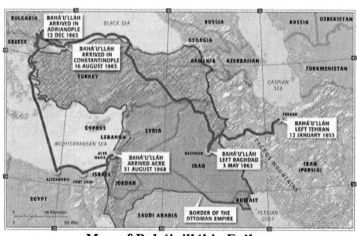

Map of Bahá'u'lláh's Exiles
© *Bahá'í International Community*

The scene of Bahá'u'lláh's departure from Adrianople was similar to His departure from Baghdad; He had so endeared Himself to the townspeople that many wept to see Him leave. The Turkish governor deplored his own government's decision to banish Bahá'u'lláh. Some of the foreign consuls in Adrianople offered Bahá'u'lláh their assistance, which He refused.

AKKA—THE LAST EXILE

In 1868, Bahá'u'lláh's party of seventy to eighty family members and close companions arrived by ship at Haifa, in the Holy Land, and crossed the bay north to the city of Akka, the most dreaded penal colony in the Turkish Empire.

Historically, Akka was known in ancient times as Achor, or Accho, in Jesus' time as Ptolemais, and in the time of the Crusaders, one thousand years later, as the fortified city of St. Jean d'Acre. Napoleon's army had been unable to breach its thick walls. Now, the city had degenerated into a place that was notorious for its unhealthy air and water. It was the site of the harshest prison in the Empire, reserved for the most dangerous criminals and unrepentant enemies of the government. The Turkish authorities fully believed that the terrible conditions Bahá'u'lláh would have to endure there would kill Him. Bahá'u'lláh called this confinement the *Most Great Prison*.

For the first two years, the exiles suffered greatly from their harsh treatment. Several of them died in prison. In 1870, the Bahá'ís had to move to a confinement in nearby rented housing when the prison was needed as military barracks. Despite the initial public prejudice against the *Bahá'í renegades from the true faith* which existed at the time of their arrival, Bahá'u'lláh's influence now began to make itself felt. Sympathetic prison officials reduced the number of guards; the harsh treatment was eased.

Siyyid Muhammad, Mirza Yahya's main adviser, was one of the Adrianople Bahá'ís exiled with Bahá'u'lláh when Yahya was sent to Cyprus. Siyyid Muhammad was frustrated by his inability to corrupt the loyal Bahá'ís with whom he was confined. As soon as they were moved from their close prison confinement,

Siyyid Muhammad and a few of his accomplices began to connive with some of Akka's disreputable elements to attack Bahá'u'lláh's house in hopes that He would be injured or killed. Seven of the Bahá'ís loyal to Bahá'u'lláh, unable to bear any longer Siyyid Muhammad's constant treachery, staged a fight in which Siyyid Muhammad and his accomplices were killed.

Bahá'u'lláh had repeatedly counseled His followers to avoid any deed that bore, no matter how remotely, any resemblance to retaliation. He was extremely saddened by this rejection of His teachings among these well-meaning but mistaken followers. In a letter written by Shoghi Effendi, Bahá'u'lláh was quoted:

My captivity can bring on Me no shame. Nay, by My life, it conferreth on Me glory. That which can make Me ashamed is the conduct of such of My followers who profess to love Me, yet in fact follow the Evil One.[98]

The Kitab-i-Aqdas—In the midst of the tribulations afflicting Bahá'u'lláh by acts of both His enemies and His erring followers, He revealed the most important book of His Revelation, the Kitab-i-Aqdas (the Most Holy Book). Described later by Shoghi Effendi as *a treasury enshrining the priceless gems of His Revelation*, the Kitab-i-Aqdas provides all of the key elements needed to guide humanity toward the destiny that the earlier Revelations had prophesied.

In this Most Holy Book, Bahá'u'lláh proclaims His Station as a Manifestation of God, outlines His plan for the Administrative Order (See Chapter Nine—The Administrative Order), and prescribes the obligations of each individual to promote his own spiritual growth. Bahá'u'lláh noted the connection between this book and the earlier Revelations. **"Verily, it is My weightiest testimony unto all people... In such a manner hath the Kitab-i-Aqdas been revealed that it attracteth and embraceth all the divinely appointed Dispensations... So vast is its range that it hath encompassed all men ere their recognition of it."**[99]

CALL FOR WORLD UNITY

While He was in prison, Bahá'u'lláh again took up His letters to *the kings of the earth*, which He did not have time to complete in Adrianople. His letters not only exhorted the world's leaders to strive for world unity, but also outlined a number of steps to be taken in order to achieve this goal.

Among the steps that must be taken to achieve world peace, He wrote, are:

▶ Creation of an international tribunal with authority to decide on disputes between nations.

▶ Creation of an international police force maintained by member states to enforce peaceful resolution of international disputes.

▶ Creation of an international auxiliary language so that every society could maintain its own cultural identity and still communicate with all other races and nations.

▶ A compulsory educational system to assure worldwide literacy.

▶ The application of basic democratic principles of government in the conduct of internal national affairs.

▶ Taxation that is now used for military expenditures should be drastically curtailed in favor of social welfare.

By present day standards, such advice in the mid-nineteenth century coming from anyone would be considered impertinent, disrespectful, audacious and presumptuous. As for the imperious, egotistical world leaders of that time, any advice, especially advice requiring the surrender of a portion of their power, and from a powerless Turkish prisoner, a negative reaction was almost certain. None of these letters received any significant response.

But in the eyes of Bahá'ís, such missives from a Manifestation of God carried spiritual powers that could not be denied. One such was the second letter that Bahá'u'lláh wrote from His prison cell to Napoleon III, the Emperor Louis Napoleon of France, at that time considered the most powerful European monarch. In this letter, Bahá'u'lláh warned the emperor that because of his abuse of power and his hypocrisy, **"thy kingdom shall be thrown into confusion and thine**

empire shall pass from thy hands, as a punishment for what thou hast wrought... Hath thy pomp made thee proud? By my life! It shall not endure..."[100]

In less than two years, the Franco-Prussian War ended the reign of Louis Napoleon. Of the major rulers listed above, only the British monarch, Queen Victoria, was not charged with gross abuse of power. Bahá'u'lláh even commended her for the recent British edict abolishing slavery. All the other rulers did not survive and their governments were overthrown.

The Turkish sultan and the Persian shah, the eastern rulers who actively opposed Bahá'u'lláh, were explicitly told that their thrones were forfeit for their crimes against their people. All of Bahá'u'lláh's predictions came true shortly thereafter.

Bahá'u'lláh remained confined in Akka, a prisoner by the sultan's decree, until 1877. During this time, His stream of visitors grew, as they had in Baghdad and Adrianople. The spiritual beauty radiating from Bahá'u'lláh attracted people from all walks of life—dignitaries, clergy of all faiths, rich, poor, visitors from all parts of Palestine and travelers from other countries.

The Mufti of the city, the leading Muslim authority, became a Bahá'í. The governor of Akka would not enter Bahá'u'lláh's presence before removing his shoes, as a sign of respect. At Bahá'u'lláh's request, the governor had an ancient aqueduct reconstructed to provide fresh water for the city.

Though still technically a prisoner of the sultan, no objection would have been raised had Bahá'u'lláh wished to leave. 'Abdu'l-Baha later wrote in His memoirs how Bahá'u'lláh was persistently urged by friends and followers to leave His prison.[101]

It wasn't until a devoted friend, an Arab Shaykh, on his knees and with tears in his eyes, implored Him to leave that He agreed to move to Mazra'ih, a country estate outside Akka. Two years later, He moved again, to Bahji, a mansion on the outskirts of Akka, where He lived for the remainder of His life. From the time He left the prison in Akka, Bahá'u'lláh revealed a vast body of writings that are now part of the Bahá'í Scriptures.

THE PERSON OF BAHÁ'U'LLÁH

Some individuals who attained Bahá'u'lláh's presence have recorded their impressions of the transcendental majesty of His person. A Bahá'í, Haji Mirza Haydar-Ali, who saw Bahá'u'lláh numerous times, wrote an account of his own pilgrimage to Akka:

Outwardly He was a prisoner, condemned and wronged, but in reality He was the Sun of Glory, the Manifestation of grandeur and majesty... Although He showed much compassion and loving-kindness, and approached anyone who came to His presence with tender care and humbleness, and often used to make humorous remarks to put them at ease... no one, whether faithful or disbelieving, learned or unlettered, wise or foolish, was able to utter ten words in His presence in the usual everyday manner. Indeed, many would find themselves to be tremulous with an impediment in their speech.

Some people asked permission to attain His presence for the sole purpose of conducting arguments and engaging in controversies. As a favor on His part... He gave these permission... As they entered the room, heard His voice welcoming them in, and gazed at His countenance beaming with the light of grandeur, they could not help but prostrate themselves at His door... When He showed them where to sit, they would find themselves unable to utter a word or put forward their questions. When they left they would bow to Him involuntarily. Some would be transformed through the influence of meeting Him and would leave with the utmost sincerity and devotion, some would depart as admirers, while others would leave His presence, ignorant and heedless, attributing their experience to pure sorcery.

[T]o what can it be attributed when one enters into His presence as an antagonist and leaves as a believer, or comes in as an enemy but goes out as a friend, or comes to raise controversial arguments, but departs without saying anything and, due to willful blindness, attributing this to magic? ...the bounties which were vouchsafed to a person as a

result of attaining His presence were indescribable and unknowable. The proof of the sun is the sun itself.[102]

It was in Bahji, His final residence, that Bahá'u'lláh received Professor E.G. Browne, the British scholar and orientalist, a non-Bahá'í, who recorded his impressions of this meeting:

I found myself in a large apartment, along the upper end of which ran a low divan, while on the side opposite to the door were placed two or three chairs. Though I dimly suspected whither I was going and whom I was to behold (for no intimation had been given to me), a second or two elapsed ere, with a throb of wonder and awe, I became definitely conscious that the room was not untenanted. In the corner where the divan met the wall sat a wondrous and venerable figure, crowned with a felt head-dress of the kind called a taj by dervishes (but of unusual height and make), round the base of which was wound a small white turban. The face of him on whom I gazed I can never forget, though I cannot describe it. Those piercing eyes seemed to read one's very soul; power and authority sat on that ample brow... No need to ask in whose presence I stood, as I bowed myself before one who is the object of a devotion and love kings might envy and emperors sigh for in vain!

A mild dignified voice bade me be seated, and then continued:—"Praise be to God that thou hast attained... Thou hast come to see a prisoner and an exile... We desire but the good of the world and the happiness of the nations; yet they deem us a stirrer up of strife and sedition worthy of bondage and banishment... That all nations should become... as brothers; that the bonds of affection and unity between the sons of men should be strengthened; that diversity of religion should cease, and differences of race be annulled—what harm is there in this... Yet so it shall be; these fruitless strifes, these ruinous wars shall pass away, and the 'Most Great Peace' shall come... Do not you in Europe need this also? Yet do we see your kings and rulers lavishing their treasures more freely on means for the destruction of the human race than on that which would conduce to the happiness of mankind... These strifes and this bloodshed and discord must cease, and all men be as one kindred and one family... Let not a man glory in this, that he loves his country; let him rather glory in this, that he loves his kind..."[103]

THE POWER OF BAHÁ'U'LLÁH

Jesus, through His own spiritual return, was the same Promised One Who earlier appeared as Moses, later as Muhammad, and more recently as Bahá'u'lláh. It is understandable that even believers might discount persistent reports about miraculous feats like striking water from rocks or walking on water. Such miracles were part of the mystique surrounding each Manifestation.

Among the many unusual powers attributed to Him, Bahá'u'lláh is reported to have revealed His tablets with such rapidity as to keep a number of scribes continuously busy. He moved back and forth, from one to the other, dictating to each, *without error and with matchless eloquence*, the correct portions of the torrent of thoughts that flowed effortlessly through Him.

Like His chosen Predecessors, Bahá'u'lláh was more than simply a great teacher or reformer. His claim as a Messenger of God combined not only the Message, or the teachings of God for *this day*, but also the divine energy—called by some the Holy Spirit—which conferred the power to put these teachings into effect.

In the past, empires and civilizations blossomed forth as a result of the spiritual power emanating from earlier Manifestations. **Bahá'ís believe it is this divine impulse that has enabled every past revelation to create a new and higher civilization.**[104]

The political, social and scientific developments of the mid-nineteenth century heralded changes that Bahá'u'lláh promised would exceed anything achieved in the past. We are presently experiencing some of these promised changes. Politically, socially and scientifically, humanity is moving, despite the enormous dangers that encircle us, in the direction of wonders we can as yet barely imagine. The occurrence of these changes will vary in their impact on human progress according to humanity's willingness to accept the new teachings from God as revealed by Bahá'u'lláh.

FINAL YEARS

In His final years, Bahá'u'lláh spent more of His time writing and less time with visitors. The total of His writings, He said, exceeds the combined scriptures of all the previous Manifestations of God. He left the day-to-day affairs of the Bahá'í community to His eldest son and appointed successor, Abbas Effendi, who preferred to be called 'Abdu'l-Baha.[105] In the latter part of 1891, Bahá'u'lláh told His companions that His work was done and that He wished to depart from this world. Soon after, He contracted a fever and after a brief illness, passed away on May 29, 1892, at the age of seventy-five.

A distinguishing feature of the Bahá'í Faith is its explicit manner of transferring authority, a procedure that is designed to insure its unity and protect it from division into sects. In Judaism, in Christianity, and in Islam, the disagreements among the followers over their respective Founder's message, which was the Word of the one and same God, gave rise to various groups, each claiming the correct interpretation. Thus the Word of God became unclear, distorted, and was eventually corrupted. The differences among these groups, or sects, were magnified into enmity and, in some instances, led to wars and killing over their disagreements. There are now, literally, hundreds of sects in every major religion, and although they are not always killing each other, the differences remain, and the true meaning of the Word of God has become lost.

In the entire religious history of mankind, only the Bahá'í Faith has been able to maintain its unity. After more than 150 years, there are still no sectarian groups in the Bahá'í world community. This does not mean, of course, that there are no differences of understanding or interpretation among individuals. Any differences can always be settled because there is only one recognized authority for the Bahá'í teachings—the Universal House of Justice. Bahá'u'lláh took great care before His death to appoint 'Abdu'l-Baha His successor and sole interpreter of His teachings. The Universal House of Justice was designated by Bahá'u'lláh to be formed and to serve as the perpetual authority for the Bahá'í community. It does not have the authority to interpret the teachings, but it can elucidate specific teachings by calling attention to sacred texts and interpretations left by Shoghi Effendi. The Universal House of Justice may not make any changes in the Bahá'í scriptures, though it may legislate on matters not expressly revealed in the sacred texts.

Entrance, Shrine of Bahá'u'lláh, Akka, Israel
© *Bahá'í International Community*

CHAPTER REVIEW—Bahá'u'lláh

Summary
▶ Bahá'u'lláh was an active follower of the Bab.
▶ Bahá'u'lláh was imprisoned as a leader of the Babi community.
▶ Bahá'u'lláh was exiled four successive times, a prisoner for forty years.
▶ During His third exile, Bahá'u'lláh called for the major world rulers to establish world unity.
▶ Bahá'u'lláh selected His son, 'Abdu'l-Baha, to lead the Bahá'í community after Him.

Discussion
1. Describe conditions in the Siyah-Chal.
2. Identify major events of Bahá'u'lláh's exile in Baghdad.
3. Describe three major writings during His first exile.
4. Why was the second exile in Istanbul so short?
5. What was the theme of Bahá'u'lláh's 'Tablets to the Kings'? How did 'the kings' respond?
6. Discuss some of the specific proposals in these tablets.
7. Identify some main themes of the Kitab-i-Aqdas.
8. How are the teachings brought by a Manifestation of God superior to those of an ordinary teacher?
9. What was a common characteristic behavior of anyone admitted to the presence of Bahá'u'lláh?
10. Discuss the concept of justice in Bahá'u'lláh's injunction against 'retaliation'. Compare this with the Torah's teaching of 'an eye for an eye'.
11. What evidence is there that the unity theme taught by Bahá'u'lláh, and changes in political, social and scientific development are growing ever closer?

Research Topics
A. Explain the significance of the '1260 Days' referred to in Revelation 11:3? (Chapter 2, Islam)
B. Explain the calculations by which this number is obtained.

CHAPTER FIVE—'Abdu'l-Baha

'Abdu'l-Baha, the eldest son of Bahá'u'lláh, was Bahá'u'lláh's chosen successor and sole interpreter of His Father's Faith. He ranks, after the Bab and Bahá'u'lláh, as the third most important figure in Bahá'í history. Shoghi Effendi[106], in his history of the first century of the Bahá'í Faith, *God Passes By*, described 'Abdu'l-Baha as the completion of the Heroic Age and His passing as the beginning of the Formative Age[107] of the Bahá'í Faith.

'Abdu'l-Baha was born on May 23, 1844, the very same night of the Bab's declaration to Mulla Husayn. His entire life was devoted to His Father's Cause. Although 'Abdu'l-Baha was not a Manifestation of God, He is considered by Bahá'ís to be the exemplar of the perfect man, an example of the spiritual development to which all human beings might aspire.

He grew up in the shadow of His Father, and shared all of His trials, imprisonment and afflictions. He served as Bahá'u'lláh's secretary, confidant and official representative. Not only was 'Abdu'l-Baha the heir to Bahá'u'lláh's leadership of the Bahá'í community, but He also inherited, in His leadership position, the persecution and the enmity of the Persian and Turkish authorities.

After Bahá'u'lláh's death, 'Abdu'l-Baha remained a prisoner. It took the collapse of the Turkish Empire to end more than forty years of imprisonment and exile for 'Abdu'l-Baha. His crime was being the son of Bahá'u'lláh and the designated head of the Bahá'í community.

'Abdu'l-Baha, more than any of His Father's closest companions, had an opportunity to absorb and put into practice Bahá'u'lláh's teachings and principles of personal behavior. He radiated a spiritual purity that drew others. The qualities of selflessness, intellect and humility which He displayed, plus Bahá'u'lláh's obvious admiration for His son, won for 'Abdu'l-Baha the title of *the Master*, a term which is used even today by Bahá'ís in referring to 'Abdu'l-Baha.

COVENANT OF BAHÁ'U'LLÁH

The idea of a covenant, or agreement, between God and man is familiar to other religions. Jews believe that God made a covenant with Abraham, and Christians are taught that Jesus entered into a new covenant with His followers. The Universal House of Justice clarified the idea of a covenant in the religious sense as **"a binding agreement between God and man, whereby God requires of man certain behavior in return for which He guarantees certain blessings."**[108]

The Bahá'í Faith teaches that Bahá'u'lláh made a two-part covenant with His followers. The first part, *the Greater Covenant*, calls for His followers to accept God's chosen Messenger, the next Manifestation, when He appears.

The second part, *the Lesser Covenant*, is the agreement that they will accept Bahá'u'lláh's appointed immediate successor. The Universal House of Justice noted that the Faith can remain united if its followers accept the Lesser Covenant. If not, **"the Faith becomes divided and its force spent. It is a (Lesser) Covenant of this kind that Bahá'u'lláh made with his followers regarding 'Abdu'l-Baha and that 'Abdu'l-Baha perpetuated through the Administrative Order."**[109]

CENTER OF THE COVENANT

The Lesser Covenant of Bahá'u'lláh is the name given to 'Abdu'l-Baha's appointment as His Father's successor. Bahá'u'lláh carefully documented this appointment to avoid the disunity and dissension that occurred in earlier religions soon after the death of their Founders. Bahá'u'lláh, in His *Will and Testament*, uniquely strengthened the authority of succession.

Bahá'u'lláh's Will also conferred upon 'Abdu'l-Baha the sole authority to interpret Bahá'u'lláh's writings. This made 'Abdu'l-Baha the focal point for Bahá'u'lláh's followers—'Abdu'l-Baha was termed the *Center of the Covenant*. By virtue of this authority, 'Abdu'l-Baha, in His own *Will*, appointed His eldest grandson, Shoghi Effendi, to serve as the *Guardian of the Faith* after His death.

In the past, each Manifestation of God left His teachings (His revelations of the Word of God) to posterity, and these teachings served, after they were written down, as the Holy Books of the respective religions. The followers were free to interpret the teachings as they pleased. Soon after the Founder's departure, disagreements arose in interpreting these teachings. These disagreements would soon lead to the rise of divisive groups—movements, denominations, cults or sects within each religion, e.g. the Catholic, Protestant and Eastern Orthodox in Christianity; the Orthodox, Conservative and Reform in Judaism; and the Sunni and Shiah in Islam. Within each of these groups, sub-groups quickly multiplied. Within Christianity alone, it has been estimated that there are now more than 25,000 different groups and sub-groups, and there are numerous divisions in all the other religions as well. All, that is, except the Bahá'í Faith. After more than one hundred years since Bahá'u'lláh's death, the Bahá'í Faith is still united under one recognized authority, the Universal House of Justice.

For Bahá'ís, the Lesser Covenant of Bahá'u'lláh is of major importance because it guarantees the unity of the Faith. To be faithful to the Covenant means to accept the authority of Bahá'u'lláh's appointed successor, 'Abdu'l-Baha (as well as His appointed successor, Shoghi Effendi). To break the Covenant is to reject the authority of this line of succession and, in effect, the authority of Bahá'u'lláh.

Some envious relatives and other individuals tried to break the Covenant and discredit 'Abdu'l-Baha (and later, Shoghi Effendi) in order to usurp their positions, but none could achieve their ends. Ultimately, each effort disintegrated with the death of its leader.

THE MASTER

Like Bahá'u'lláh, 'Abdu'l-Baha's magnetic personality and leadership qualities impressed both Bahá'ís and non-Bahá'ís. Numerous reports, anecdotal recollections, biographical accounts, and books about Abdu'l-Baha amply testify to the admiration and high esteem in which He was universally extolled by both friends and foes. An enemy of the Faith once announced from the pulpit that **"if there was one proof by which Bahá'u'lláh could substantiate His claims to Prophethood, it would be that He reared such a Son as 'Abbas Effendi** ('Abdu'l-Baha)."[110]

Professor E.G. Browne, the Cambridge scholar and a non-Bahá'í who was granted an audience with Bahá'u'lláh in 1890 wrote of 'Abdu'l-Baha, whom he later came to know well:

Seldom have I seen one whose appearance impressed me more. A tall, strongly-built man holding himself straight as an arrow, with white turban and raiment, long black locks reaching almost to the shoulder, broad powerful forehead indicating a strong intellect combined with an unswerving will, eyes keen as a hawk's, and strongly-marked but pleasing features—such was my first impression of Abbas Effendi, the Master, as he par excellence is called by the ...[Bahá'ís]. Subsequent conversation with him served only to heighten the respect with which his appearance had from the first inspired me. One more eloquent of speech, more ready of argument, more

`Abdu'l-Bahá as a young man
© *Bahá'í International Community*

apt of illustration, more intimately acquainted with the sacred books of the Jews, the Christians, and the Muhammadans, could, I should think, scarcely be found even amongst the eloquent, ready, and subtle race to which he belongs. These qualities, combined with a bearing at once majestic and genial, made me cease to wonder at the influence and esteem which he enjoyed even beyond the circle of his father's followers. About the greatness of this man and his power no one who had seen him could entertain a doubt.[111]

END OF IMPRISONMENT

For sixteen years after the death of Bahá'u'lláh, 'Abdu'l-Baha remained a prisoner in Akka. During this time, 'Abdu'l-Baha had guided the affairs of the Bahá'í community from his confinement in Akka, through letters and direct contact with visiting believers.

In the Turkish capital of Istanbul the corrupt government of Sultan 'Abdu'l-Hamid was encountering increasing pressure from various groups for political reform. In 1908, a group called the *Young Turks* demanded and finally won from the sultan the restoration of the Turkish constitution, which the sultan himself had suspended thirty years earlier. As a result, all political and religious prisoners in the empire were set free, including 'Abdu'l-Baha, now broken in health after forty years of exile and imprisonment.

He moved His residence from Akka across the bay to the seaport city of Haifa, near Mount Carmel, in the vicinity Bahá'u'lláh had selected years earlier for the future administrative and religious headquarters of the Bahá'í Faith.

EARLY NORTH AMERICAN BAHÁ'ÍS

The Bahá'í community at this time was concentrated in Persia and in India. In order to establish the Faith as a worldwide community, 'Abdu'l-Baha recognized the need for concentrated teaching efforts in the West—in Europe, and in North America. The wide attention given in the West to the dramatic story of the Bab, especially among the artistic and intellectual circles in Western Europe, was a positive indication of considerable interest in the Bahá'í message.

In America, the first public reference to the Bahá'í Faith was made at the Chicago World Fair, in 1893. Within a few years, teachers sent by 'Abdu'l-Baha to conduct Bahá'í classes listed hundreds of Bahá'í believers just in the area around Chicago.

Among the early American believers were several individuals who later became some of the most effective teachers of the Faith. One of these was Lua Getsinger, formerly Louisa A. Moore, who traveled throughout the United States lecturing to interested groups. So successful was she that Shoghi Effendi in later years acknowledged her as the *mother teacher of the West*.

One of her students, Mrs. Phoebe Hearst, a philanthropist millionaire, organized the first party of Western pilgrims to visit the Holy Land, where they met 'Abdu'l-Baha in 1898. This meeting with 'Abdu'l-Baha was a rare spiritual experience for them, and their visit to the Holy Land proved to be a great stimulus to the growth of the Faith in the West.

So impressed were the Western pilgrims with the spiritual radiance of 'Abdu'l-Baha that some were convinced He was Himself the Messiah. In a reply to a letter from some American believers, He publicly stated that He is not to be acclaimed as the return of Jesus Christ, the Son Who will come **"in the glory of the Father. You have written that there is a difference among the believers concerning the 'Second Coming of Christ.' Gracious God! Time and again this question hath arisen, and its answer hath emanated in a clear and irrefutable statement from the pen of 'Abdu'l-Bahá, that what is meant in the prophecies by the 'Lord of Hosts' and the 'Promised Christ' is the Blessed Perfection (Bahá'u'lláh) and His holiness the Exalted One (the Bab). My name is 'Abdu'l-Baha** (Servant of Baha). **My qualification is 'Abdu'l-Baha. My reality is 'Abdu'l-Baha. My praise is 'Abdu'l-Baha. Thralldom to the Blessed Perfection** (Bahá'u'lláh) **is my glorious and refulgent diadem, and servitude to all the human race my perpetual religion... No name, no title, no commendation have I, nor will ever** have, except 'Abdu'l-Baha... This is my greatest yearning. This is my eternal life. This is my everlasting glory."[112]

The visit of the Hearst party was the beginning of a steadily growing stream of Western visitors that continued for twenty-three years, until 'Abdu'l-Baha's death in 1921. It was interrupted only for the duration of World War I and for His absence in the Holy Land during His memorable visit to the West.

VISIT TO THE WEST

In 1910, 'Abdu'l-Baha decided to make the long-cherished visit to the West. After a preliminary stop in Egypt for a needed rest to prepare Himself physically for the rigors of His forthcoming journey, 'Abdu'l-Baha sailed for Marseilles in August of 1911. This twenty-eight-month mission throughout the Western world proved to be one of the highlights of 'Abdu'l-Baha's lifelong service to the Cause of Bahá'u'lláh and a major milestone in the worldwide expansion of the Faith.

'Abdu'l-Baha's first public address was in London, at City Temple in Holborn. He had never before given a sermon or addressed an audience anywhere. His Father's extensive teachings had been ingrained in 'Abdu'l-Baha throughout His life. These now came to mind in topics appropriate for the occasion. This was the beginning of an intensive sequence of public contacts carrying the message of Bahá'u'lláh to the people of the West.

For the next five months 'Abdu'l-Baha maintained a continuing round of public addresses in London and Paris, as well as in numerous side trips. In addition to daily talks to assembled visitors at His hosts' homes, He met with prominent people in government, industry, education and religion. By December of that year, it was decided that the next phase of His journey, to America, would have to be postponed long enough to reduce the energy drain this teaching schedule had made upon His strength. He returned to Egypt for a three-month rest, and on March 25, 1912, in His sixty-eighth year, 'Abdu'l-Baha boarded the ocean liner S.S. Cedric in Alexandria, headed for New York.

As expected, 'Abdu'l-Baha's eight months in the

United States and Canada turned out to be the most physically taxing of His travels. They were also the most rewarding in terms of the impetus it gave to the expansion of the Faith. His busy schedule, more intense than His earlier visit to Europe, consisted of talks, press interviews, public meetings, conferences and gatherings. He visited more than forty cities, chiefly in the areas around New York, Washington D.C., Chicago, San Francisco and Montreal.

He laid the cornerstone of the first Bahá'í Temple in the West, at Wilmette, near Chicago. Among the numerous prominent public figures He met are: Theodore Roosevelt, former president of the United States; Alexander Graham Bell, inventor of the telephone; Andrew Carnegie, renowned financier and philanthropist; John James Audubon, renowned botanist; Samuel Gompers, labor leader; Josephine Hull and W.E.B. DuBois, social reformers.

The respect and honor `Abdu'l-Bahá was given wherever He appeared in public reflected a society that was receptive to His message. At Stanford University near San Francisco, the university president, Dr. David Starr Jordan, introduced `Abdu'l-Bahá to an assembled crowd of two thousand: **"...`Abdu'l-Bahá will surely unite the East and the West: for he treads the mystic way with practical feet."**[113]

`Abdu'l-Bahá

Throughout His tour of North America, from April to December, 'Abdu'l-Baha received extensive coverage from major newspapers. The speeches, talks and interviews He gave dealing with social, theological and moral issues as well as economic, racial and political questions from the standpoint of Bahá'í teachings were received favorably.

He deplored the growing political unrest in Europe and warned of the coming bloodshed of World Wars I and II; but He also noted that international unity would be established before the end of the century.

Some listeners and readers mistakenly jumped to the conclusion that this was a promise of world peace and the end of war, clearly an unwarranted assumption. International unity had its shaky beginnings with the League of Nations and earlier; even military alliances were a primitive example of international unity. It is thus clear that international unity was a process—a long process of social development that has gained ground slowly, in such areas as trade, finance, scientific research, and humanitarian aid. Political unity has proceeded at a much slower pace.

Toward the end of His tour 'Abdu'l-Baha's energy-draining speaking schedule, sometimes numbering five or six in one day, was taking a heavy toll on His strength. At times, He would have to sit or even lie down during His talks, but He would not consent to a cancellation of any planned meeting just because He needed to rest. Visitors were constantly calling, at His hotel or at the home of a host, to talk to Him, to ask an important question or request advice, or just to be close to Him and feel the spirit of His presence.

Love of mankind, a key principle of Bahá'í teachings, was part of 'Abdu'l-Baha. He would never turn anyone away; His limited time for proclaiming Bahá'u'lláh's message, He said, was too precious to waste on relief of His own mere physical discomfort or weakness.

The public addresses of 'Abdu'l-Baha in North America were compiled from stenographic notes in a book entitled *The Promulgation of Universal Peace, Talks Delivered by 'Abdu'l-Baha During His Visit to the United States and Canada in 1912*. These talks were described as "**...one of the most strenuous teaching journeys in all recorded religious history, the more remarkable because it was accomplished by a man of sixty-eight Whose health was broken by long years of deprivation and imprisonment.**"[114]

In its introduction, the book described this journey as a *'loving service to mankind.'* 'Abdu'l-Baha refused remuneration for any of His addresses in promoting the Cause of Bahá'u'lláh. On the contrary, He often donated to needy churches and other charitable institutions.

Standing in the doorway of Bowery Mission one night He distributed two hundred dollars in silver to a long line of poor, disconsolate men, speaking words of uplift and encouragement as they passed before Him. Under all circumstances 'Abdu'l-Baha refused to accept money for Himself and the Cause He represented. When the Bahá'ís of this country received word of His intended visit, the sum of eighteen thousand dollars was subscribed toward the expense of His journey. He was notified of this action, and a part of the money forwarded to Him by cable. He cabled in answer that the funds contributed by His friends could not be accepted, returned the money and instructed them to give their offering to the poor.[115]

'Abdu'l-Baha left New York on December 5, 1912. A week later He arrived in Liverpool on the first leg of His return to Haifa. He resumed the teaching schedule of His earlier visit, this time visiting Edinburgh, Scotland for several days. As before, His audiences were large and enthusiastic, His words uplifting and inspiring. Towards the end of January, 1913, He moved on, to Paris, where He also maintained a heavy speaking schedule.

While in Paris, 'Abdu'l-Baha took a month off to visit eager Bahá'í friends in Stuttgart, Germany. From Germany He traveled a bit farther, to Vienna and Budapest, where His words and spirit reached out to all. He returned to Paris and several weeks later He left for Marseilles where He boarded a steamer for Egypt and later for the Holy Land and Haifa.

'Abdu'l-Baha's historic tour of the West was over. His journey had the effect of establishing the Bahá'í Faith as a major new force for social reform and religious renewal. Bahá'u'lláh's message had been proclaimed in the industrialized world and a new generation of firm believers had now been enlisted.

But the physical drain of the journey was evident; 'Abdu'l-Baha had aged visibly. For almost the entire period of His tour the physical body had been driven by spiritual power that permitted no rest in spreading the message of Bahá'u'lláh to receptive souls hungry for that message. The cumulative fatigue of the past twenty years of His leadership of the Faith weighed heavily upon Him. In a tablet to the Bahá'í community He wrote:

Friends! The time is coming when I shall be no longer with you... I have served the Cause of Bahá'u'lláh to the utmost of my ability... all the years of my life. O how I long to see the loved ones taking upon themselves the responsibility of the Cause... O how I yearn to see the friends united even as a string of pearls, as the brilliant Pleiades...[116]

The stream of pilgrims and visitors continued to grow. 'Abdu'l-Baha, concerned that the storm which He had predicted was about to break over Europe and over the world, stopped the flow of visitors and instructed those present to leave. The Holy Land, still a part of the Ottoman Turkish Empire, now had to suffer the unrest and instability of a nation at war.

WAR YEARS

The Ottomans, the despotic dynasty that had ruled Turkey with an iron fist for the past few centuries, was now but a shell of its former glory. The empire was a patchwork of diverse territories and cultures, each clinging to its own languages and customs, and commonly resentful of each other and of their own harsh treatment by the central government.

The sultan and his corrupt advisors, greedy and distrustful of each other, knew no other way to deal with their own people except by harsh suppression. Under these adverse conditions, they led their people into a pact with Germany and Austria-Hungary in a war against Britain, France and Russia (and later, the United States).

The war years in the Holy Land worsened the normal poverty and poor living conditions which most of the people had to endure. Scarce food supplies became scarcer. 'Abdu'l-Baha, who had visited and aided the poor for years, as Bahá'u'lláh had done in His time, continued His aid throughout the war years, comforting and sharing His limited supplies as best He could. In an effort to prevent a famine in the area, 'Abdu'l-Baha personally organized a large agricultural project that resulted in an increase of wheat production.

The Turkish authorities, though fully engaged in their military operations, were sympathetic to the accusations of 'Abdu'l-Baha's enemies, His own relatives who had never accepted His leadership of the Bahá'ís. 'Abdu'l-Baha was accused of secretly aiding the British and serving as a contact for military information. The Turkish general for that region, Jamal Pasha, vowed to hang 'Abdu'l-Baha after the British forces in the Middle East were defeated.

Despite the problems in the Holy Land created by the war, 'Abdu'l-Baha always had the fortunes of the Faith very much in mind. The time He spent proclaiming the teachings of Bahá'u'lláh to the Western world, especially in America, provided the means by which 'Abdu'l-Baha would open the rest of the world to Bahá'u'lláh's Message. He foresaw the role American Bahá'ís were destined to play in spearheading the growth of the Bahá'í Faith throughout the world. **"The continent of America," wrote 'Abdu'l-Bahá in February, 1917, "is, in the eyes of the one true God, the land wherein the splendors of His light shall be revealed, where the mysteries of His Faith shall be unveiled, where the righteous will abide, and the free assemble."**[117]
The American nation is equipped and empowered to accomplish that which will adorn the pages of history, to become the envy of the world, and be blest in both the East and the West for the triumph of its people... The American continent gives signs and evidences of very great advancement. Its future is even more promising, for its influence and illumination are far-reaching. It will lead all nations spiritually.[118]

Reflecting on the results of His journey to the West, 'Abdu'l-Baha recognized the pioneering spirit and unbounded energy of the North American Bahá'ís as the core of His plan to internationalize the Faith. He wrote a series of fourteen letters, later known as *The Tablets of the Divine Plan*, addressed to the believers in North America. In these letters, 'Abdu'l-Baha rallied the believers to teach and promote the principles of the Bahá'í Faith in other lands.

In December 1917, the British forces under General Allenby, moving westward from military successes in Iran and Iraq, captured Jerusalem in the course of their drive towards Turkey. Jamal Pasha, the Turkish general, now had an opportunity to make good his vow to hang 'Abdu'l-Baha as he passed through Haifa while retreating to Turkey.

Fearful for His safety, Bahá'ís in England persuaded the government to take special measures to protect the life of 'Abdu'l-Baha. General Allenby received a government cable to protect 'Abdu'l-Baha, His family and His friends when the British marched on Haifa. The British managed to take Haifa sooner than anyone expected, and General Allenby's cable said: **"Have today taken Palestine. Notify the world that 'Abdu'l-Baha is safe."**[119] Guards were posted around 'Abdu'l-Baha's house and word was passed through enemy lines that stern retribution would follow any attempt on the life of the great Persian master or any of His household.

With the end of the war, the Republic of Turkey was established to replace the Ottoman government. The former empire lost its Middle East territories and the Holy Land was assigned to the protection of the British Empire by the newly-formed League of Nations. 'Abdu'l-Baha, now a local hero because of His service to the Haifa community during the war, was held in high esteem by the British governing officials. He was later awarded a knighthood by the British Empire.

FINAL YEARS

No longer isolated by wartime restrictions, the stream of Bahá'í pilgrims to the Holy Land from both East and West resumed, together with letters and requests for another visit from the Master. 'Abdu'l-Baha was once again fully occupied with the steadily increasing volume of leadership responsibilities, which taxed His strength to its limits.

He was also gaining recognition on the world stage. As the leader of a growing religious movement advocating world government as one of its goals for world peace, international statesmen and world leaders often consulted 'Abdu'l-Baha on the formation of the League of Nations.

Despite His busy schedule, 'Abdu'l-Baha's charm and spiritual magnetism were evident. In 1919, Dr. John E. Esslemont was a guest of 'Abdu'l-Baha. In Esslemont's book, *Bahá'u'lláh and the New Era*, there was a description of an average day in the life of the Master:

At that time, although nearly seventy-six years of age, he was still remarkably vigorous, and accomplished daily an almost incredible amount of work... [H]is services were always at the disposal of those who needed them most. His unfailing patience, gentleness, kindliness and tact made his presence like a benediction...

From early morning until evening... he was busily engaged in reading and answering letters from many lands and in attending to the multitudinous affairs of... the Cause. In the afternoon he usually had a little relaxation in the form of a walk or a drive, but even then he was usually accompanied by one or two, or a party of, pilgrims with whom he would converse on spiritual matters...

Both at lunch and supper he used to entertain a number of pilgrims and friends, and charm his guests with happy and humorous stories as well as precious talks on a great variety of subjects. "My home is the home of laughter and mirth," he declared, and indeed it was so. He delighted in gathering together people of various races, colors, nations and religions in unity and cordial friendship around his hospitable board. He was indeed a loving father not only to the little community of Haifa, but to the Bahá'í community throughout the world.[120]

The Tablets of the Divine Plan, the series of fourteen letters 'Abdu'l-Baha had addressed to the North American believers two years earlier, now began to bear fruit. Hardy souls, eager to find some way to show their devotion to God, found in 'Abdu'l-Baha's letters the inspiration they needed. Clara and Hyde Dunn, he in his sixties, left their home in California and set out for Australia. Before he died, in 1941, Hyde Dunn saw the establishment of an active, growing Bahá'í community in the South Pacific. Clara Dunn remained in Australia and worked for the Faith until her death in 1960.

Another intrepid Bahá'í pioneer, Martha Root, a journalist, went to South America. This was the start of a twenty-year travel mission, writing articles, speaking to large groups, meeting royalty, statesmen, eminent scholars and other people of all types. She tirelessly pursued her travel mission, visiting all parts of the world, until her death in 1939.

The spiritual seeds she planted in the hearts of thousands of people bore fruit in later years. Queen Marie of Rumania declared her acceptance of the Bahá'í Faith as a result of her contacts with Martha Root.

In 1908, 'Abdu'l-Baha had outlined the plan for implementing the administrative structure Bahá'u'lláh had conceived for building the Kingdom of God on earth. The Scriptures of all the earlier religions included statements and prophecies about this Kingdom, but without the details of how it would be done. Bahá'u'lláh, who proclaimed Himself the Promised One of all the earlier religions, had begun the process of fulfilling these prophecies.

The central institutions of the administrative order which Bahá'u'lláh had identified as the governing bodies for the affairs of the Bahá'í Faith, were designated by 'Abdu'l-Baha as the **Guardianship** and the **Universal House of Justice**. The Guardian of the Bahá'í Faith, Shoghi Effendi Rabbani, was later appointed by 'Abdu'l-Baha as the sole interpreter of the Bahá'í teachings. The Universal House of Justice was designated as the primary legislative and administrative authority for the Bahá'í Faith, responsible for all international Bahá'í activities. The Guardian would assume authority upon the death of 'Abdu'l-Baha, but the House of Justice would not come into existence until the prerequisites for its creation (described later in this book) were in place.

By now the pressures of His activities were visible in 'Abdu'l-Baha's weakened appearance and movements, but His will and sense of responsibility kept Him going. He prayed for His own release from this world:

O Lord! My bones are weakened... and I have now reached old age, failing in my powers... No strength is there left in me wherewith to serve Thy loved ones... O Lord, my Lord! Hasten my ascension unto Thy sublime threshold... and my arrival at the door of Thy grace beneath the shadow of Thy most great mercy.[121]

On the morning of November 28, 1921, 'Abdu'l-Baha passed away in His seventy-eighth year. Despite a lifetime of persecution, imprisonment, hardship and suffering, 'Abdu'l-Baha demonstrated, through devoted service to others and unswerving loyalty to the spiritual principles His Father had instilled in Him, the level of spiritual achievement to which an ordinary human being can hope to attain.

After His release from the repressive restrictions of the Turkish government, 'Abdu'l-Baha's spiritual qualities radiated to others and brought Him the love, honor and adulation which now poured in from around the world. Without seeking any recognition, 'Abdu'l-Baha had become revered as a sage, philanthropist and holy man by all the religious communities in Palestine, as well as by numerous people and groups throughout the world.

His funeral, held the day after His death, drew a respectful crowd estimated at more than ten thousand. It included prominent members of every religious group in the Holy Land, in addition to the British High Commissioner, governors and many other public officials. When word of His passing reached distant parts of the world, newspapers printed lengthy obituaries, and solemn public and private observances were held in 'Abdu'l-Baha's memory.

In the words of Shoghi Effendi and Lady Blomfield:

The eyes that had always looked out with loving-kindness upon humanity, whether friends or foes, were now closed. The hands that had ever been stretched forth to give alms to the poor and needy,

the halt and the maimed, the blind, the orphan and the widow, had now finished their labour. The feet that, with untiring zeal, had gone upon the ceaseless errands of the Lord of Compassion were now at rest. The lips that had so eloquently championed the cause of the suffering sons of men, were now hushed in silence. The heart that had so powerfully throbbed with wondrous love for the children of God was now stilled. His glorious spirit had passed from the life of earth, from the persecutions of the enemies of righteousness, from the storm and stress of well nigh eighty years of indefatigable toil for the good of others.[122]

`Abdu'l-Bahá, Formal Portrait
© *Bahá'í International Community*

CHAPTER REVIEW—'Abdu'l-Baha

Summary
▶ 'Abdu'l-Baha shared with His father more than forty years of exile and imprisonment.

▶Bahá'u'lláh appointed 'Abdu'l-Baha as the Center of the Covenant and His successor to lead the Bahá'í community.

▶ 'Abdu'l-Baha's twenty-eight-month visit to the West was a major step in the international growth of the Bahá'í Faith.

▶His Tablets of the Divine Plan, addressed to the North American believers, provided the impetus for carrying the Bahá'í message throughout the world.

Number in chronological order
___ His first meeting with Professor E.G. Browne.
___ Outbreak of the First World War.
___ His talk at Stanford University.
___ The visit of the first party of Western pilgrims.
___ Queen Marie of Rumania declared her belief in Bahá'u'lláh
___ 'Tablets of the Divine Plan' sent to the North American believers.
___ His visit to Stuttgart, Germany.

Discussion
1. Why was 'Abdu'l-Baha kept a prisoner in the Holy Land after the death of Bahá'u'lláh?
2. How was the unity of the Bahá'í Faith maintained after the death of Bahá'u'lláh?
3. Describe the development of the Bahá'í Faith in America, from its earliest introduction, to 'Abdu'l-Baha's 'Visit to the West'.
4. How did the Covenant of Bahá'u'lláh safeguard the integrity of the Bahá'í teachings?
5. What is 'Abdu'l-Baha's role in the Covenant of Bahá'u'lláh?
6. How did 'Abdu'l-Baha respond to those who thought of Him as the Messiah?
7. Enumerate the highlights of the 'Visit to the West.'
8. Describe 'Abdu'l-Baha's 'Tablets of the Divine Plan'?
9. What connection did 'Abdu'l-Baha have with the League of Nations?

CHAPTER SIX—Shoghi Effendi

EDUCATION AND TRAINING

The Bahá'í community, stunned by the devastating loss of their revered and beloved leader, looked toward Haifa for guidance. Thanks to 'Abdu'l-Baha's careful planning in His will and testament, His successor, Shoghi Effendi, was clearly identified.

At this time Shoghi Effendi was a student attending the University of Oxford, in England. Fortunately, his beloved great-aunt, Bahiyyih Khanum[123], 'Abdu'l-Baha's devoted sister, was present at 'Abdu'l-Baha's death and she filled in for her brother until Shoghi Effendi could return from England and assume his duties as Guardian of the Bahá'í Faith.

Shoghi Effendi was born in Akka on March 1, 1897, in the home of his grandfather, 'Abdu'l-Baha. Like the bond that united 'Abdu'l-Baha with Bahá'u'lláh, Shoghi Effendi enjoyed a special tie with his grandfather. Perhaps it was fortunate for Shoghi Effendi that 'Abdu'l-Baha dared not display fully the intense love He felt for His first grandson for fear that enemies of the Cause might use this relationship to further their own nefarious ends. No one but 'Abdu'l-Baha recognized the role destined for Shoghi Effendi when the Master insisted that the

Shoghi Effendi
© *Bahá'í International Community*

respectful title, *Effendi* (sir or mister), be used when addressing little Shoghi, even as a small child.

The process in which the spiritual qualities and values 'Abdu'l-Baha absorbed and developed as a result of His close association with Bahá'u'lláh was repeated in the special closeness Shoghi Effendi enjoyed with his grandfather. Although they both shared similar spiritual qualities, their personalities were quite different. Shoghi Effendi was shy and sensitive compared to 'Abdu'l-Baha's outgoing magnetism that drew people to Him.

In preparation for his future role in serving the Cause, Shoghi Effendi's education was carefully supervised by 'Abdu'l-Baha. The schools he attended emphasized the mastery of foreign languages, and the young Shoghi Effendi worked hard to add English to his already fluent Arabic, French, Persian and Turkish. During school vacations Shoghi Effendi translated 'Abdu'l-Baha's letters and served as His secretary. In 1918, Shoghi Effendi was awarded a Bachelor of Arts degree from the American College in Beirut.

In order to serve his grandfather more effectively, especially through his command of English, Shoghi Effendi decided to pursue more intensively his study of English and in 1920 he reluctantly left his grandfather to pursue his studies in England, at Balliol College, Oxford University. His grief was profound when he received word of 'Abdu'l-Baha's death a year later.

EARLY YEARS

The Bahá'í Faith during Shoghi Effendi's early years as Guardian was very vulnerable. Small in numbers, scattered among many countries, and having just lost a charismatic guide and Holy Father figure, the believers were like children who had just been orphaned.

The awesome responsibility 'Abdu'l-Baha had placed upon Shoghi Effendi's young shoulders was bearable only because of his great love for his adored grandfather. The devastating shock of losing his grandfather was equal only to the complete surprise of his appointment as Guardian.

The years he had spent at the side of 'Abdu'l-Baha,

watching how He dealt with people in all walks of life, from ministers and government officials of high rank to enemies of the Faith, enabled Shoghi Effendi to gradually settle into the role his destiny had assigned to him.

Enemies of the Faith, mainly his own family members, tried to usurp his position by claiming what they felt were their rights. Letters were arriving from all over the world requesting advice and interpretation of Bahá'í teachings. To all of these, the young Shoghi Effendi now had to respond with maturity, wisdom and tact.

Bahá'u'lláh cultivated the soil and prepared the foundation for the Kingdom of God. 'Abdu'l-Baha designed and established the machinery for building this Kingdom. And it was Shoghi Effendi who was the master builder and engineer, the organizer who followed the master plan and supervised the building of its basic structures.

'Abdu'l-Baha's summons to the North American believers through the Tablets of the Divine Plan spurred the geographical spread of the Bahá'í community. Shoghi Effendi now proceeded to tighten the bonds uniting the Bahá'í world through a continuous stream of letters on Bahá'í teachings covering issues from family life to world government. These letters stimulated the growth of the Faith and served as a continuing source of encouragement and support.

Shoghi Effendi also strengthened the organization of the administrative order by encouraging the formation of local Houses of Justice (called Local Spiritual Assemblies) wherever there were sufficient numbers of Bahá'ís. And from these Local Spiritual Assemblies were formed National Spiritual Assemblies.

His letters provided guidance on the system and procedures for elections and group decision-making. These elected bodies also served as distributing points for the dissemination of his messages to the individual believers, although he continued to answer specific correspondence from individuals.

Unlike the role of loving father which 'Abdu'l-Baha displayed to the believers as leader of the Bahá'í Faith,

Shoghi Effendi subordinated his personal function as Guardian and emphasized the institution of the Guardianship as the object of respect, love and allegiance for all Bahá'ís.

He forbade any commemoration of his birthday or other event in his life; he discouraged photographs of himself. His goal was to wean the Bahá'í community from dependence on anyone except God. Their attention was to be focused on the institutions of the Faith. This was a first step in the growing up process for the Bahá'í world community.

The numerous letters Shoghi Effendi wrote to the believers stressed the equality and the brotherhood of man, and he referred to himself in terms of an equal (and not a father figure). He signed his letters, *'Your true brother, Shoghi.'* The Heroic Age of the Bahá'í Faith, he said, had passed with the Bab, Bahá'u'lláh and 'Abdu'l-Baha. They created the foundation from which God's Kingdom on earth would arise. Now was the beginning of the Formative Age, the building of that new world society, called the Golden Age of the Kingdom of God on earth, when the religion of God would transform all of mankind into one loving family.

During the thirty six years of his ministry as Guardian until his death in 1957, Shoghi Effendi poured forth enormous energy, skill, love and administrative genius that transformed the Faith from a tiny, unknown, religious movement into a global, unified religion with a message of universal appeal. With the breadth of vision of a gifted chief executive, Shoghi Effendi conducted his campaign of developing the Faith on all fronts.

He established the Bahá'í World Center, and united the Bahá'í community with his inspiring letters and brilliant translations of the Bahá'í writings. He directed the efforts of the North American Bahá'í believers in spreading the message of Bahá'u'lláh to all parts of the world through the implementation of 'Abdu'l-Baha's Tablets of the Divine Plan.

Bahá'u'lláh had instructed 'Abdu'l-Baha where the final resting-place of the Bab was to be located on the slope of Mount Carmel in Haifa. 'Abdu'l-Baha and later Shoghi Effendi undertook the purchase of land and the construction, not only for the Bab's shrine but also for what was to become the Bahá'í World Center. Over the simple mausoleum block built by 'Abdu'l-Baha in 1908, in which were placed the Bab's earthly remains, Shoghi Effendi later personally supervised the construction of the beautiful golden-domed *Shrine of the Bab*. This now commands a majestic view of Haifa's harbor, and forms the central point of the magnificent buildings and terraced gardens covering the entire slope of Mount Carmel.

This is the Bahá'í World Center, home of the Universal House of Justice and other Bahá'í administrative institutions and buildings. The Bahá'í World Center is now one of Israel's major tourist attractions. For Bahá'ís, it is the site on *God's holy mountain*, from which divine guidance flows to humanity.

GUARDIAN'S LITERARY OUTPUT

Shoghi Effendi's literary contributions to the growth and unity of the Bahá'í Faith cannot be overestimated. The numbers alone are impressive. More than 26,000 letters which he wrote to individual believers as well as local and national spiritual assemblies are in the Bahá'í archives at the World Center. English was his preferred language. Shoghi Effendi's mastery of English is in a class with the most celebrated authors in the English language.

His translations of the writings of the Bab, Bahá'u'lláh and 'Abdu'l-Baha, are considered by world scholars to be literary masterpieces. His book, *God Passes By*, is generally recognized as the most complete and authoritative work, the definitive history of the first hundred years of the Bahá'í Faith.

He packed so much information into each sentence that some people complained that his writing was sometimes difficult to understand. He refused to water down his writing to accommodate lazy readers; he insisted that the length of his sentences would require more concentration by the reader and help develop a sharper mental focus.

Because he was the ultimate authority for interpreting the Bahá'í writings, Shoghi Effendi's

English translations of the Bahá'í writings are sometimes used for study by religious scholars together with the original scriptures in Persian and Arabic.[124]

The letters Shoghi Effendi sent out for dissemination to all Bahá'ís were not merely words of advice and encouragement. They were also powerful teaching tools that helped to deepen believers in understanding the teachings of Bahá'u'lláh and 'Abdu'l-Baha.

In a series of letters later published under the title, *The World Order of Bahá'u'lláh*, Shoghi Effendi explained why the Bahá'í Faith had been able to resist the forces of division and disagreement that have endlessly plagued Christianity and Islam. He first depicted the religious hierarchies of the Christian Papacy, the Islamic Caliphate, and all of their *attending ecclesiastical orders* as similar to the Bahá'í Guardianship and the Universal House of Justice. How, he argued, could the Bahá'í institutions escape *the deterioration in character, the breach of unity, and the extinction of influence, which have befallen all organized religious hierarchies*, as exemplified by the Christian and Islamic institutions?

Where and how does this Order established by Bahá'u'lláh, which to outward seeming is but a replica of the institutions established in Christianity and Islam, differ from them?... What can possibly be the agency that can safeguard these Bahá'í institutions,...[similar] **in some of their features, to those which have been reared by the Fathers of the Church and the Apostles of Muhammad...? Why should they not eventually suffer the self-same fate that has overtaken the institutions which the successors of Christ and Muhammad have reared?**[125]

Shoghi Effendi pointed out that the earlier institutions were developed without the specific guidance of the Founder and were thus subject to the inherent weaknesses of every man-made institution. The institutions of the Bahá'í Faith, however, rest on the authority of Bahá'u'lláh's explicit writings and its unity is thus ensured.

[T]he fundamental reason why the unity of the

Church of Christ was irretrievably shattered, and its influence was in the course of time undermined, was that the edifice which the Fathers of the Church reared after the passing of his first Apostle was an edifice that rested in nowise upon the explicit directions of Christ himself. The authority and features of their administration were wholly inferred, and indirectly derived... from certain vague and fragmentary references which they found scattered amongst his utterances as recorded in the Gospel. Not one of the sacraments of the Church; not one of the rites and ceremonies... reposed on the direct authority of Christ, or emanated from his specific utterances...

Had it been possible for the Church Fathers... to refute the denunciations heaped upon them by quoting specific utterances of Christ regarding the future administration of his Church, or the nature of the authority of his successors, they would surely have been capable of quenching the flame of controversy, and preserving the unity of Christendom. The Gospel, however, the only repository of the utterances of Christ, afforded no such shelter to these harassed leaders of the Church,... helpless in the face of the pitiless onslaught of their enemy, and who eventually had to submit to the forces of schism which have invaded their ranks.

In the Muhammadan Revelation... [Muhammad] gave no written, no binding and conclusive instructions to those whose mission it was to propagate his Cause.... the Qur'an... gives no definite guidance regarding the Law of Succession, the source of all the dissensions, the controversies, and schisms which have dismembered and discredited Islam.

Not so with the Revelation of Bahá'u'lláh... Both in the administrative provisions of the Bahá'í Dispensation, and in the matter of succession... the followers of Bahá'u'lláh can summon to their aid such irrefutable evidences of Divine Guidance that none can resist, that none can belittle or ignore. Therein lies the distinguishing feature of the Bahá'í Revelation. **Therein lies the strength of the unity of the Faith, of the validity of a Revelation that claims not to destroy or belittle previous Revelations, but to connect, unify and fulfill them.**[126]

In one of his most dramatic and powerful messages, *The Promised Day Is Come*, addressed to the Bahá'ís of the West, Shoghi Effendi explained and clarified the meaning of the crisis of this age. It was written in 1941, during World War II, but its significance for today, in a time of social breakdown and degenerating moral values, is equally relevant.

The power of Shoghi Effendi's literary eloquence is evident in the following excerpt from *The Promised Day Is Come*. He dramatically selects quotations from Bahá'u'lláh's warnings (written in Adrianople) to the earth's rulers, before His final exile to Akka, and paints a frightening picture of the destruction mankind is bringing upon itself. This destruction, however, is not total, as it is serving a beneficial purpose, a spiritual cleansing that will prepare mankind for entrance into its *Golden Age*:

A tempest, unprecedented in its violence, unpredictable in its course, catastrophic in its immediate effects, unimaginably glorious in its ultimate consequences, is at present sweeping the face of the earth. Its driving power is remorselessly gaining in range and momentum. Its cleansing force, however much undetected, is increasing with every passing day. Humanity, gripped in the clutches of its devastating power, is smitten by the evidences of its resistless fury. It can neither perceive its origin, nor probe its significance, nor discern its outcome. Bewildered, agonized and helpless, it watches this great and mighty wind of God invading the remotest and fairest regions of the earth, rocking its foundations, deranging its equilibrium, sundering its nations, disrupting the homes of its peoples, wasting its cities, driving into exile its kings, pulling down its bulwarks, uprooting its institutions, dimming its light, and harrowing up the souls of its inhabitants.

'The time for the destruction of the world and its people,' Bahá'u'lláh's prophetic pen has proclaimed, 'hath arrived.' 'The hour is approaching... when the most great convulsion will have appeared.' "The promised day is come, the day when tormenting trials will have surged above your heads, and beneath your feet, saying: 'Taste ye what your hands have wrought!' 'Soon shall the blasts of His chastisement beat upon you, and the dust of hell enshroud you!'... 'And when the appointed hour is come, there shall suddenly appear that which shall cause the limbs of mankind to quake.' "The day is approaching when its (civilization's) flame will devour the cities... 'The day will soon come,' He... has written, 'whereon they will cry out for help and receive no answer.' 'The day is approaching,' He... prophesied, 'when the wrathful anger of the Almighty will have taken hold of them... He shall cleanse the earth from the defilement of their corruption, and shall give it for an heritage unto such of His servants as are nigh unto Him.'

Dear friends! The powerful operations of this titanic upheaval are comprehensible to none except such as have recognized the claims of both Bahá'u'lláh and the Bab. Their followers know full well whence it comes, and what it will ultimately lead to. Though ignorant of how far it will reach, they clearly recognize its genesis, are aware of its direction, acknowledge its necessity, observe confidently its mysterious processes, ardently pray for the mitigation of its severity, intelligently labor to assuage its fury, and anticipate, with undimmed vision, the consummation of the fears and hopes it must necessarily engender.

This judgment of God... is both a retributory calamity and an act of holy and supreme discipline. It is at once a visitation from God and a cleansing process for all mankind. Its fires punish the perversity of the human race, and weld its component parts into one organic, indivisible, world-embracing community. Mankind... is... being simultaneously called upon to give account of its past actions, and is being purged and prepared for its future mission. It can neither escape the responsibilities of the past, nor shirk those of the future. God... can... neither allow the sins of an unregenerate humanity... to go unpunished, nor will He be willing to abandon His children to their fate, and refuse them that culminating and blissful stage in their long, their slow and painful evolution throughout the ages, which is at once their inalienable right and their true destiny.[127]

BUILDING THE ADMINISTRATIVE ORDER

A crowning achievement of Shoghi Effendi's Guardianship was the establishment of the Bahá'í Administrative Order as the governing process for the Bahá'í world community. It does not threaten or infringe upon the authority or power of any national government. It does not interfere with the civic loyalty of Bahá'í citizens of any country upholding human rights.

Shoghi Effendi
© *Bahá'í International Community*

As a result of His historic tour of the West, 'Abdu'l-Baha was impressed with the energy and pioneer spirit He saw in America. He chose the North American believers, and especially the United States community, which Shoghi Effendi aptly described as the *cradle of the Administrative Order* to spearhead its building. Shoghi Effendi called upon the administrative talents of the American Bahá'ís to form local spiritual assemblies, following the Bahá'í principles outlined by 'Abdu'l-

Baha. This would later lead to the formation of the national spiritual assembly.

Through his letters to the American believers, Shoghi Effendi guided their efforts in organizing and forming their spiritual assemblies. These were then used as a model for developing Bahá'í administrative structures in other countries.

Bahá'í communities in other countries were encouraged to follow the example of the American spiritual assemblies.

Following the guidelines in 'Abdu'l-Baha's Tablets of the Divine Plan, and spurred by the eloquence of Shoghi Effendi's inspirational messages, the North American believers pioneered to other lands to spread Bahá'u'lláh's message and to guide new believers in taking their first steps in forming spiritual assemblies in the embryonic Administrative Order.

The field is indeed so immense, the period so critical, the Cause so great, the workers so few, the time so short, the privilege so priceless, that no follower of the Faith of Bahá'u'lláh... can afford a moment's hesitation. That God-born Force, irresistible in its sweeping power, incalculable in its potency, unpredictable in its course, mysterious in its workings, and awe-inspiring in its manifestations... acting even as a two-edged sword, is, under our very eyes, sundering, on the one hand, the age-old ties which for centuries have held together the fabric of civilized society, and is unloosing, on the other, the bonds that still fetter the infant and as yet unemancipated Faith of Bahá'u'lláh.[128]

It was a learning process for everyone, for the Bahá'í administrative process included a key spiritual element, *Bahá'í consultation*, (described in Chapter Nine—The Administrative Order). With the comforting and loving support of Shoghi Effendi to guide the believers in their first halting steps, the Bahá'í Administrative Order, as well as the number of new believers, grew in strength and effectiveness. This gradual evolution and maturation of the Administrative Order was bringing the Bahá'í community ever closer to the number of national assemblies Shoghi Effendi felt was required for the creation of the Universal House of Justice.

To help him with the increasing volume of work necessitated by the growth of the Bahá'í community, Shoghi Effendi followed the examples of Bahá'u'lláh and 'Abdu'l-Baha. In 1951 he appointed certain distinguished believers as *Hands of the Cause of God*, to assist him in his responsibilities as Guardian to teach the Faith and protect its institutions. Some of these *Hands* were appointed to the *International Bahá'í Council*, a forerunner of the Universal House of Justice.

In 1953, Shoghi Effendi launched the *Ten-Year Plan*, a world crusade to bring the message of Bahá'u'lláh to more and more people, and to reach more than one hundred thirty countries and territories where the Bahá'í Faith was still unknown. Halfway through the Ten-Year Plan, in November 1957, the Bahá'í world was stunned by the announcement that Shoghi Effendi had succumbed to a heart attack while on a buying trip to London to purchase furnishings for the new Bahá'í Archives building on Mount Carmel.

According to 'Abdu'l-Baha's Will and Testament, the Guardian was authorized to name his successor to the Guardianship, but Shoghi Effendi did not leave a will, and the only other authorized institution was the Universal House of Justice, which was not yet in existence.

In one of his letters to the Bahá'ís, Shoghi Effendi had described the Hands of the Cause as the *Chief Stewards of the Faith*. Their responsibility was to protect the unity of the Faith, and to collaborate closely with the National Spiritual Assemblies in carrying out the goals of the Ten-Year Plan.

On this basis, the Hands of the Cause took over the Guardian's duties and served as an interim authority while the Ten-Year Plan was in effect. By the end of the Plan, in 1963, all the goals of the Ten-Year Plan had been achieved or surpassed, including the election of thirty-three new national spiritual assemblies. And so, exactly one hundred years after Bahá'u'lláh proclaimed His mission, the first Universal House of Justice was elected and assumed its duties.

Shoghi Effendi achieved a phenomenal growth record for the Faith during the thirty-six years of his leadership, and he set a pattern that is continuing. At the time of Bahá'u'lláh's passing, the believers numbered about 50,000; at 'Abdu'l-Baha's death, its numbers had doubled, to about 100,000. When Shoghi Effendi died, there were approximately 400,000, and less than fifty years later, at the close of the century, the number of Bahá'ís was approaching six million.

Despite his efforts to avoid his own exaltation, Shoghi Effendi's stupendous achievements as leader of the Bahá'í Faith transcended his natural humility. His outstanding record of service made him an object of profound respect and high regard. Shoghi Effendi was the foremost figure of the Formative Age.

Through his selfless service to the Cause of God, he won the love and gratitude of the Bahá'í world community (who referred to him as *the Beloved Guardian*), as well as the respect and admiration of the non-Bahá'ís with whom he came in contact.

HANDS OF THE CAUSE OF GOD

The institution of the Hands of the Cause of God grew from the appointment, as a mark of honor by Bahá'u'lláh, of several dedicated Bahá'ís who devoted their lives to the Cause. 'Abdu'l-Baha did not appoint any living Hands of the Cause, but He did so honor posthumously four people. In His Will and Testament, 'Abdu'l-Baha described the superlative spiritual qualities of the Hands, and their important duties to protect and preserve the Faith. After 'Abdu'l-Baha, only the Guardian was authorized to appoint Hands of the Cause.

At the time of Shoghi Effendi's death, there were twenty-seven Hands, all distinguished and dedicated Bahá'ís, who were currently serving the Cause. Nine of these formed the International Bahá'í Council in Haifa to function in place of the Guardian while the others were scattered in various parts of the world as liaisons with the National Spiritual Assemblies. At the end of the Ten-Year Plan, the Hands of the Cause called for the election of the Universal House of Justice, and declared themselves ineligible for election.

The Universal House of Justice, after its election, announced that, according to 'Abdu'l-Baha's Will and Testament, only the Guardian had the right to appoint Hands of the Cause. This meant that no one would hold this rank after the present Hands died. In view of their exalted rank and their special functions, the House of Justice stated further that it would be inappropriate for the Hands of the Cause to be elected or appointed to administrative institutions.

Although the House of Justice barred the appointment of any more Hands, their primary functions, to protect and preserve (or propagate) the Faith, had proved invaluable to the needs of the world Bahá'í community. The House, therefore, created a new institution, *Continental Boards of Counselors*, to assume these functions. Counselors were appointed to serve as guides and consultants in matters of the Faith for the Bahá'í communities in the various continents where they were assigned. The House of Justice appoints counselors to five-year terms whereas the Hands of the Cause were appointed for life. At the time of this writing, there were three Hands of the Cause still living.[129]

CHAPTER REVIEW—Shoghi Effendi

Summary
▶From childhood, Shoghi Effendi prepared himself for a life of service to the Bahá'í Faith.
▶At age twenty-four he assumed the position of Guardian of the Bahá'í Faith.
▶Shoghi Effendi guided the formation of the institutions of the Bahá'í Administrative Order.
▶His letters to the Bahá'í community served the dual purpose of deepening its members in their understanding of Bahá'í teachings, and of bonding a diverse global group into one society.
▶He personally supervised the design and construction of the Bahá'í World Center.
▶His English translations of the Bahá'í writings served to establish standards for translations into other languages as well.

Discussion
1. Describe Shoghi Effendi's preparation for his future role as 'Guardian of the Bahá'í Faith'.
2. How was Shoghi Effendi's role as leader of the Bahá'í community different from that of 'Abdu'l-Baha?
3. Describe some of the achievements of Shoghi Effendi's tenure as Guardian of the Bahá'í Faith.
4. What was the significance of Shoghi Effendi's masterful translations of the Bahá'í writings?
5. What were the main functions of the Hands of the Cause of God prior to the inauguration of the Universal House of Justice?
6. Read separately each paragraph excerpted in Chapter Six from Shoghi Effendi's The Promised Day Is Come. Discuss its meaning and its social impact.
7. Identify the following Shoghi Effendi publications as books, translations or letters:
    a. World Order of Bahá'u'lláh
    b. God Passes By
    c. Promised Day Is Come
    d. Hidden Words
    e. Kitab-i-Iqan (The Book of Certitude)
8. What were the results of Shoghi Effendi's Ten-Year-Plan?
9. How did Shoghi Effendi's unexpected death affect the process of succession to the leadership of the Bahá'í world community?

CHAPTER SEVEN—Fundamentals

A Bahá'í view is given on topics relating to the nature of man, the material universe, and the concepts of God and the world of the spirit. In some respects these views may differ from the views of other religions. Bahá'u'lláh's descriptions and explanations of these topics are more explicit and detailed than the expressed views of the other religions, but they are not in conflict with the teachings of their Founders.

ONENESS

The concept of unity is simple and complex—simple because everyone has some notion of its nature, and complex because it demands a total reorientation of views concerning practically every aspect of life.[130]

The principle of unity, or oneness—the oneness of God, the oneness of mankind, and the oneness of religion, is the basic concept underlying the Bahá'í teachings.

ONENESS OF GOD

All the religions teach that God is One. In some religions, such as Hinduism, Christianity and Zoroastrianism, various names have been given to forms or aspects of the one God. In Hinduism, God is said to appear in three aspects: Brahma, the Creator; Vishnu, the Preserver; and Shiva, the Destroyer. In Christianity, the trinity of the Father, the Son and the Holy Spirit are all aspects of the one God. In Zoroastrianism, Ahura Mazda and Ahriman, deities representing the duality of good and evil, are later interpretations of the one God, which was taught by Zoroaster, the Founder.

Bahá'u'lláh explained that human beings with finite (limited) minds could never fully understand the nature of an infinite God. Shape and form, race and gender, location and condition—none of these terms can be applied to God. An anthropomorphic concept of the essence of God is inappropriate and unacceptable in this age. We are created in the likeness of God, but God is not created in our image.[131]

The capacity of a lower form of life is less than the capacity of higher forms. Vegetables do not have the capacity to understand (or make use of) the motive power of animals, and animals lack the capacity to understand the reasoning power of human beings. Similarly, human beings lack the capacity to understand the infinitely greater powers of God.

GENDER

Many of the misconceptions concerning God are related to the shortcomings of language. Describing God as He or She is an oxymoron; God can have no gender. Gender implies procreation through a pairing of the male and female functions. The attributes of God's oneness and eternality preclude this implication. God creates but need not procreate.

Capitalizing the gender pronoun by referring to God as He or She (instead of 'he' or 'she') exalts the Divine, but in the process creates greater confusion. An example of this confusion is the tripartite God of the Christian Trinity, which many Christian believers do not understand clearly. God the Father, God the Son, and God the Holy Spirit may be viewed as different functions of one Being, a concept the other religions reject. The use of the masculine Father, masculine Son, and neuter Holy Spirit adds to the confusion. A genderless God referred to as He (or She, or even It) is an inadequacy of language. Masculine superiority, common in many languages, including English, is a reflection of the social inequalities that existed, and which still exist, in the primitive and immature societies of the past and present.

RECOGNIZING GOD

Our inability to understand the greater powers of God reflect some of the differences in interpretation of His nature. The Word of God, the Spirit of God, the Messenger of God—all represent God, but they are not the Essence of God, just as the rays of the Sun represent the powers of the Sun but are not the Sun itself. Through our contacts with His representations

(His Word, Spirit, and Messengers), we obtain our knowledge of God, but we can never know God Himself—what Shoghi Effendi describes as the innermost Spirit of Spirits or the Eternal Essence of Essences. God's true nature is unknowable, even to a Manifestation of God.

When Moses asked God to reveal Himself, God answered, **"you cannot see my face, for no one may see me and live."** (Exodus 33:20)

From time immemorial... He... hath been veiled in the ineffable sanctity of His exalted Self, and will everlastingly continue to be wrapt in the impenetrable mystery of His unknowable Essence... Ten thousand Prophets, each a Moses, are thunderstruck upon the Sinai of their search at God's forbidding voice, 'Thou shalt never behold Me!'; whilst a myriad Messengers, each as great as Jesus, stand dismayed upon their heavenly thrones by the interdiction 'Mine Essence thou shalt never apprehend!'[132]

These Tabernacles of holiness, these primal Mirrors which reflect the light of unfading glory, are but expressions of Him Who is the Invisible of the Invisibles. By the revelation of these gems of divine virtue all the names and attributes of God, such as knowledge and power, sovereignty and dominion, mercy and wisdom, glory, bounty and grace, are made manifest... These attributes of God are not and have never been vouchsafed specially unto certain Prophets, and withheld from others. Nay, all the Prophets of God, His well-favoured, His holy, and chosen Messengers, are, without exception, the bearers of His names, and the embodiments of His attributes. They only differ in the intensity of their revelation, and the comparative potency of their light.[133]

From a Deist perspective, we can contemplate the world around us and infer God as the Creator. But everything else we know of God must come from the Manifestation of God, His Chosen Messenger Who embodies His Word and His Spirit. Each Manifestation of God speaks with the authority of God. Hearing Him is like hearing God; seeing Him is like seeing God.

ONENESS OF MANKIND

All human beings are members of one family, *the family of man*. We are one species, distinct from all others, the most highly evolved of all life forms. No other species has the capacity to be aware of God's existence.

Having created the world and all that liveth and moveth therein, He... chose to confer upon man the unique distinction and capacity to know Him and to love Him—a capacity that must needs be regarded as the generating impulse and the primary purpose underlying the whole of creation.[134]

This distinctive capacity is true of all human beings, the entire family of man, regardless of color of skin, hair and eyes, of ethnic background or of any other superficial difference. The similarities of human capacities are much more significant in understanding the nature of man than the minor differences of physical or cultural features. Therefore, the Bahá'í Faith rejects unconditionally all of the man-made (and false) prejudices of racial superiority which have tended to blur the concept of the unity of mankind.

Bahá'u'lláh's message of unity seeks to create a worldwide social awareness of the oneness of mankind. The society of man has evolved through a series of social institutions, from family and clan to tribe, city-state and nation. It is now in a position to enter the next stage of its development—a society encompassing all mankind—a planetary society.

Shoghi Effendi did not mince any words in a strongly worded statement rejecting outworn traditions that are no longer appropriate for the times. He called for support of a principle and a plan that will measure up to the world's requirements for a new worldview of mankind:

The call of Bahá'u'lláh is primarily directed against all forms of provincialism, all insularities and prejudices. If long-cherished ideals and time-honored institutions, if certain social assumptions and religious formulae have ceased to promote the welfare..., if they no longer minister to the needs of a continually evolving humanity, let them be swept

away and relegated to the limbo of obsolescent and forgotten doctrines. Why should these, in a world subject to the immutable law of change and decay, be exempt from the deterioration that must needs overtake every human institution? For legal standards, political and economic theories are solely designed to safeguard the interests of humanity as a whole, and not humanity to be crucified for the preservation of the integrity of any particular law or doctrine.

Let there be no mistake. The principle of the Oneness of Mankind—the pivot round which all the teachings of Bahá'u'lláh revolve—is no mere outburst of ignorant emotionalism or an expression of vague and pious hope... Its implications are deeper, its claims greater than any which the Prophets of old were allowed to advance... It implies an organic change in the structure of present-day society, a change such as the world has not yet experienced... It calls for no less than the reconstruction and the demilitarization of the whole civilized world... It represents the consummation of human evolution...

The principle of the Oneness of Mankind, as proclaimed by Bahá'u'lláh, carries with it no more and no less than a solemn assertion that attainment to this final stage in this stupendous evolution is not only necessary but inevitable, that its realization is fast approaching, and that nothing short of a power that is born of God can succeed in establishing it.[135]

In earlier times, such statements would be impossible to consider seriously. *World government*, which these words call for, is a goal that is receiving support from an increasing number of people with vision, among them statesmen, scholars and people of influence.

Technologically, world government is now a feasible concept. Politically, considering the growing instability of almost every society in the world, it is, as Shoghi Effendi noted, *not only necessary but inevitable*. The world government concept represents the highest form of social institution mankind can create on the planet.

It is a sign of mankind's approaching maturity.

> **The Revelation of Bahá'u'lláh... should... be regarded as signalizing... the coming of age of the entire human race. It should be viewed... as marking the last and highest stage in the stupendous evolution of man's collective life on this planet. The emergence of a world community, the consciousness of world citizenship, the founding of a world civilization and culture— should... be regarded... as the furthermost limits in the organization of human society, though man, as an individual, will... continue indefinitely to develop.**[136]

The Bahá'í world community may be viewed as a model of the future world civilization envisioned above, though still in an embryonic stage. Bahá'ís, as individuals following the teachings of Bahá'u'lláh, are learning to live and think in terms of the unity of all mankind. These values and standards influence their life goals, their vision of the future, and their daily activities.

ONENESS OF RELIGION

Each of the major religions emphasizes the teaching of one important divine attribute, a central concept. The central concept underlying the Bahá'í teachings is *unity*, just as the central concept of Judaism is *justice* (the law), in Islam, *submission* (to the will of God), and in Christianity, *love* (for God and fellow-man). 'Abdu'l-Baha noted that there is **"a unity of mankind which recognizes that... all are servants of one God."** There is also a spiritual unity, which can create in mankind a willingness to make sacrifices for each other.

Another unity He identified is the unity underlying progressive revelation, the unity of the Manifestations of God. He affirmed that Abraham, Moses, Zoroaster, Buddha, Jesus, Muhammad, the Bab and Bahá'u'lláh are one in spirit and reality. Moreover," He said, **"each Prophet fulfilled the promise of the one who came before him and likewise each announced the one who would follow..."**[137]

In some ways, the Qur'an eulogizes Jesus even more

than does the Gospel. 'Abdu'l-Baha related how Muhammad urged His followers:

Why have you not believed on Jesus Christ? Why have you not accepted the Gospel? Why have you not believed in Moses? Why have you not followed the precepts of the Old Testament... You must know the Old and the New Testaments as the Word of God...[138]

The unity of all religions is a reflection of the unity of the one God. If all the religions acknowledge the existence of only one God, then it is the same God, regardless of the names He is called. And if the teachings of each religion are claiming the same Source, then they, too, must be in agreement, and therefore, must be essentially the same.

These principles and laws "**...have proceeded from one Source and are the rays of one Light. That they differ from one another is to be attributed to the varying requirements of the ages in which they were promulgated.**"[139]

[T]he sovereign remedy and mightiest instrument for the healing of all the world is the union of all its peoples in one universal Cause, one common Faith...[140]

The decline in the influence of religion has been paralleled by social and ethical degradation such as the replacement of holiday spirit with increasing commercialization, and environmental endangerment caused by reckless waste and abuse. Without the bond of community created by religion and the spirit of service arising from it, people are left increasingly empty and without any higher purpose than their own needs and desires. Such a motivational base is inherently selfish...[141]

The purpose of the Revelation brought by each Manifestation of God was the renewal and fulfillment of the Revelation that preceded it. Their messages were the same. The differences among the teachings of the various religions were owing to the particular audience for whom they were intended. These differences involved the temporary, or social, laws. They were appropriate only for the people of that particular time, and they were changed when the next Manifestation of

God announced new social laws for a later time and different living conditions. This illustrates the concept of *progressive revelation*, which is discussed earlier in this book.

The independent and mutually exclusive divisions and subdivisions that are found in all of the earlier religions have been compared to the nations, kingdoms and empires which continue to maintain their political independence and exclusivity in a world that is crying for political unity. Differences among the smaller groups can often be minimized by the unifying influence of their larger parent group. The same principle holds true for the smaller subdivisions of religious sects that lack the unifying influence of their larger parent group. Such disunity existing within these religions has diluted the spiritual powers contained within the revelations of their Founders. **"The human explanation of a truth has been substituted for the truth itself... Sectarianism in essence is not freedom of religion. It is an opportunity to abandon the way of life revealed from on high and substitute... ritual for virtue... (and) creed for understanding..."**[142]

The permanent laws, those that do not change, are also taught by each Manifestation of God. These laws do not change, although they may differ in the depth and fullness of explanations, depending on the capacity of the people to understand.

...in every dispensation the light of Divine Revelation hath been vouchsafed unto men in direct proportion to their spiritual capacity.[143]

Every Manifestation of God acclaimed His predecessor in superlative terms, whereas His followers did not consider the earlier Prophet the equal of their own. Bahá'ís view each Manifestation of God as having the same status and the same powers. None is superior in any way to any of the others. Only Their revelations are different, because they are tailored to Their particular audiences.

All the Prophets of God abide in the same tabernacle, soar in the same heaven, are seated upon the same throne, utter the same speech, and proclaim the same Faith... They differ only in the

intensity of their revelation and the comparative potency of their light.[144]

...Consider the sun. How feeble its rays the moment it appears above the horizon. How gradually its warmth and potency increase as it approaches its zenith, enabling meanwhile all created things to adapt themselves to the growing intensity of its light... [I]f the Sun of Truth[145] were suddenly to reveal, at the earliest stages of its manifestation, the full measure of [its powers, everything]... would waste away and be consumed...[146]

In a spiritual sense, all the Manifestations of God may be viewed as One, in Their same stations as the Word of God and the Revealer of His message. Through Moses in the Old Testament, God spoke as "**I, thy Lord.**" Muhammad is recorded as saying, "**I am the embodiment of the prophets,**" and in another passage, "**I am Noah, I am Abraham, I am Moses, I am Christ.**" Jesus said, "**Before Abraham was, I am.**" When He spoke of His return, Bahá'ís interpret Jesus as referring to later Manifestations.[147]

MATERIAL EXISTENCE

We are familiar with invisible forces that cause objects to move. Electromagnetic forces, gravitational forces, and forces of atomic radiation are part of scientific explanations for many natural phenomena. Scientists are aware of other cosmic forces in the universe that are yet part of the unknown. Forces we can detect but not control, coming from remote parts of the galaxy, pass through our bodies constantly; but their effects, if any, are unknown.

The term *spirit* is sometimes used to denote a force, or power. Bahá'u'lláh describes the phenomenon of life as varying levels of spirit that animate all forms of matter. In God's creation, the spirit of life is expressed as motion. A moving object is a living object, and anything that is motionless or inert is as dead. Not dead—*as* dead.

The Greek philosopher, Aristotle, described creation in terms of different states (or kingdoms) of matter— the *mineral kingdom*, the *vegetable kingdom*, the *animal kingdom*, and the *human kingdom*. **"Each of these levels displays a particular evolution of matter, its particular population manifesting both identifiable physical and spiritual limits..."**[148]

In our material universe nothing is stationary. Using the atomic conception of the universe, every created thing (or being) is alive if it is in the process of composition, of coming together. Even elemental dust particles in interstellar space are attracted together to form larger bodies, according to natural laws.

In the Bahá'í concept of evolution, the existence of life is a matter of degree, i.e., a degree below a higher degree is like non-existence, or death. A mineral is dead compared to a vegetable. In a mineral there is a moving force, a power of attraction (a cohesive force) that holds the atoms of the mineral together. Thus, the *life force* of the mineral kingdom is the power (or spirit) of cohesion, or attraction. The vegetable, a higher degree of existence, has, in addition to the cohesive spirit of the mineral, the power (or spirit) of growth and reproduction. The animal, the next higher kingdom of creation, or level of life, contains the animal spirit which includes, in addition to the powers of the mineral and vegetable spirits, the spirit of the senses, or movement and survival intelligence.

The highest degree, the human being, has, in addition to the spiritual powers of the animal (which includes the vegetable and mineral powers), the intelligent, contemplative, or conscious reasoning power of the human spirit. The power of each life form includes all the powers of the lower kingdoms plus the distinguishing power(s) identifying its degree.

The whole physical creation is perishable. These material bodies are composed of atoms; when these atoms begin to separate decomposition sets in, then comes what we call death. This composition of atoms... is temporary. When the power of attraction, which holds these atoms together, is withdrawn, the body, as such, ceases to exist.[149]

Each degree of existence is as dead when compared to a higher degree. A human being in a deep coma is said to be in a *vegetative state*; he is as dead. When the life forms in the higher degrees of existence, i.e., vegetable, animal and human, cease exercising their respective spiritual powers, they die (through the process of decomposition) and return to the lowest degree, the mineral, to begin anew the evolutionary life cycle. The human being, however, is a special case, as we shall see.

Each degree of existence can evolve into a more perfect example of that degree, but it can never evolve into a higher degree. A vegetable can never become an animal. The most perfect animal can never attain the human spirit (reasoning power), though it can exceed the human in animal powers (strength, speed of movement, sensory awareness, etc).

Look at this mineral. However far it may evolve, it only evolves in its own condition; you cannot bring the crystal to a state where it can attain to sight... It is true that coal could become a diamond, but both are in the mineral condition, and their component elements are the same.[150]

DUAL NATURE OF MAN

Of all the degrees of existence described above (mineral, vegetable, animal and human), it is only the human that has a dual reality. The cohesive power of the mineral spirit, the growth power of the vegetable spirit, and the sensory powers of the animal spirit are materially-oriented in that they control conditions of material existence.

The body of man **"grows and develops through the animal spirit."**[151] But the distinguishing feature of the human spirit—reason and conscious intelligence, is part of a higher order of spirit; this spirit deals with conditions of nonmaterial existence such as feelings, ideas, thought and imagination. This higher order of the human spirit signifies man's spiritual reality.

Thus, man straddles two kingdoms of reality. Physically he is a member of the animal kingdom and spiritually he is part of the human kingdom. The material nature of man (his lower nature) includes the powers of his animal spirit, but it is his spiritual nature (the higher human nature) that is his true spirit, the quality that makes him superior to the animal. Bahá'u'lláh explained that the life of the flesh is common to both men and animals, but the true life of man is of the spirit.[152]

Even though man's animal powers (strength, speed of movement, etc.) may be inferior to the animal powers of some animals, man can develop his higher human powers to invent tools and machines which enable him to exceed the powers of any animal. Thus, if man applies his human powers to satisfy his animal (lower) nature, he will be like a super-animal. But this would be a misuse of his human powers and contrary to the direction of evolution. 'Abdu'l-Baha noted that man approaches God through his higher (spiritual) nature; in his lower (animal) nature he lives only for the material world.

Man has the power both to do good and to do evil; if his power for good predominates and his inclinations to do wrong are conquered, then man in truth may be called a saint. But if... he rejects the things of God and allows his evil passions to conquer him, then he is no better than a mere animal.[153]

HUMAN EVOLUTION

The human embryo goes through developmental stages that resemble lower life forms before it becomes a fetus showing distinctive human characteristics. But at all times during this growth process it is a member of the human species. The embryos of animals and humans may look similar at different stages of development, but the animal embryo never can develop, under the best possible conditions, the capacities of reasoning and the other distinctive human qualities that the human embryo can naturally develop.

The Bahá'í teachings accept the evolutionary history of man going back millions of years.

Starting from a very simple, apparently insignificant form, the human body is pictured as developing stage by stage, in the course of untold generations, becoming more complex... until the man of the present day is reached... The human embryo may at one time resemble a fish with gill-slits and tail, but it is not a fish. It is a human

embryo.[154]

Just as other animals and plants have evolved over millions of years from primitive to more advanced forms, so have human beings evolved over long periods of time. The Old Testament story of creation is an allegory revealed by Moses more than three thousand years ago to a people who could not have understood the concept of geological time spans that underlie current evolutionary theory. If He so wished, God could have created the world in one day, or instantly. The Biblical six days of creation representing millions of years of evolution are a truer allegorical picture of creation according to God's natural laws than is a literal interpretation of a story that is contrary to all reason and logic. Denying the evidence of our greatest bounty from God, our reasoning powers, is a sad betrayal of this most precious gift.

Man is at the highest point of material evolution and at the beginning of spiritual evolution. He is the most complex and advanced of material life forms. Although his material capacities have evolved and may evolve further, he was and always will be man. The human brain, where the conscious and reasoning power of the human spirit, the mind, abides, represents the peak of man's material evolution.

Because man is at the beginning of spiritual evolution, he has the freedom to develop spiritually within the human kingdom. It is his spiritual development, the improvement of his distinctive spiritual qualities that bring man closer to perfection as a human being.

The goal of evolution is to achieve ever-greater perfection. Perfection for man is viewed as a process rather than an endpoint. Human beings can never achieve absolute perfection because no matter how much we progress there is always room for improvement. It is the striving to achieve ever-higher levels of perfection in God's perfect creation that brings us closer to God.

'Abdu'l-Baha eloquently describes man's material life as a necessary learning experience in his efforts to achieve spiritual perfection.

Man must walk in many paths and be subjected

to various processes in his evolution upward. Physically he is not born in full stature but passes through consecutive stages of fetus, infant, childhood, youth, maturity and old age. Suppose he had the power to remain young throughout his life. He then would not understand the meaning of old age and could not believe it existed. If he could not realize the condition of old age, he would not know that he was young. He would not know the difference between young and old without experiencing the old. Unless you have passed through the state of infancy, how would you know this was an infant beside you? If there were no wrong, how would you recognize the right? If it were not for sin, how would you appreciate virtue? If evil deeds were unknown, how could you commend good actions? If sickness did not exist, how would you understand health? Evil is nonexistent; it is the absence of good. Sickness is the loss of health; poverty, the lack of riches... Without knowledge there is ignorance; therefore, ignorance is simply the lack of knowledge. Death is the absence of life.[155]

SOUL

"Man—the true man—is soul, not body; though physically man belongs to the animal kingdom, yet his soul lifts him above the rest of creation."[156] The soul is the essence of the human spirit. The mind is one aspect of this spiritual entity called the soul. The soul can live without the body, but the body dies without the soul.

The soul, Bahá'u'lláh noted, is created at the same time as the body. The soul of man, therefore, begins its spiritual (and eternal) existence at conception. The soul, which includes the mind and the consciousness of the individual, is man's true reality, the true individual. Like the embryo, the soul starts out as a single entity, without spiritual attributes but with the capacity for acquiring them within its human lifetime through its own efforts. After material death, in a purely spiritual state, it is, therefore, conscious of other souls, and can recognize those it has known in the physical life.

The growth of limbs and organs in the embryonic life... [may be compared with] **the development of spiritual qualities by the soul... But there is a major difference. The growth of the embryo is involuntary and dictated by nature, while the soul has freedom of choice.**[157]

Unlike the embryo that continually subdivides as it develops limbs and organs from its beginnings as one cell, the soul is composed of one substance and remains a single entity as it grows spiritually, both in this world and the hereafter. Testimony to the soul's eternal existence is found in the sacred scriptures of other religions as well as the Bahá'í Faith:

Know thou of a truth that the soul, after its separation from the body, will continue to progress... It will endure as long as the Kingdom of God... (Gleanings, Writings of Bahá'u'lláh, pp. 155-56)

(At death) **he will be united with me. Be certain of that.** (Bhagavad-Gita 8:4)

Then shall the dust return to the earth as it was: and the spirit shall return unto God who gave it. (Old Testament: Ecclesiastes 12:7)

Soon ye return to us: and we will let you know what ye have done... For unto God shall be the final gathering. (Qur'an 10:24; 35:19)

All men have proceeded from God and unto Him shall all return. (Selections from the Bab, p.157)

Verily, we are from God and to Him shall we return. (Bahá'u'lláh: Seven Valleys & Four Valleys, p.17)

The weaknesses of the body have no effect on the soul; it is independent of sickness and disease. To a question about the consciousness of souls after death, Bahá'u'lláh responded: **"They that are of the same grade and station are fully aware of one another's capacity, character, accomplishments and merits. They that are of a lower grade, however, are incapable of comprehending adequately the station, or of estimating the merits, of those that rank above them... They that are the followers of the one true God shall, the moment they depart out of this life, experience such joy and gladness as** would be impossible to describe..."[158]

Thus, man's true reality is spiritual. He lives in (and communicates with) the material universe by means of his material body. The association of the soul with the body may be compared to light and a mirror. The light is reflected in the mirror, but it is not *in* the mirror. If the mirror is removed, the light remains unaffected. When the material mirror (the body) wears out (decomposes, or dies), the spiritual light (soul) remains and lives on in the world of the spirit.

DEVELOPING SPIRITUALITY

The body and the soul begin their existence together as an embryonic human being in the material world. As noted earlier, the human body *grows and develops through the animal spirit*. The human spirit, which contains the powers of the lower kingdoms, also possesses *potentially* the distinguishing human powers of reason, intellect and imagination.

The human being is already equipped with the animal powers required for bodily growth and development. But to be a fully functioning human being he must develop his higher spiritual qualities. This each person must do *in this material environment, and to the degree of his own efforts.*

How does a person develop spiritual qualities? How does one attain spirituality? In a society that is dominated by materialistic forces that are presently **"undermining the foundations of man's moral and spiritual life"**, the obstacles appear formidable.

Shoghi Effendi noted that the **"spirit of the age, taken on the whole, is irreligious... the core of religious faith is that mystic feeling which unites Man with God. This state of spiritual communion can be brought about and maintained by means of meditation and prayer. And this is the reason why Bahá'u'lláh has so much stressed the importance of worship. It is not sufficient for a believer merely to accept and observe the teachings. He should, in addition, cultivate the sense of spirituality which he can acquire chiefly by means of prayer. The Bahá'í Faith, like all other Divine Religions, is thus fundamentally mystic in character. Its chief goal is** the development of the individual and society, through the acquisition of spiritual virtues and powers. It is the soul of man which has first to be fed. And this spiritual nourishment prayer can best provide."

Laws and institutions, as viewed by Bahá'u'lláh, can become really effective only when our inner spiritual life has been perfected and transformed. Otherwise religion will degenerate into a mere organization, and becomes a dead thing. The believers... should therefore fully realize the necessity of praying. For prayer is absolutely indispensable to their inner spiritual development...[159]

Spiritual development is a lifelong process that is perfected by degrees over time and with continuing effort. It is not enough to understand each spiritual quality; we must internalize these qualities and make them part of ourselves.

Conduct and behavior reflect our true feelings more than words. Bahá'u'lláh said, **"Let deeds, not words, be your adorning."**[160]

SPIRITUAL EXISTENCE

"The world beyond is as different from this world as this world is different from that of the world of the womb."[161] If the fetus could understand you, how would you describe this world? The colors of the rainbow, the beauty of the flower, the vastness of the ocean, all are beyond the comprehension of one who knows only what is moist, dark and warm.

We are living in the second stage of a three-stage existence:

(1)   The world of the womb
(2)   The material world we live in
(3)   The world of the spirit

At first the infant finds it very difficult to reconcile itself to its new existence. It cries as if not wishing to be separated from its narrow abode and imagining that life is restricted to that limited space. It is reluctant to leave its home, but nature forces it into this world. Having come into its new conditions, it finds that it has passed from darkness into a sphere of radiance;

from gloomy and restricted surroundings it has been transferred to a spacious and delightful environment. Its nourishment was the blood of the mother; now it finds delicious food to enjoy. Its new life is filled with brightness and beauty; it looks with wonder and delight upon the mountains, meadows and fields of green, the rivers and fountains, the wonderful stars; it breathes the life-quickening atmosphere; and then it praises God for its release from the confinement of its former condition and attainment to the freedom of a new realm.

This analogy expresses the relation of the temporal world to the life hereafter - the transition of the soul of man from darkness and uncertainty to the light and reality of the eternal Kingdom. At first it is very difficult to welcome death, but after attaining its new condition the soul is grateful, for it has been released from the bondage of the limited to enjoy the liberties of the unlimited. It has been freed from a world of sorrow, grief and trials to live in a world of unending bliss and joy. The phenomenal and physical have been abandoned in order that it may attain the opportunities of the ideal and spiritual. Therefore, the souls of those who have passed away from earth and completed their span of mortal pilgrimage... have hastened to a world superior to this. They have soared away from these conditions of darkness and dim vision into the realm of light. These are the only considerations which can comfort and console those whom they have left behind.[162]

It is in the womb that man received the capacity and endowment for the reality of human existence. "The forces and powers necessary for this world were bestowed upon him in that limited condition. In this world he needed eyes; he received them potentially in the other. He needed ears; he obtained them there in readiness and preparation for his new existence. The powers requisite in this world were conferred upon him in the world of the matrix so that when he entered this realm of real existence he not only possessed all necessary

functions and powers but found provision for his material sustenance awaiting him."[163]

A thin barrier separates the world of the womb and this world. In the same way that the fully developed fetus is preparing to leave the womb for the vastness of this world, the individual in this world is preparing for entrance into the spiritual world, a world of *the invisible realms of God*, a world which we cannot yet understand. The fetus develops sensory organs and limbs in the womb whose functions can't be understood because they can't be used until birth in the next stage of its existence. If this birth did not occur, the limbs and organs would be useless and irrelevant. In the same way, we must develop spiritual qualities in this world in preparation for *our birth in the next existence*, the many worlds of God.

In this context Bahá'u'lláh spoke of the vastness of the next world as spiritual realms. Current scientific theories regarding the probability of countless numbers of planets in the material universe are matched by Bahá'u'lláh's description of the universe as God's creation. **"Know thou of a truth that the worlds of God are countless in their number, and infinite in their range... the creation of God embraceth worlds besides this world, and creatures apart from these creatures. In each of these worlds He hath ordained things which none can search except Himself, the All-Searching, the All-Wise."**[164]

The life we live as purely spiritual beings begins when the soul leaves the body, at the moment of material death. The doubts and uncertainties about a spiritual existence that we may have held during a material existence no longer remain because we are part of a new reality. We see with spiritual eyes—we no longer need the material eyes we left in our material bodies. The words we use, geared to a material reality, may appear somewhat awkward when used in a spiritual sense. In a spiritual world the ability to see takes on added meaning, by the use of spiritual qualities developed in an earlier existence.

Our birth in the next world (our death in this world) will occur in due time. If the spiritual qualities needed for functioning in the next world are not adequately developed, we will be *born with spiritual handicaps* (we may *see* less clearly.) Though our development in the womb is involuntary and requires no effort, our spiritual development in this world is voluntary and does require effort, through prayer and religious study.

A friend asked 'Abdu'l-Baha: **"How should one look forward to death?" He replied, "How does one look forward to the goal of any journey? With hope and expectation. It is even so with the end of this earthly journey. In the next world, man will find himself freed from many of the disabilities under which he now suffers."**[165]

GOD'S CREATION

In addition to our material universe (the world of matter), God's creation consists of a spiritual universe (the world of the spirit), which is related but superior to the material universe we now inhabit. While both universes are part of God's single perfect creation, the spiritual universe is perfect and our material universe is in the process of (evolving toward) perfection.

The term *Kingdom of God* is used in two ways in the Bahá'í writings. One is spiritual, the other material. The first refers to the *spiritual Kingdom of God*, or the *world of the spirit*, which is inhabited by spiritual beings. **"... the Kingdom is not a material place... It is a spiritual world... To be limited to place is a property of bodies and not of spirits. Place and time surround the body, not the mind and spirit."**[166]

The second interpretation of the *Kingdom of God* refers to the physical world. Such phrases as *the last days*, the *end times*, the *end of the world*, and *Kingdom Come* have often been used to describe the major changes that are promised in the scriptures of the earlier religions. From the Lord's Prayer, the Gospels affirm, **"Thy kingdom come, Thy will be done, On earth as it is in heaven."**[167]

During His visit to London, 'Abdu'l-Baha responded to a question from a visitor who asked whether *'this misery-laden world would ever attain happiness.'* He said, **"It is nearly two thousand years since His Holiness the Lord Christ taught this prayer (the**

Lord's Prayer) to His people... Thinkest thou that He would have commanded thee to pray for that which would never come? That prayer is also a prophecy."[168] **From time immemorial God has guided us toward one collective goal: the unity of the human race in a society that reflects divine qualities. This goal, the establishment of the Kingdom of God on earth, is not a utopian dream. It will not be thrust upon humanity suddenly and completely through divine intervention. Nor will it be simply the outcome of political or economic development.**[169]

This is the Kingdom Bahá'u'lláh has proclaimed as the one mankind is now ready to build in the material world. It is now time for the *world of man* to become the *world of God*. The prophecies of all the religions over the past thousands of years have reached their time for fulfillment, not in a magical transformation, but through man's efforts and with God's inspiration.

SPIRITUAL EVOLUTION PICTORIAL

This diagram is believed to have been prepared with 'Abdu'l-Baha's guidance by Lua Getsinger, one of the first American believers and a prominent teacher of the Bahá'í Faith. The diagram may be helpful in clarifying the Bahá'í view of the evolution of the soul.

All created beings move through a cycle of existence that begins with God. The process of material evolution as explained by scientific theory is acceptable to Bahá'ís only within each kingdom of matter; Bahá'ís do not accept the evolutionary process between two kingdoms. A vegetable can never become an animal. The most perfect animal can never attain the human spirit (reasoning power), though it can exceed the human in animal powers (strength, speed of movement, sensory awareness, etc).

The human being at birth begins life in the company of a newly created soul. 'Abdu'l-Baha noted that the human being has the power of all the other worlds of matter and has attained the furthest point and the most distant from God. He (or she) has passed through all the conditions of the material side of the circle by the hidden power of God. The first side, or descending circle, is the natural or material worlds of matter; the second or ascending circle is the world of the Spirit. The first half is the night, the second half the day. The human world is the point furthest away from God, but the rays of God may shine directly on man. The world is in darkness, but on the side of the ascending circle light appears.

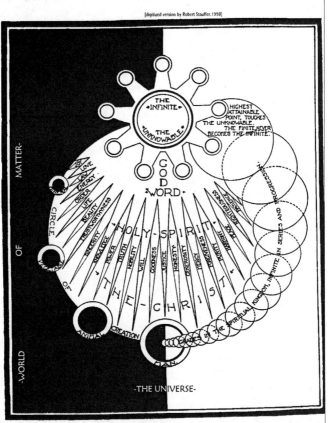

The person who turns to the light sees the Manifestation of God who mirrors the Light of God (through God's Teachings.) Leaving the material world marks the beginning of the spiritual journey back to God in the worlds of the Spirit.

CHAPTER REVIEW—Fundamental Concepts
Summary
▶The principle of unity is the basic concept underlying the Bahá'í teachings.
▶The unity of the one God worshipped in all the religions defines the unity of these religions; having the same source makes of humanity but one family.
▶Material existence encompasses life forms in four levels, or degrees: mineral, vegetable, animal and human.
▶The Kingdom of God already exists spiritually; materially, it is in the process of formation.
▶Man has both a material and a spiritual reality; it is his spiritual reality that he must develop for eternal life.
▶Each individual prepares for a life after death which cannot be understood clearly until it is experienced, in the same sense that a person blind from birth could never understand a verbal description of color.

Discussion
1. How is the sun used to explain the nature of God?
2. Describe the social evolution of mankind in terms of its social institutions.
3. Discuss the Bahá'í interpretation of the quotation from the Old Testament, Exodus 33:20—"...you cannot see my face; for man shall not see me and live."
4. How can the 'social laws' of the religions differ, yet all come from the same Source?
5. What are the differences in the permanent laws of the major religions? Identify.
6. Identify the characteristic powers of the various life forms.
7. How can a mineral be said to be alive?
8. How can a vegetable be said to be alive and dead at the same time?
9. How is the reality of man different from the other life forms—animal, vegetable, and mineral?
10. Discuss the analogy of the fetus in the womb to explain the circumstances of the soul in this world.
11. Explain man's animal nature in relation to his dual reality.
12. What is the point of striving for perfection if there is always room for improvement?
13. If the goal of evolution is to strive for ever-greater perfection, why is old age a process of decline (imperfection), in mind as well as in body?
14. How can God, a non-physical spiritual essence, rule the human subjects of a physical 'Kingdom of God on earth'?
15. Explain God's creation using the diagram at the end of the chapter text.

CHAPTER EIGHT—Basic Teachings

The basic teachings include those principles that will prepare mankind to live and be a part of the Kingdom of God on earth as promised by all the religions.

This kingdom is neither a supernatural supraterrestrial place nor a metaphor for the abode of the deceased, but it is a kingdom on this planet. It is none other than the realization of the unity of mankind and of world peace...[170]

The essential theme of the Bahá'í teachings, *unity*, provides the connecting link for the basic teachings discussed in this chapter.

INDEPENDENT INVESTIGATION OF TRUTH

In a talk He gave in Montreal, Canada, 'Abdu'l-Baha said that man is responsible for using his own God-given talents to investigate for himself the fundamental realities. He especially praised the American people for their initiative in assuming this responsibility:

..man must endeavor... to investigate the fundamental reality. If he does not independently investigate, he has failed to utilize the talent God has bestowed upon him. I am pleased with the American people because, as a rule, they are independent seekers of the truth...[171]

Human reason is the distinguishing feature of mankind as the highest life form of the material world. It is this same reasoning power that is one of the connecting links between the material world and the world of the spirit. None of the lower levels of existence (mineral, vegetable, and animal) has such a power, and nothing less is adequate to investigate spiritual reality.

Religious authorities in past religions taught that it was unnecessary (and in some cases forbidden) for the individual seeking truth to investigate for himself. He was told what to believe and how to behave. But ultimately it is each individual who must decide for himself what he believes and how he will behave—because regardless of what he is told, each person must bear ultimate responsibility for his own beliefs and actions.

The Bahá'í Faith has no clergy. It has elected institutions (Spiritual Assemblies and the Universal House of Justice) and appointed consultants (Counselors and their assistants.) It is the responsibility of each individual to decide for himself what is truth. Further, each individual is encouraged to read, study, consult others (people, religions, etc.) and investigate for himself, and then make his own decisions. Each person's responsibility for what he believes and how he behaves, is solely between that person and God, and no others.

Among the series of letters that Bahá'u'lláh wrote to the world's most powerful kings and religious leaders were those He wrote to the chief authorities of the major religions. He called for a return to the principles taught by their own religions. It was the religious leaders especially, those who were most familiar with their own scriptures, who best should be able to interpret correctly the teachings and prophecies, and guide their own people. But each time a new Prophet appeared, it was the clergy who led the opposition to His recognition.

It was the Jewish priests who led the Jews to reject Jesus, and the Christian clergy who opposed Muhammad, and the Islamic leaders who most fanatically persecuted the Bab and Bahá'u'lláh. Because these leaders were false to their obligations, because the kings ignored His messages and the clergy opposed Him, Bahá'u'lláh curtailed their power. **"From two ranks amongst men power hath been seized: kings and ecclesiastics."**[172]

Bahá'u'lláh's judgment on the fate of autocratic kingship has been essentially fulfilled. His judgment on the influence and power of religious institutions is still in the process of fulfillment. Shoghi Effendi described the devastating power behind this judgment. **"... the ecclesiastical hierarchies of both Sunni and Shiah Islam... shall be turned into the most abject abasement, and this pomp and might converted into the most complete subjugation..."**[173]

[Bahá'u'lláh's] **numerous and repeated**

exhortations and warnings to the entire Christian world... directed particular messages... to the heads ...of the ecclesiastical orders of Christendom..."[174] We have... to appreciate the steady deterioration of their influence, the decline of their power, the damage to their prestige, the flouting of their authority, the dwindling of their congregations, the relaxation of their discipline, the restriction of their press, the timidity of their leaders, the confusion in their ranks...[175]

Shoghi Effendi emphasized that Bahá'u'lláh's judgment against the ecclesiastical hierarchies, the clergy, does not imply the slightest disrespect or criticism of the Manifestations of God, Whose teachings the clergy have distorted, nor of those religious leaders who are faithful to their vows:

The [Bahá'í] Faith... disclaims any intention to belittle any of the Prophets gone before..., to whittle down any of their teachings, to obscure... the radiance of their Revelations, to oust them from the hearts of their followers, to abrogate the fundamentals of their doctrines, to discard any of their revealed books, or to suppress the legitimate aspirations of their adherents.[176] Nor... [do] the followers of Bahá'u'lláh either seek to degrade or even belittle the rank of the world's religious leaders, whether Christian, Muslim, or of any other denomination, should their conduct conform to their professions, and be worthy of the position they occupy.[177]

'Abdu'l-Baha deplored the misinterpretations of their scriptures that led to disagreements among the religions and their various sects. This was most often due to blind imitation of ancestral beliefs. Differences in ceremony and ritual were given precedence over the more important principles of love, unity, and the fellowship of humanity, which were common to all.

Too often, religion has been a heritage descending from father to son. If your father is a Jew, then you are a Jew, a Muslim is born of a Muslim, a Buddhist is a Buddhist because his father was a Buddhist... People have imagined that the law of God demanded blind imitation of ancestral forms of belief and worship... Therefore, hatred and hostility have appeared... Even contact and communication have been considered contaminating.[178]

'Abdu'l-Baha commented further on the search for truth, in talks given in Paris. Each religion considers itself the only guardian of the truth and every other religion is composed of errors.

We must distinguish between dogma, superstition and prejudice on the one hand, and truth on the other. No one truth can contradict another truth. Light is good in whatsoever lamp it is burning. 'Abdu'l-Baha cautioned, "We must not allow our love for any one religion or any one personality to so blind our eyes that we become fettered by superstition."[179] If the divine light of truth shone in Jesus Christ it also shone in Moses and in Buddha. 'Seek the truth, the truth shall make you free.' So shall we see the truth in all religions, for truth is in all, and truth is one.[180]

With the decline of the clergy, the importance of independent investigation becomes an essential part of the requirement that each individual must make the effort for his own spiritual development. We are each part of humanity's approaching spiritual maturity. We must each make this effort, though only God will know to what extent we have succeeded.

But how does one go about investigating the truth of the Divine? Investigating the truths of the world around us, such as the laws governing the various scientific disciplines, often demands that we manipulate the object of our study, i.e. place it under a microscope, so to speak. As the investigators, we are relatively superior to the object of our study, and we can therefore impose on the study-object whatever conditions or circumstances we find necessary to conform to the criteria for our investigation.

With God, this is no longer possible. The superiority relationship is now reversed; the investigator is inferior to the object of study. As God may not be manipulated, we must prepare ourselves to be worthy investigators for this study; we must become spiritually receptive. It is necessary that we **"learn** how to discern expressions of God's will for us and respond adequately to them. It is we who now must become (consciously acquiescing) instruments for God's purposes."[181]

The differences among religions, in the Bahá'í view, are differences of interpretation and not scriptural truth. As the various Scriptures are all from one source—God, they cannot disagree. Therefore, an examination of any interpretation in the light of any or all of the Scriptures should uncover the truth.

The Scriptures of all the religions are equally valid. This validity is strongly supported by a key Bahá'í concept—the Manifestation of God. For purposes of this discussion, the reader should review this topic in Chapter One—Manifestation of God, before continuing with this line of thought.

ONENESS OF MANIFESTATIONS OF GOD

Bahá'ís view each of God's Messengers (Manifestations) as being one in spirit, though different in body. Their missions were the same—to deliver God's message. Bahá'u'lláh said, **"There is no distinction whatsoever among the Bearers of My Message. They all have but one purpose..."**[182]

Every human being has a material and a spiritual nature, the spiritual side being the true measure of the individual (see Chapter Seven—The Dual Nature of Man).

The Manifestation, created as a human being, also has a dual nature, or reality, His spiritual side being the true Individual. It is this spiritual side that represents the Voice of God Himself. When He speaks, it is the same as God speaking. Jesus displayed this power, as did Moses, Muhammad, Buddha, and all of the other Manifestations.

How can the same powers belong equally to each Manifestation? What comparisons can be made if they are all the same spiritually? Bahá'u'lláh answered these questions simply. He said that They **"are all sent down from the heaven of the Will of God, and as they all arise to proclaim His irresistible Faith, they therefore are regarded as one soul and the same person"**[183]

This is the crux of Bahá'u'lláh's argument in the Kitab-i-Iqan (Book of Certitude). The Manifestations may have different names and different physical bodies, even different human realities, but inwardly (spiritually) they are the same person reappearing in a different outward guise.

From this perspective, Jesus, Moses, Muhammad, and the other Manifestations always were one and always will be the same person. That *person* is the Divine Spirit who returns with each appearance of a Manifestation of God, or, as Christianity would put it, *the one universal Christ who reappears from age to age.*

One other question needs clarification regarding the oneness of the Manifestations. Are the Manifestations the same as God? From the perspective of serving as *the voice of God*, Bahá'ís would answer in the affirmative. However, the true nature of God can never be fully understood. Bahá'u'lláh stated that **"the Unseen can in no wise incarnate His Essence and reveal it unto men. He is, and hath ever been, immensely exalted beyond all that can either be recounted or perceived."**[184] This statement is found throughout the Bahá'í writings, that God's infinite Essence can never be limited to a physical form, nor can anyone but God fully understand its nature, not even a Manifestation of God.

The Manifestation of God, in His outward aspect, has a human body, a human soul, and a human mind. Inwardly, however, He is the Primal Will, the universal divine mind, in human form. The Primal Will, it should be emphasized, is not the Essence of God, but it is the Mind of God, or the Self of God. In the sense that all Manifestations embody or incarnate the same *Mind or Self*, they are one and the same person. *The Manifestation is thus God in spirit, though not in essence.*

Christianity has more adherents and is geographically more widespread than any other religion. As readers of various faiths are more likely to be commonly familiar with Christian concepts than they are of any other faith besides their own, an examination of a few Christian concepts has been selected as examples for this investigation.

WAS JESUS REALLY GOD?

Perhaps the single most controversial Christian belief, for all other religions and also for many Christians, is *the dogma of exclusivity*. This dogma asserts the claim that:

(1) Jesus is unique and eternally supreme,

(2) He is equal to God (the incarnation of God, or God in human form), and

(3) salvation can come only through Jesus.

These claims, which elevate Christianity above all others, and which deny the validity of any other religious position, make it difficult for any Christian to investigate any other religion without bias or feelings of superiority.

In support of Jesus' supremacy above all others, Christians often present these quotations from the Bible:

..for God so loved the world that He gave His only Son. (John 3:16)

The Word was God...and the Word became flesh. (John 1:1, 14)

Jesus himself stated, "I and the Father are One." (John 10:30)

I am the way, and the truth, and the life; no man comes to the Father, but by me. (John 14:6)

The Bible, however, clearly rejects this supremacy theory with equally authoritative quotations affirming that Jesus and God are not the same:

He who believes in me, believes not in me, but in him who sent me. (John 12:44)

The words that I say to you I do not speak on my own authority... (John 14:10)

...and the word which you hear is not mine but the Father's who sent me. (John 14:24)

And a ruler asked him, saying, "Good Teacher, what shall I do to inherit eternal life?" And Jesus said to him, "Why do you call me good? No one is good but God alone." (Luke 18:18-19)

I can do nothing on my own authority; as I hear I judge; and my judgment is just; because I seek not my own will, but the will of him who sent me. (John 5:30)

...the Father is greater than I.[185](John 14:28)

(Jesus) was faithful to him who appointed him, just as Moses was faithful... (Hebrews 3:2)

But of that day (the Day of Judgment) or that hour no one knows, not even the angels in heaven, nor the Son, but only the Father. (Mark 13:32)

In support of Jesus as the only avenue to salvation, Christians may quote:

...for there is no other name under heaven given among men, by which we must be saved. (Acts 4:12)

He who believes and is baptized will be saved; but he who does not believe will be condemned. (Mark 16:16)

For there is one God, and there is one Mediator between God and men, the man Christ Jesus. (1Timothy 2:5)

The Christian interpretation of these Biblical quotations reflects puzzling discrepancies in light of the "dogma of exclusivity."

The Bahá'í concept of the "oneness of the Manifestations" can accept without discrepancy or conflict the same Biblical quotations. Moses, Zoroaster or any of the other Manifestations could have made similar statements about Their relationship to God with equal validity. Each spoke with the power and authority of God because spiritually all were the same individual. Although the Messenger is God's creation and not God Himself, He manifests God's perfections, acts entirely in concert with the will of God and speaks the Word of God; He is one with God. Bahá'u'lláh explained, **"whosoever... hath recognized and attained unto the presence of these glorious, these resplendent and most excellent Luminaries, hath verily attained unto the 'Presence of God' Himself..."**[186]

The belief that only Jesus is the key to salvation is itself inconsistent with Christian teachings.

Is it credible that the loving God and Father of all people, "the true light which lighteth every man" (John 1:9), who desires "all men to be saved" (1 Timothy 2:4), who "love(s) them that love me" (Proverbs 8:17)... has decreed that only those born within one particular thread of history shall be saved? The manifest injustice of an exclusive

access to salvation has even been apparent to the [Christian] **church for some time...** [This] **is evident in the statement from** [a Christian Missionary Congress in 1960]: "Since...[World War II] **more than one billion souls have passed into eternity and more than half of these went to the torment of hell fire without even hearing of Jesus Christ, who he was, or why he died on the cross...**"[187]

If we consider that these so-called contradictions are based upon fallible human interpretations of infallible sacred scripture, then it is the human interpretations that must be at fault, not the scripture. Scripture may be metaphoric or literal but as truth it may not be inconsistent with other truths.

DID JESUS DIE FOR OUR SINS?

The scriptures of the Western religions use the terms *life and death* as symbols related to the condition of the soul (See Chapter Seven—The Dual Nature of Man).

We can be physically alive in this world yet spiritually dead. Heaven and hell are terms that can be applied both to life here and the condition of the soul after physical death.[188]

In the case of the soul, existence after physical death is eternal, whether in heaven (unending bliss) or hell (untold suffering and torment). Eternal existence in hell is no better than (and perhaps worse than) death, or even non-existence.

Salvation is generally defined as a means of being saved or protected from harm, risk or loss. In theological terms, it is deliverance from the consequences or penalty of sin.

The Christian View. Many Christians believe that Jesus gave His life as a sacrifice for the sins of mankind. Further, they believe that this was necessary for our salvation, and that only Jesus could have made this sacrifice. This belief reflects the Christian view of *atonement*.

A sin is a violation of God's law, and the Bible teaches that *the wages of sin is death* (Romans 6:23). Sinners who are not saved before they die are believed to be condemned to eternal hell. Since all people are sinners deserving of death according to God's justice, out of His mercy, God sent His son as a ransom for humanity's sins. A sinless Jesus offered Himself as a sacrifice to save a sinful humanity.

But God accepts this sacrifice (of Jesus for humanity) only for those who:

(1) repent,

(2) believe that Jesus is the Christ (Messiah), and

(3) accept Him as their Savior.

Good people who do not meet these three qualifications will not be saved, regardless of their goodness; good deeds, charitable giving, helping the poor, or volunteer services are not enough for this definition of salvation.

The Bahá'í View. Salvation is for the person (or the soul) who obeys God, and develops those higher spiritual qualities which will be useful in a spiritual existence. These spiritual qualities are powerful enough to dominate, tame and control his lower animal nature. Bahá'u'lláh describes the soul as **"the first among all created things to declare the excellence of its Creator... If it be faithful to God, it will reflect His light, and will, eventually, return unto Him. If it fail, however, in its allegiance to its Creator, it will become a victim to self and passion, and will, in the end, sink in their depths."**[189]

There are some points of agreement with the Christian view. Bahá'ís believe that:

(1) Jesus did sacrifice Himself for mankind,

(2) Jesus Himself was sinless and voluntarily accepted His sacrifice for love of God and mankind, and

(3) man cannot save himself by good deeds alone.

The Bahá'í view disagrees with the exclusivity of the Christian view. Bahá'ís believe salvation (or closeness to God) was attained through **all** of the Manifestations of God. They believe that:

(1) all Manifestations of God sacrifice Themselves for mankind,

(2) all Manifestations accept persecution (including death, as in the case of Jesus and the Bab) in order to spread the Word of God, and

(3) the current Manifestation of God (at present,

Bahá'u'lláh) is the key to salvation.

The concept of hell as a place of eternal suffering is rejected by Bahá'ís. The Bahá'í concept of heaven and hell is equated, respectively, with *the condition of being spiritually near to or far from God.* The soul who was distant from God during material life can still gain the blessings of heaven (closeness to God), but only through God's mercy, not His justice.

Bahá'u'lláh said that the two requirements for salvation are:

(1) recognizing the current Manifestation of God, and
(2) following His teachings.

He noted that **"These twin duties are inseparable. Neither is acceptable without the other."**[190] Words and actions must reflect each other.

A Bahá'í prayer refers to these requirements: **"...thou hast created me to know Thee** (God) **and to worship Thee."**[191] Recognizing God (through His Manifestations) as 'all-powerful', 'all-merciful', all-forgiving', etc. implies the advisability and good sense to worship Him as the key to salvation. To worship God implies the desire to do His bidding (as revealed through His Manifestations.)

RESURRECTION OF JESUS

The Bahá'í view of resurrection can be succinctly summarized by two quotations, one from Shoghi Effendi, and the other from the Universal House of Justice.

The "Risen Christ" is the consciousness that came to His disciples, grieving over His death, of His living reality; it was not a physical thing but a spiritual realization.[192]

Concerning the Resurrection of Christ you quote the twenty-fourth chapter of the Gospel of St. Luke, where the account stresses the reality of the appearance of Jesus to His disciples who, the Gospel states, at first took Him to be a ghost. From a Bahá'í point of view the belief that the Resurrection was the return to life of a body of flesh and blood, which later rose from the earth into the sky is not reasonable, nor is it necessary to the essential truth of the disciples' experience,

which is that Jesus did not cease to exist when He was crucified (as would have been the belief of many Jews of that period), but that His Spirit, released from the body, ascended to the presence of God and continued to inspire and guide His followers and preside over the destinies of His dispensation.[193]

RELIGION AND SCIENCE AGREE

There is a widespread belief that science and religion are unalterably opposed—specifically that science rejects the teachings of religion about spiritual concepts, and that religion denies certain scientific statements.

This was not always so. It was not until the mid-nineteenth century that the scientific revolution burst forth with major discoveries, inventions and theories that transformed human society.

The enthusiasm, energy, and optimism brought by almost continuous scientific breakthroughs gave mankind wings and hope for an undreamed-of world of comfort, wealth and well-being. Science was elevated to a level of respect and adulation that challenged and threatened the dominance of the religious establishment, especially in the Western world. The social changes resulting from man's newfound power over nature gave rise to confrontations between science and religion as to *which truth was truer.*

Initially, the masses and the clergy clung to their belief in God, and the supporters of science challenged that belief, and argued for *a rational and scientific approach to the study of natural phenomena.*

A century later, many scientists of repute were believers in God. Despite all the scientific advances, it was a humbling experience for many scientists to realize that each new advance opened up ever-greater mysteries which science now had to explore. The masses, on the other hand, succumbed to the doubts about God's existence raised a century earlier, which they now felt were still fashionable.[194]

As in any disagreement, both sides, religion and science, have points to make, and all must be scrutinized carefully and honestly before making any judgments.

SCIENTIFIC METHOD

Science is not just a body of knowledge, a mere accumulation of facts. It does, however, include a body of knowledge, statements of facts that were developed according to a certain process we call *the scientific method*.

It is this method of science that is important—*the way scientific statements are generated*. A statement (hypothesis) is proposed that will explain a number of events, occurrences or conditions. Then experiments or observations are made to test the truth of the statement. If the statement holds true for these tests, then it gradually becomes accepted as a scientific statement or theory. This is essentially the scientific method. In order to be recognized as scientific, a statement must be generated by the scientific method, no matter what question is to be explored.

Scientific truths (statements or theories) are tentative, subject to continuing tests that either prove their validity or their falsity. Strictly speaking, no scientific test can prove that a scientific statement (theory) is unconditionally true because there is always the possibility that later tests using better measuring instruments will find that statement to be false. The best that can be hoped for a statement or theory is that the test shows (at least for the moment) that it is not false. If proven false by a later test, such *'truths'* become false theories and may then be either discarded and replaced by new theories that overcome the objections of the invalidating tests, or the older theories can be modified and improved so that they can satisfy the new test requirements.

This is an ongoing process; scientific statements, or theories, are always subject to retesting. This is a simple (and incomplete) description of a complicated process, but it will serve for the purposes of this discussion.

The ongoing process of testing and retesting of scientific statements is generally considered to date from the time of the Renaissance, about the 14th or 15th centuries. But the modern scientific age, the age sometimes called *the scientific revolution*, goes back no further than the mid-nineteenth century. The methods of science newly developed at that time came into conflict with ancient religious teachings that were already long past their prime and burdened with outdated traditions, obsolete examples, and misinterpretations both honest and politically inspired.

In the eyes of thinking men, the fresh new ideas of science, which were bringing visible benefits to society, completely outmatched the objections of religion with its old rules that were difficult to understand and which appeared to perpetuate the social evils of the past. It was like the story of David and Goliath—the scientific young David against the powerful old Goliath, the giant establishment of the Church.

The means of self-correction is part of the scientific process but it is lacking in the earlier religious institutions. When, for example, a Darwin or an Einstein **"proclaims theories which modify our ideas it is a triumph for science. We do not go about saying that there is another defeat for science, because its old ideas have been abandoned. We know that another step of scientific insight has been gained."**[195]

It is interesting to note that science seeks to know everything and that religion claims to have all the answers. But the truth of science and the truth of religion are both part of the truth of one reality—if they are both true, they cannot contradict each other, they can only support each other. They are both part of our reality:

Acceptance without proof is the fundamental characteristic of western religion. Rejection without proof is the fundamental characteristic of western science... religion has become a matter for the heart and science has become a matter for the mind. This... does not reflect the fact that, psychologically, one cannot exist without the other. Everybody needs both. Mind and heart are only different aspects of us.[196]

TESTIMONY OF LEADING SCIENTISTS

Leading scientists of the twentieth century recognize

that science and religion both have a role to play in man's search for truth. If we admit that there can be only one truth, then we must also admit that scientific truth and religious truth cannot contradict each other. Some world-renowned scientists are quoted:

There can be no conflict between science and religion. Science is a reliable method of finding truth. Religion is a search for a satisfying way of life. Science is growing; yet a world that has science needs, as never before, the inspiration that religion offers. (Arthur H. Compton, physicist)

The probability of life originating from accident is comparable to the probability of the unabridged dictionary resulting from an explosion in a printing shop. (Edwin Conklin, biologist)

If a universe could create itself, it would embody the powers of a creator, and we should be forced to conclude that the universe is itself a God.
(George Davis, physicist)

I believe in an immortal soul. Science has proved that nothing disintegrates into nothingness. Life and soul, therefore, cannot disintegrate into nothingness, and so are immortal.
(Wernher von Braun, rocket scientist)

Religion without science is blind. Science without religion is lame. The man who regards his own life and that of his fellow creatures as meaningless is not merely unfortunate but almost disqualified for life. My religion consists of a humble admiration of the illimitable superior spirit who reveals himself in the slight details we are able to perceive with our frail and feeble minds. That deeply emotional conviction of the presence of a superior reasoning power, which is revealed in the incomprehensible universe, forms my idea of God.
(Albert Einstein, theoretical physicist)

Science cannot solve the ultimate mystery of nature. And that is because, in the last analysis, we ourselves are part of nature, and therefore, part of the mystery we are trying to solve.
(Max Planck, theoretical physicist)

TRUE RELIGION AND SCIENCE ARE TRUE

Bahá'í teachings assert that human society has evolved through progressive stages of development because of the influence of the Manifestations of God. The power to influence the progress of humanity is necessarily impressive; anyone who has such power must be greater than an average human being, and is certainly worthy of recognition and support.

But until we are sure He is genuine, we must investigate Him. Taking someone else's word for it is not enough—we must be convinced heart and soul. A number of studies suggest how the scientific method can be applied to examine Bahá'u'lláh's claim to be a Manifestation of God. If it appears that He is indeed a Manifestation of God, then anything He says must be true.

We must see if we can render these assertions considerably more acceptable than their negations. In the case of Bahá'u'lláh, we have many things which we can test empirically.[197] **Bahá'u'lláh made predictions. Did they come true...? In His teachings are found statements concerning the nature of the physical world. Has science validated these...? He engaged in extensive analysis of the nature of man's organized social life. Does His analysis accord with our own scientific observations of the same phenomena?**[198]

Bahá'u'lláh made many detailed prophecies. Have they been fulfilled or have any been contradicted by subsequent events? He described scientific facts that were unknown in His lifetime. Have these been verified, or have any been decisively refuted during this past century?[199]

Let us examine briefly some of Bahá'u'lláh's statements concerning the physical universe. Towards the end of His life, Bahá'u'lláh, noting the growing activity of the Western powers in developing weapons for war, warned of dangers still hidden involving atmospheric changes and lethal contamination. In one tablet, He foreshadowed the development of atomic weapons when He wrote:

Strange and astonishing things exist in the earth but they are hidden from the minds and the

understanding of men. These things are capable of changing the whole atmosphere of the earth and their contamination would prove lethal.²⁰⁰

'Abdu'l-Baha, too, referred to this same awesome power when, in 1911, He met in Paris with the Japanese ambassador to Spain, Viscount Arawaka.

There is in existence a stupendous force, as yet, happily, undiscovered by man. Let us supplicate God... that this force be not discovered by science until spiritual civilization shall dominate the human mind. In the hands of men of lower material nature, this power would be able to destroy the whole earth.²⁰¹

In 1920, 'Abdu'l-Baha wrote to a group of students in Tokyo, "In Japan the divine proclamation will be heard as a formidable explosion..."²⁰²

'Abdu'l-Baha expressed the Bahá'í views of religion and science as fully compatible with each other. Reason and logic, the distinguishing feature of God's highest level of creation, the human being, cannot be cast aside in the search to understand his true higher nature. How can science and religion contradict each other if they are both true? The moral teachings of all the religions are logical and are not opposed by science. Religion and science, said 'Abdu'l-Baha, are the two wings upon which man's intelligence can soar into the heights.

It is not possible to fly with one wing alone! Should a man try to fly with the wing of religion alone he would quickly fall into the quagmire of superstition, while on the other hand, with the wing of science alone he would also make no progress, but fall into the despairing slough of materialism.²⁰³

The disagreements among the various religions, churches and sects are primarily due to differences in rites and ceremonial practices rather than the fundamental teachings of their Founders. The resulting discord, hatred and dissension among these groups have convinced many cultured people that religion and science have no common ground, that religion is a blind adherence to certain teachers and their own special dogmas and precepts. Both religion and science, 'Abdu'l-Baha stated, are the measure of our understanding. **"Put all your beliefs into harmony with science; there can be no opposition, for truth is one."**[204]

The story of *Adam and Eve* is a common example of the rejection by science and reason of a Biblical truth. A literal interpretation is unacceptable to man's intelligence, much less the Divinity of God.

We must reflect a little: if the literal meaning of this story were attributed to a wise man, certainly all would logically deny that... this invention could have emanated from an intelligent being. Therefore, this story of Adam and Eve who ate from the tree, and their expulsion from Paradise, must be thought of simply as a symbol. It contains divine mysteries and universal meanings, and it is capable of marvelous (and numerous) explanations.[205]

THE DIFFERENCES ARE NOT SCIENTIFIC

We have pointed out the distinguishing features of science and the emphasis that has been placed upon its so-called conflict with religion. What are the circumstances surrounding these disagreements? We must first admit that, like most participants in a disagreement, there may be fault on both sides. Both science and religion, as they are described above, do not deny reason as a judge of their truth. What we have found as the shortcomings of religion must be due to the misinterpretations of fallible human beings because the religious teachings themselves are, by definition, from God. So let us examine our understanding of science for any misjudgments that may contribute to the apparent disagreements.

Through its phenomenal successes, science has gained a remarkable reputation for discovering truth. Some people are so impressed that they feel science can explain everything, and anything that it cannot explain (or cannot prove) is simply not true.

By definition, science must test any question or statement before drawing a scientific conclusion as to its truth or falsity. Are there any questions or statements that science cannot test (and therefore not prove to be true or false)? The answer, of course, is yes—anything that is infinite, or without limits. Science can test only that which has limits—that which can be defined. Therefore, the question whether the universe is finite or infinite cannot be determined by scientific testing; God's existence cannot be scientifically determined because God is, by definition, infinite in all of His aspects.

These ideas cannot be tested by science. No scientific proof or claim can be made—*neither for nor against*. Any statement or claim that is made on these (or similar) topics can be no more than beliefs, not scientific truths. A noted research physicist, Anjam Khursheed, wrote:

It is unavoidable that we should make suppositions about matters lying beyond the scope of science. What is to be avoided is the misapprehension that these suppositions are scientific, and the misapprehension that everything worth saying is scientific. As Karl Popper expresses it... 'science does not make assertions about ultimate questions—about the riddles of existence, or about man's task in the world... The fact that science cannot make any pronouncement about ethical principles has been misinterpreted as indicating that there are no such principles, while in fact the search for truth presupposes ethics.'[206]

In his book *The Limits of Science*, Peter Medawar makes a similar point. He said that those questions that are beyond the power of science to answer are a reflection of the limits of science.

These are the questions that children ask—the 'ultimate questions' of Karl Popper... such questions as: How did everything begin? What are we all here for? What is the point of living? Doctrinaire positivism (an obsolete and discredited belief that only our human senses reveal what is real)... dismissed all such questions as nonquestions or pseudo-questions such as only simpletons ask and only charlatans... profess to be able to answer. This peremptory dismissal leaves

one empty and dissatisfied because the questions make sense to those who ask them, and the answers, to those who try to give them; but whatever else may be in dispute, it would be universally agreed that it is not to science that we should look for answers.[207]

Other limits of science may include intellectual shortcomings. Human intelligence itself may have limits beyond which we simply cannot perceive.

Just as the vegetable world cannot comprehend the animal world, or the animal world comprehend the human world, so too perhaps the human intellect may not be able to comprehend or confirm the existence of other (spiritual) worlds. Another way of illustrating this is to liken the human mind to a fishing net. A fishing net is restricted to catching fish larger than the mesh comprising it, and in the sea of life the human mind may also be restricted in what it can perceive and what it can comprehend. Indeed, to assume it is not runs contrary to experience: all forms of life are restricted and limited in some way. It is important at least to acknowledge that this possibility exists.[208]

THE COMPLEX COMPUTER ANALOGY

Khursheed presents an analogy illustrating the error of believing that there can be no plan or grand design for creation.

Imagine an infinitely complex computer whose circuitry is hidden from human sight except through a small number of portholes. On looking through these holes one may observe a limited number of semiconductor switches operating in certain sequences. If measurements of electrical signals on these switches were made, one would detect two signals. Firstly... some computer-operating signals which represent the running of the computer; but since only a small part of the computer's circuitry can be observed, these signals would be mysterious, and their purpose could not be completely known.

Secondly, one would detect the presence of

random electrical fluctuations, known as electrical noise. If one were to conclude that the whole computer did not have any purpose, purely from the detection of random electrical fluctuations (electrical noise), one would be in great error... It is equivalent to saying that the computer-operating signals in the analogy are generated and entirely accounted for by the presence of electrical noise.

Experience shows, however, that electrical noise or any other such random effect always averages out and does not produce large signals of its own accord. The question of purpose can obviously not be settled by gaining partial glimpses of the computer's circuitry, particularly if that circuitry is infinite in complexity, making it impossible to gain complete knowledge of its operation, even in principle.[209]

The results of our investigation of science and religion indicate that any problem we encounter in our understanding of their characteristics may well be due to our own human misperceptions rather than to real differences. Our obligation, then, is to be extremely careful in our interpretation of what is truth.

EQUALITY OF MEN AND WOMEN

The Bahá'í principle of the equality of men and women is a natural extension of the basic theme of unity. It is one of the social laws that mankind is now qualified to accept as part of the dawning of a socially mature society. This is the first time in history that the founder of a world religion has explicitly stated this equality.

Although the functional and biological differences of the sexes are evident in themselves, it is the essential human characteristics of their spiritual realities that are equal in the eyes of God. 'Abdu'l-Baha, in one of His talks during His visit to the United States, said that as all are created in the (spiritual) image of God, those who best reflect the divine attributes are closest to God, irrespective of gender.

In the animal and vegetable kingdoms, all plants, trees and animals are subject to functional differences by creation, but among themselves there is absolute equality without further distinction as to sex. In the human kingdom, women's lack of educational opportunities have kept hidden their equal capacities, and perpetuated an inequality that is unjust and contrary to natural law.

Achievement of full equality for women will require some difficult changes for our present societies. Both men and women have been conditioned by an attitude of paternalism and male domination that has held women to be inferior socially.[210] **The Universal House of Justice deplores this social inequality that has discriminated against half the world's population. Such an injustice has permeated family, workplace, politics and international relations. It has no moral, practical or biological grounds on which it can be justified.** [211]

The world in the past has been ruled by force, and man has dominated over woman by reason of his more forceful and aggressive qualities both of body and mind. But the balance is already shifting; force is losing its dominance, and mental alertness, intuition, and the spiritual qualities of love and service, in which woman is strong, are gaining ascendancy. Hence the new age will be an age less masculine and more permeated with the feminine ideals, or, to speak more exactly, will be an age in which the masculine and feminine elements of civilization will be more evenly balanced.[212]

As women are offered opportunities for development and advancement, equality of the sexes will become a reality. Imagine the advance of human progress when both men and women can contribute in equal measure to the welfare of the human race.

'Abdu'l-Baha applied His two wings analogy to men and women in the world of humanity. Both wings must be equally developed for the bird to fly, He said. The creation of a peaceful and sustainable world civilization will be impossible without the full participation of women in every arena of human activity.[213]

The statement of this equality by Bahá'u'lláh more than one hundred years ago was the beginning of a process that is still underway. The many women's suffrage and human rights movements since that time, especially in the West, are an indication of the spiritual forces that were released to energize the changes that have been won. Many more changes have yet to be fought and won to achieve full equality for women.

ELIMINATION OF PREJUDICE

The principal Bahá'í theme of unity proclaims the ultimate oneness of mankind. From the standpoint of the unity of mankind, any distinction of race, class, ethnic origin or national identity has no real significance. Such distinctions do not stand up to any reasonable examination.

Differences between individuals and groups are inevitable. It is their biased negative targeting that is reprehensible. The tendency to make negative judgments based on illogical and faulty perceptions of these differences lead to stereotypes. Such individuals and groups suffer unwarranted censure, ignominy and even attack for unfair and often unreal shortcomings resulting from misperceptions of fact. This is prejudice.

The desire to exalt oneself above others is a very deep root cause of all kinds of prejudice. People want to be at the top of the heap, with the most money or biggest house or prettiest face... Thus prejudice against the overweight, the short and the ugly arises in a very real sense from the same motivation that inspires racial prejudice: a desire to be superior.[214]

Among the various kinds of prejudice mankind has yet to overcome, the odious practice of racial prejudice is considered by many to be one of the major worldwide social problems. Shoghi Effendi, in numerous letters to the Baha'i world community, warned of the dangers of this evil practice as a darkness surrounding humanity.[215]

It has been calculated that every person alive today is at least a 50th-cousin of every other person in the world. It is highly unlikely that any living individual does not have some trace of ethnic, tribal, national or racial mix in his heritable background. If we are all blood relations in the family of man, upon what can we base any feelings of superiority? Differences in economic condition, education, intelligence or physical appearance are accidental and/or too temporary to maintain or justify as intrinsically distinctive or special.

"God maketh no distinction between the white and the black. If the hearts are pure both are acceptable unto Him."[216] **Speaking through Bahá'u'lláh, the voice of God proclaims: "O CHILDREN OF MEN! Know ye not why We created you all from the same dust? That no one should exalt himself over the other...**[217] **Close your eyes to racial differences, and welcome all with the light of oneness..."In the estimation of God," He states, "all men are equal. There is no distinction or preference for any soul, in the realm of His justice and equity." "God did not make these divisions," He affirms; "these divisions have had their origin in man himself. Therefore, as they are against the plan and purpose of God they are false and imaginary."** [218]

UNIVERSAL LANGUAGE

The fundamental principle of unity requires that there be full and open communication among all members of the human race. Bahá'u'lláh called on all nations to select one common language:

Select ye a single language for the use of all on earth, and adopt ye likewise a common script... This will be the cause of unity... and the greatest instrument for promoting harmony and civilization...[219]

At one of His talks given in Paris, 'Abdu'l-Baha noted that not only unity would be strengthened by a universal language. The need for numerous languages and translations would be eliminated by the adoption of a single language, whether it was one already in common use worldwide, such as English, or an invented one, such as Esperanto.

With more than eight hundred languages used throughout the world, and the geographical shrinking of distances by technology, it is necessary that all people be able to communicate and develop closer ties. The mother tongue and the universal language are the only two languages that need be learned for everyone to communicate freely throughout the world.

'Abdu'l-Baha proposed an international Congress to develop a new language or choose an existing one. He said, **"Difference of speech is one of the most fruitful causes of dislike and distrust that exists between nations... If everybody could speak one language, how much more easy would it be to serve humanity!"**[220]

UNIVERSAL EDUCATION

Education is an essential teaching of all the religions. Acquiring knowledge is one of the highest priorities of every religion:

ISLAM To acquire knowledge is binding on all believers, both men and women. (Ibn Maja)

BAHÁ'Í Knowledge is as wings to man's life, and a ladder for his ascent. Its acquisition is incumbent upon everyone. (Tablets of Bahá'u'lláh)

JUDAISM Apply your heart to instruction, and your ears to words of knowledge. (Proverbs)

HINDUISM In this world, there is no purifier like knowledge. (Bhagavad Gita)

BUDDHISM He who in early days was unwise but later found wisdom, he sheds a light over the world like that of the moon when freed from clouds. (Dhammapada)

CHRISTIANITY Be transformed by the renewing of your mind. Then you will be able to test and approve what God's will is... (Romans)

The reason for the importance of education is not difficult to understand. In order to follow the teachings of God, humanity must be taught what these teachings are. Education comprises three elements— the one who educates (the educator, or teacher); the one who is educated (the learner); and the connecting process. In terms of religion, the one who educates is God (through His chosen Appointee, the Manifestation of God). The one who is educated (the learner) is all of humanity; and the connecting process is the transfer (of the teachings, or scriptures) between the educator (God, through His Manifestation) and the learner (humanity).

Bahá'u'lláh explained that the reason God wants us to follow His teachings is the purpose of our lives on earth. When we were ready, we moved individually from *the world of the womb* to this physical world. The time we spend in this world is but a preparation for the spiritual world. In the world of the womb, we developed the physical powers we needed for this world; in this life our purpose is to develop spiritual attributes, qualities we will need in our next life (the world of the spirit).

The Prophets of God have been sent, the Holy Books have been written, so that man may be made free. Just as he is born into this world of imperfection from the womb of his earthly mother, so is he born into the world of spirit through divine education.[221]

DIVINE EDUCATOR

'Abdu'l-Baha describes three kinds of education: material, human and spiritual. *Material education* applies to both animals and man, and is concerned with the knowledge of the body and its needs, such as obtaining food, comfort, and safety. *Human education* has to do with the knowledge of human civilization and progress; examples are government, the arts, the sciences, inventions, natural law—all that contribute to human living, both individually and socially. *Spiritual education* is the knowledge and development of those qualities that are appropriate for spiritual beings—another name for *divine education*. Because spiritual or divine education is the highest level of education, it encompasses the lower levels as well. Human beings can learn (and have learned) both material and human education by experience, but they cannot learn divine education without a qualified (divine) teacher.

'Abdu'l-Baha emphasized the key role of the divine educator in the education process. Such a teacher must be knowledgeable in material and human education as well as in spiritual areas. His behavior must reflect this knowledge, so he must be distinguished above all men; if he were like the rest of humanity, he could not be their educator. A teacher of spiritual qualities must display those same qualities, and must serve as an example for those he teaches. [222]

Every Manifestation of God was a divine educator. The teachings of each Manifestation, coming from the same source, could not contradict the teachings of any other Manifestation; indeed, He could only reinforce and affirm them.

AGREEMENT AMONG DIVINE EDUCATORS

The Manifestations of God, bringing their messages from the same source, have never denounced each other. An early Western Bahá'í, J.E. Esslemont, wrote to this point:

It is the unworthy followers of these great world teachers— worshippers of the letter but not of the spirit of their teaching—who have always been the persecutors of the later prophets... They have studied the light of the particular revelation which they hold sacred, and have defined its properties and peculiarities as seen by their limited vision, with the utmost care and precision. That is for them the one true light... If God in His infinite bounty sends fuller light from another quarter, and the torch of inspiration burns brighter than before from a new torchholder, instead of welcoming the new light and worshipping with new gratitude the Father of all lights they are angry and alarmed. This new light does not correspond with their definitions. It has not the orthodox color, and does not shine from the orthodox place, therefore it must at all costs be extinguished lest it lead men astray into the paths of heresy! Many enemies of the Prophets are of this type— blind leaders leading the blind, who oppose new and fuller truth in the supposed interests of what they believe to be the truth.[223]

'Abdu'l-Baha noted that the Jewish clergy of Jesus' time denounced Him as a destroyer of the Mosaic Law. They proclaimed Him a violator of the holy Sabbath and destroyer of the Temple of

Solomon. Nevertheless, Jesus honored the memory of Moses. Through Christ's message, the Old Testament was translated into six hundred languages and was spread to every part of the world. Moses became widely known as a Prophet of God and His book the Book of God because of Christianity's influence.[224]

JUSTICE AND MERCY

The divine attributes are spiritual qualities that have been taught by all of the divine educators. Possessing these qualities is a matter of degree for everyone. We display these qualities in a manner that shows how well we have made them part of us—that is, how well we have mastered the teachings of the divine educator.

Spiritual qualities are appropriate for groups and societies as well as for individuals. Trying to display evidence of all of our spiritual qualities at all times to the greatest extent possible reflects an immature and superficial understanding of their nature. Although they are all good in themselves, spiritual qualities, if used improperly, can be harmful. For example, the spiritual quality of justice demands that wrongdoing deserves punishment. The spiritual quality of mercy is forgiveness of wrongdoing without deserved punishment. These two spiritual qualities are contradictory unless they are balanced properly.

In an analysis of punishment both in theory and practice, retribution (the retributivist view) and social utility (the utilitarian view) are identified as the main conflicting principles justifying punishment in human society. The retributivist says justice demands that a wrongdoer must be punished, whereas the utilitarian opposes punishment for a wrong unless it benefits society. Generally, mercy would carry more weight in the utilitarian view than it would for the retributivist.[225]

The decline of religion in recent years has been accompanied by a corresponding growth in a pseudo-religious philosophy called *humanitarianism, or humanism.* **"It is basically a nonreligion in that it makes humankind rather than a higher power central to life and thought."**[226] Because this philosophy ranks the good of human beings in this world as paramount, the humanitarian would say that the spiritual quality of mercy takes precedence over justice.

Those who break the law are generally punished, but there is a humanitarian tendency in many societies to show compassion and to reduce sentences as much as possible. Blame for criminal action is often placed on society rather than the individual perpetrator. The criminal is viewed as a victim of circumstances, and so he is shown mercy and pardon rather than justice and punishment for his actions. **"Leniency and compassion in the courts of law, supported by modern theories aimed at forgiveness and clemency have increased the reign of violence in the world to alarming proportions."** [227]

Contrary to this utilitarian/humanitarian view, Bahá'u'lláh categorically insists that **"those who apply the law should not show mercy to a criminal, nor become compassionate when punishing him, for if they do, they will undermine the foundations of justice."** [228] 'Abdu'l-Baha cautions that kindness to a wrongdoer **"encourages him to become worse... The more kindness you show to a liar the more apt he is to lie, for he thinks that you know not, while you do know, but extreme kindness keeps you from revealing your knowledge."** [229]

Because the humanitarian view is mainly concerned with this life and not with life after death, mild punishments and plenty of compassion and even educational rehabilitation are preferred to punishment. No concern is shown for the consequences of an individual's actions on the progress of his soul in the next life, whereas the Bahá'í view of this world as a transitory stage in man's eternal life is of major importance.

Bahá'u'lláh's mission of world unity requires a human society to be established upon the principles of justice. **"O SON OF SPIRIT! The best beloved of all things in My sight is Justice... Verily justice is My gift to thee and the sign of My loving-kindness. Set it then before thine eyes."** [230]

In every civilized society law and order are the basis

of peace and security. The breaking of laws, therefore, must incur some punishment. **"The bonds which unite individuals are love, compassion and forbearance, but what binds nations together... is justice."**[231]

It should be noted that the Bahá'í view of justice does not condone vengeance or personal retaliation as acceptable punishment because it only compounds the crime.

...If a man strikes another, and he who is struck takes revenge by returning the blow, what advantage will he gain...? In truth the two actions are the same, both are injuries; the only difference is that one occurred first and the other afterwards... The law of the community will punish the aggressor but will not take revenge... But if he who has been struck pardons and forgives, he shows the greatest mercy. This is worthy of admiration.[232]

Unfortunately, there is little distinction made today between individuals and society regarding the display of spiritual qualities. For individuals, the Bahá'í teachings rank the quality of mercy over the demands of justice because the cement of unity requires compassion, love and brotherhood.

But society, the institution that must apply the laws of humanity, must maintain justice above all, to protect equally all the members of society. **"So there is a vast difference between a Baha'i outlook on life and that of humanists. The former strives to use the opportunities of this life to reap a rich harvest in the next, while the latter exerts all efforts to prosper while on this earth. It is these contrasting views that constitute the basis for Bahá'u'lláh's emphasis on punishment and the humanist view on leniency and compassion."**[233]

METAPHORICAL PROCESS

The metaphor is one of the most powerful teaching strategies that can be used to develop understanding of unfamiliar concepts and relationships, especially for such abstract concepts as the divine or spiritual teachings.

The metaphorical process is an extremely valuable educational device for explaining the unfamiliar in terms of the familiar, or the abstract in terms of the concrete.

Hatcher describes the metaphor as an analogical equation in which an unknown factor is compared to a known factor in order to explain the unknown factor. As an example, he uses the metaphor, *Jane is a lovely flower*.[234] The unknown Jane is compared to the known flower. The metaphorical process requires that each person must exercise his own judgment in determining the meaning of Jane as presented in the statement.

Another use of the metaphorical process, especially in the area of religion is its protection against **"literalism and hence against imitation and dogmatism. For example, when Christ states that he is the "bread of life" (John 6:35), he means something positive by it, that he is valuable, essential, a source of sustenance, of spiritual nutrition. But there is no one 'correct' meaning or translation of the equation. Unless we realize that Christ's statement is metaphorical, we may end up believing that Christ was a piece of bread."**[235]

'Abdu'l-Baha offered additional examples in His explanations of the use of the metaphor. He described two kinds of human knowledge, or reality—sensory and intellectual. Sensory knowledge refers to things that are perceptible to one or more of the senses. Examples would be the sun, thunder, perfume, food and heat.

Intellectual reality has no form or place; it is imperceptible to the senses. Examples would be God, nature, thought, happiness and love. 'Abdu'l-Baha described these as realities of the intellect. To explain intellectual realities, we must resort to material, or sensory, terms. 'Mary is making great progress', even though she is still in one place. 'Harry is bursting with joy', although he continues to live.

'Abdu'l-Bahá noted that the *dove* that descended upon Christ was not a material dove. In the Old Testament, when God appeared as a pillar of fire, it was not a material reality, but an intellectual reality.

Intellectual realities are expressed by sensory images.
Christ says, "The Father is in the Son, and the Son is in the Father." Was Christ within God, or God within Christ...? On the contrary, this is an intellectual state which is expressed in a sensible figure...[236]

The importance of the metaphorical process in religion cannot be overestimated. Ceremonies, rites and rituals are sensory symbols representing spiritual truths. We speak of spiritual things that are outside of our material experience only in material terms that are part of our present experience. The concerns of religion are mainly spiritual concerns. **"Unfortunately, religion, which in its youthful vitality and purity is able to open man's inward eye to these spiritual truths, gradually loses this inner strength. The spiritual truths become obscured or forgotten while the symbols which represent them, the rites and rituals, become the all-important thing."**[237]

Take, for example, from the Christian scriptures, the verse from John 14:9-10, in which Jesus says, **"He who has seen me has seen the Father,"** and **"The words that I say to you I do not speak on my own authority; but the Father who dwells in me does his works."** The failure of the Christian authorities to recognize the metaphorical process in these verses is seen in the Nicene Creed, an early statement of Christian beliefs, which declared that Christ was equal to God.

In 325 AD, at the Council of Nicaea, in Asia Minor, leaders of Christianity met to decide between the arguments of Athanasius, an Egyptian theologian who said that Jesus and God were the same, and Arius, a Libyan bishop who argued that Jesus was not God, but the chosen Messenger of God. Arius, who was defeated by the Council's vote, was condemned as a heretic by the church authorities and the followers who supported his position became known as *the Arian heresy*, a major source of opposition to the unity of the Catholic Church.

Bahá'u'lláh poetically applies metaphor in an instructive prayer to promote spiritual growth:
Intone, O My servant, the verses of God that have

been received by thee, as intoned by them who have drawn nigh unto Him, that the sweetness of thy melody may kindle thine own soul, and attract the hearts of all men. Whoso reciteth, in the privacy of his chamber, the verses revealed by God, the scattering angels of the Almighty shall scatter abroad the fragrance of the words uttered by his mouth, and shall cause the heart of every righteous man to throb. Though he may, at first, remain unaware of its effect, yet the virtue of the grace vouchsafed unto him must needs sooner or later exercise its influence upon his soul. Thus have the mysteries of the Revelation of God been decreed by virtue of the Will of Him Who is the Source of power and wisdom.[238]

TEACHING THE FAITH TO OTHERS

The goal of the educative process is the transmission of knowledge to the learner. Bahá'u'lláh's message, intended for all of humanity, now offers Bahá'ís the opportunity to put into practice some of the lessons they gleaned from listening to that message. The Faith they were taught must now be taught to others. Bahá'ís show their love for God by sharing this love with their fellow human beings. What greater gift can one give another than to share one's own most precious possession?

Not everyone, however, is prepared to receive this gift. Tied to the duty of proclaiming His message is a firm caution against proselytism. Teaching others is encouraged, but not if the learner is unwilling to be taught. The excesses of proselytism reflected in the butchery of the Spanish Inquisition, the Crusades and the Islamic conquests were a violation of both Christian and Islamic teachings.

Bahá'ís are faced with a delicate task—they are required to teach the Word of Bahá'u'lláh to all of humanity but without proselytizing.

Teach ye the Cause of God, O people of Baha, for God hath prescribed unto every one the duty of proclaiming His Message...[239] We should never insist on teaching those who are not really ready for the Cause. If a man is not hungry you cannot

make him eat.[240]

These restrictions do not absolve Bahá'ís from their duty to teach others. Until they know that their audience is receptive, Bahá'ís will, without pressure, offer the message tactfully and in small doses.

WORLD GOVERNMENT—WORLD PEACE

The unity of mankind, as Bahá'u'lláh describes it, must be a spiritual unity that is developed within the fundamental concepts taught by all the earlier religions. Thus, the unity of the human race would be achieved within a spirit of justice, as taught by Moses; within a spirit of love, as taught by Jesus; within a spirit of submission to the will of God, as taught by Muhammad.

All are equally important and necessary to achieve this spiritual unity. It is abundantly clear that no organized society in the world, today or in the past, has been able to manifest and sustain sufficiently even one of the fundamental concepts described above. All attempts at social organization based on justice, for example, eventually developed deep pockets of injustice.

GLOBAL ECONOMY

In one of His tablets, Bahá'u'lláh outlined His vision for the next stage of mankind's social development. **"The time must come,"** He declared, **"when the imperative necessity for the holding of a vast, an all-embracing assemblage of men will be realized. The rulers... of the earth... should resolve, for the tranquility of the peoples of the earth, to be fully reconciled among themselves. Should any king take up arms against another, all should unitedly arise and prevent him. If this be done, the nations of the world will no longer require any armaments, except for the purpose of preserving the security of their realms and of maintaining internal order within their territories. This will ensure the peace and composure of every people, government and nation. We fain would hope that the kings and rulers of the earth, the mirrors of the gracious and almighty name of God, may attain unto this** station, and shield mankind from the onslaught of tyranny."[241]

Bahá'u'lláh noted that humanity has now reached a critical turning point in its social evolution. **The historic principle of competition as the motivating factor in all of its institutions, such as language, custom, government and economy, is now in need of another motivating principle—cooperation, the unifying ingredient needed to achieve a united world.**[242]

The unity of mankind presupposes a united government and a single world economic system. It also requires a return to the ethical and moral values taught by all the religions. Both individuals and governments must be dedicated to the well being of the human race. Our loyalties must go beyond groups—it must extend to all of humanity. **"The earth is but one country and mankind its citizens. It is not for him to pride himself who loveth his own country, but rather for him who loveth the whole world."**[243]

Explaining Bahá'u'lláh's teachings, Shoghi Effendi pointed to the evolving institutions of family, tribe, city-state and nation, leading to the next stage of humanity's destiny—world unity. He noted that nation-building has come to an end. We must establish the machinery necessary for attaining the principle of the 'oneness and wholeness of human relationships'.[244]

In such a world, he said, economic organization would be directed toward the good of all humanity and not merely the interests of some limited group of people such as a class or a nation. In a united world a world currency is needed. A universal system of weights and measures is also a reasonable requirement. Raw materials must be organized for the good of the world as a whole, and markets must be coordinated in the most effective way. Bars to world trade, which now exist, will vanish, as will the greatest of all economic handicaps, *war*. There will be no wars of armaments, tariffs or quotas. The interests of mankind must take precedence over sectional interests.

Bahá'u'lláh proclaimed new laws guaranteeing a

minimum standard of life for everyone. He placed a limit on the wealth of any one individual. This would allow each person full freedom to strive for his own level of wealth within these limits, and none need be in want of the necessities.

It is necessary, said 'Abdu'l-Baha, to eliminate the extremes of poverty and wealth. Neither condition is acceptable. **"When we see poverty allowed to reach a condition of starvation it is a sure sign that somewhere we shall find tyranny."**[245]

Many of Bahá'u'lláh's teachings are concerned with the attitude towards work. For Bahá'ís, work is obligatory both for the rich and for the poor; Bahá'u'lláh warned that begging and living in idleness are both forbidden. **"Occupy yourselves with that which will profit yourselves and others besides yourselves,"** He advised.

The spirit in which work is approached should be that of a craftsman producing the best work he can in order to serve God and his fellow men. Work done in this spirit is deemed in the Bahá'í Faith equivalent to worship. **"The man who makes a piece of notepaper to the best of his ability, conscientiously, concentrating all his forces on perfecting it, is giving praise to God."**[246]

UNIFIED WORLD

The connection between the fundamental unity theme and world peace is clear and firm. A united world is necessary to establish world peace. Despite the present unstable world conditions, Bahá'ís view world peace as inevitable. The Universal House of Justice wrote in a letter

"To the Peoples of the World":
The Great Peace towards which people of good will throughout the centuries have inclined their hearts, of which seers and poets for countless generations have expressed their vision, and for which from age to age the sacred scriptures of mankind have constantly held the promise, is now at long last within the reach of the nations. For the first time in history it is possible for everyone to view the entire planet, with all its myriad

diversified peoples, in one perspective. World peace is not only possible but inevitable. It is the next stage in the evolution of this planet—in the words of one great thinker, 'the planetization of mankind'.[247]

All of the earlier Manifestations taught the cause of peace, the oneness of God and the unity of mankind. This is why there are so many prophecies about peace in all of the holy books. It was the purpose of the earlier religions to pave the way for the establishment of peace in a unified world. One of the central themes of the Bahá'í Faith is to establish that peace.

The concept of world peace taught by the earlier religions could not refer to the world in a global context because it could not be understood by the people of those earlier days. Shoghi Effendi pointed out how Christianity and Islam helped to pave the way for the establishment of world peace for a world society that is globally aware and desperately in need of unification on a global level.

Christianity, he said, stressed the individual's morality and discipline as a central theme for human society. Jesus addressed the people of His day as individuals, and not as parts of the whole of mankind. The conception of a world society in a world that was still largely unexplored could not then be understood. The people of Jesus' time were not ready for ideas involving the unity of nations or world unification.

Islam, appearing six hundred years later, developed the idea of the nation as the vital social institution for that day. World conditions and an evolving society, Shoghi Effendi continued, were appropriate for the unity of nationhood, as it was the most efficient form of social organization at that time.

In the course of their development, nation societies often misperceive threats to their own survival. Many nations fear to relinquish a portion of their national sovereignty (such as the right to make war) in order to achieve a more unified world organization. This is in some ways similar to the fears that were finally overcome by the independent American states two centuries ago to form the unified nation of the United States of America.

When the problems faced by any social group exceed the powers of that society to deal with those problems, the society itself begins to come apart. There seems to be a growing fear that society is no longer under control. As governments of sovereign nations have been unable to establish a real peace, and as they frequently endorse destructive instruments of war, the fear grows that **"governments no longer protect life and property but, on the contrary, have become the chief sources of peril to mankind..."**[248]

Bahá'ís believe that present world conditions now require the next stage of social polity after nationhood, the stage of world unity. 'Abdu'l-Baha assured us that this stage will be established within this (the twentieth) century. In this new Day **"the hostility of races and peoples, and differences among nations, will be eliminated. All men will adhere to one religion, will have one common faith, will be blended into one race, and become a single people. All will dwell in one common fatherland, which is the planet itself... Bahá'u'lláh Himself affirms... 'It is not his to boast who loveth his country, but it is his who loveth the world.'"**[249]

Shoghi Effendi described in some detail the essential administrative and economic elements of the world government that is needed to maintain world peace. The executive, legislative and judicial functions would be carried out in democratically-formed institutions, similar to current democracies, but the people selected to carry out these functions must be chosen by a divine process[250] that avoids the perils and gambles of campaigning and power-seeking which are characteristic of most current practices.

A brief listing of some of these elements barely suggest the high level of emphasis Bahá'u'lláh placed upon this aspect of His unity message.[251]

- A world commonwealth will be established in which all nations, races, creeds and classes are closely and permanently united.
- A world legislature will be formed, whose members will ultimately control the entire resources of all the component nations.
- A world executive, backed by an international

force, will carry out the decisions arrived at, and apply the laws enacted by the world legislature.
- A world tribunal will rule in all and any disputes that may arise between the various elements constituting this universal system.
- A mechanism of world inter-communication will be devised, freed from national hindrances and restrictions.
- A world metropolis will act as the nerve center of a world civilization.
- A world language will either be invented or chosen, and will be taught in the schools of all the federated nations as an auxiliary to their mother tongue.
- A world script, a world literature, a uniform and universal system of currency, of weights and measures, will simplify and facilitate intercourse and understanding among the nations and races of mankind.

As a result of a world organization as outlined in the list above, Shoghi Effendi concluded, many benefits would accrue to all of humanity:

- The economic resources of the world will be organized, its sources of raw materials will be tapped and fully utilized, its markets will be coordinated and developed, and the distribution of its products will be equitably regulated. Economic barriers and restrictions will be completely abolished.
- The press will cease to be mischievously manipulated by vested interests and will be liberated from the influence of contending governments and peoples.
- National rivalries, hatreds, and intrigues will cease.
- Racial animosity and prejudice will be replaced by racial amity, understanding and cooperation.
- The inordinate distinction between classes will be obliterated.
- Destitution on the one hand, and gross accumulation of ownership on the other, will

disappear.
- The enormous energy dissipated and wasted on war will extend the range of human inventions and technical development. Elimination of war will lead to the increase of the productivity of mankind:
   - extermination of disease
   - extension of scientific research
   - raising of the standard of physical health
   - exploitation of the unused and unsuspected resources of the planet
   - prolongation of human life

Shoghi Effendi summarized the benefits of world unification that has been destined for humanity.

A world federal system, ruling the whole earth and exercising unchallengeable authority over its unimaginably vast resources, blending and embodying the ideals of both the East and the West, liberated from the curse of war and its miseries, and bent on the exploitation of all the available sources of energy on the surface of the planet, a system in which Force is made the servant of Justice, whose life is sustained by its universal recognition of one God and by its allegiance to one common Revelation—such is the goal towards which humanity, impelled by the unifying forces of life, is moving.[252]

In the sense that such a world government does not yet exist, Shoghi Effendi's description is still a dream, but like many dreams, these are necessary before they can become a part of our reality. Coming as a prophecy and a promise from Bahá'u'lláh, a Manifestation of God, such a dream automatically becomes a goal for those who believe in Him, and a reality for those who actively dedicate themselves to its formation and construction.

THE UNITED NATIONS

It is not necessary to be a Bahá'í to believe that world government and world peace are inseparable. Since Bahá'u'lláh first proclaimed this principle in the nineteenth century, the movement towards a world outlook has gradually spread. Preliminary efforts at world organization have been made with multinational alliances and agreements, and the formation of embryonic world governments such as the League of Nations after World War I and the United Nations after World War II. Detractors and critics have deplored the weaknesses and shortcomings of these organizations much more than their promoters have publicized their progress.

The elimination of the threat of war has been one of the major arguments in favor of a world government. In the first forty years after the end of World War II, approximately sixteen million lives were lost in one hundred sixty armed conflicts.[253] Another reason for world government is the need for reducing the cost of military preparedness. Maintaining engines of war and arsenals filled with explosives and ammunition, construction of fortifications, military housing, recruitment and maintenance of large military establishments, and continuous research and development of newer weapons and strategies are a staggering economic drain on the world's resources. The following was written in 1985:

As an indication of the unbelievable hemorrhaging of the world's resources into nonproductive military budgets, just seven months' worth of world military spending would be enough to pay for supplying clean water supplies and adequate sanitation for as many as two billion people (almost half the world's population) who now lack these bare essentials of health.

Those who think that world government would be too expensive might consider the following statistic: 'The entire UN system could run for nearly two centuries on only one year's world military spending'.[254]

Rather than condemn the UN's inability to achieve all that was hoped when it was formed in 1945, it could be argued that without the UN things might have been much worse, or at least could have worsened much more rapidly than they have.

Among the UN's **successes**:

- Eradicated smallpox worldwide in 1980
- Wiped out polio in the Western Hemisphere in 1991
- Helped to end apartheid in South Africa
- Immunized 80% of the world's children (5% in 1974) against polio, tetanus, measles, whooping cough, diphtheria and tuberculosis
- Negotiated more than 300 international treaties
- UN agencies were awarded the Nobel Peace Prize five times
- Six UN dignitaries were awarded the Nobel Peace Prize

Among the world's continually **worsening problems**:

- **Population**—the world's population is increasing by one million every four days.
- **Global Warming**—500 million tons of carbon are pumped into the atmosphere each year. The atmosphere is warming and climates are changing.
- **Unemployment**—100 million jobs must be created in 20 years to give work to children already born.
- **Environment**—116 square miles of rain forest, 65 million tons of topsoil, 100-200 species are disappearing every day and is increasing.
- **Absolute Poverty**—currently more than one billion people. This is expected to at least triple in 20 years.
- **Refugees**—1.5 million in 1951. Today, there are over 20 million outside and more than 25 million displaced inside their own countries.
- **Corruption**—in many countries, foreign aid is lost through corrupt officials.

Let us note some additional world concerns by a listing of some of the UN agencies that have been created to deal with these problems:

- UN Environment Program
- World Food Program
- World Intellectual Property Organization
- UN Center for Human Settlements
- UN Conference on Trade and Development
- International Labor Organization
- International Telecommunications Union
- Food and Agricultural Organization
- UN Industrial Development Organization

- Universal Postal Union
- International Bank—Reconstruction & Development
- Universal Postal Union
- Office of UN High Commission – Refugees
- UN Development Program
- General Agreement on Trade and Tariffs
- International Monetary Fund
- UN Fund for Population Activities
- UN Children's Fund
- Intergovernmental Maritime Organization
- World Health Organization
- International Civil Aviation Organization
- UNESCO
- UN Industrial Development Organization
- World Meteorological Organization

The UN is often portrayed as inadequate to deal effectively with international problems and conflicts. The successes achieved by its efforts in these areas are, more often than not, ignored. Each of its agencies was created to solve problems that exceeded the powers of any of its member national governments. That the UN is encumbered by restrictions that limit its powers to deal with its assigned duties is a strong argument for a true, fully empowered world government.[255]

DEVELOPMENTAL PROCESS

The achievement of world peace will require a gradual process of corresponding spiritual changes in mankind. From a perspective of war and violence as a necessary prelude to political change, humanity must move toward a perspective of brotherhood, love and unity as the true path to peace.

The Bahá'í view of *the Golden Age* as termed by Shoghi Effendi, and *the Most Great Peace* promised by Bahá'u'lláh, is the same *Kingdom of God* promised in the Old Testament of Judaism and the New Testament of Christianity. It is the same Kingdom often recited in the Lord's Prayer, **"Thy Kingdom come, Thy will be done, on earth as it is in heaven."**

Bahá'u'lláh proclaimed the imminence of the changes that were to take place. **"Soon will the present-day order be rolled up and a new one**

spread out in its stead."[256]

THE LESSER PEACE

The Most Great Peace was offered to the world by Bahá'u'lláh in His *Tablets to the Kings*, the letters He wrote to the world leaders when He was in Adrianople and later in Akka. This offer was rejected. In follow-up letters He offered them *the Lesser Peace*, an interim peace that would serve as a stepping stone to the time of the promised Most Great Peace:

O Kings of the earth! We see you increasing every year your expenditures, and laying the burden thereof on your subjects... Do not rob them to rear palaces for yourselves... Your people are your treasures... By them ye rule, by their means ye subsist, by their aid ye conquer...

Now that ye have refused the Most Great Peace, hold ye fast unto this, the Lesser Peace, that haply ye may in some degree better your own condition and that of your dependents.[257]

The time frame for the achievement of the Most Great Peace is not a specific date because it comprises numerous aspects, as described above by Shoghi Effendi. The listing of the UN agencies above identifies many of these aspects. Some, such as a world intercommunications system and an international system of weights and measures are already well advanced. Other aspects are in process, e.g., the fight for civil rights, health, labor and economic reforms, some of which will be further developed during the Lesser Peace. Still other aspects may not be apparent for decades or even centuries, such as the true spiritual unity of mankind, and a world metropolis as the nerve center of a world civilization.

If we look with an evolutionary mindset at the United Nations, it can be viewed as one stage of a gradual process of development in the growth of an international order. We can then focus on its accomplishments rather than its shortcomings, and even anticipate radical discontinuities along the path of its evolving structure.[258]

The Lesser Peace, which 'Abdu'l-Baha said would occur by the end of the twentieth century, is in place, though still far from reality. It would seem that its beginnings would include an assembly of the peace-loving nations to form a true central government, with world legislative, executive, and judicial branches, plus an effective international military arm to take action against any aggressor nation, whether member or non-member states. The Universal House of Justice has referred to the Lesser Peace as 'the political unification of the world'.

Bahá'u'lláh called upon the future Universal House of Justice to support efforts to achieve the Lesser Peace. It is imperative, He said, to reduce the exorbitant military expenditures made necessary by hostilities and conflict. [259]

Shoghi Effendi described earlier in this section the world conditions necessary for the Lesser Peace. These are the beginnings of the requirements for the Most Great Peace. The Lesser Peace would still lack the spiritual unity of mankind that will mark the Most Great Peace.

Once a condition of non-aggression is attained... will humanity begin to traverse a new path... (and) **be free to proceed with examining the bounties of political, economic, racial, international, and religious unity because we will not be ensnared in the condition of perpetual war.**

We have really spent most of our history with our hands tied up in one way or another with preparations for war, actual warfare, or cleaning up the aftermath of war. It is only because wars have occurred at intervals in most parts of the globe, and not constantly, that various cultures and civilizations have had some time to flourish.[260]

CHAPTER REVIEW—Basic Teachings

Summary
▶Each person is responsible for what he believes and thus must investigate the truth for himself.
▶True religion and true science cannot be contradictory because they are both true.
▶The equality of men and women is reflected in the equality of their spiritual being.
▶Prejudice among individuals is a rejection of their essential equality.
▶A common language for all people is a prime requisite for a global community.
▶Education for spiritual beings must include that which will improve their spiritual natures.
▶A unified world economy will ensure a minimum standard of living for every individual..
▶The spiritual unity of all mankind must inevitably result in a unified world.

Discussion
1. Discuss the forms of opposition to Bahá'u'lláh from royalty and clergy, and His response to their persecution.
2. Why is 'independent investigation' emphasized as an obligation for Bahá'ís?
3. What was Bahá'u'lláh's attitude toward kingship?
4. What is the Christian 'dogma (or doctrine) of exclusivity'?
5. How do the Bahá'í teachings explain this view of exclusivity?
6. Compare the Christian and Bahá'í views of salvation.
7. Compare the Christian and Bahá'í views of 'resurrection'.
8. Explain the 'David and Goliath' relationship of science and religion. Has it changed?
9. Explain Einstein's conclusion that 'religion without science is blind and science without religion is lame'.
10. What kinds of questions are beyond the scope of scientific investigation? Give examples.
11. Explain the 'complex computer' analogy as an

217

example of scientific limitations.
12. Discuss the Bahá'í view of world unity in relation to the equality of men and women.—in relation to racial discrimination.
13. How can a world language benefit mankind?
14. Identify and describe the three kinds of education taught by a Divine educator.
15. What are the unique qualifications of the Divine educator?
16. How can justice and mercy be contradictory? How can they be reconciled?
17. How should individuals and society respond when someone commits a crime—with justice or mercy?
18. Explain 'Abdu'l-Baha's use of the terms 'sensible realities' and 'intellectual realities'.
19. Read and discuss the prayer, "Intone, O My servant..." in its metaphorical content.
20. Discuss the metaphorical process.
21. Discuss the implications of the 'elimination of the extremes of poverty and wealth', and the desire for profit.
22. How do the teachings of Judaism, Christianity and Islam support the Bahá'í teaching of world unity?
23. How are the League of Nations and the United Nations related to the idea of a world government?
24. Can war be eliminated without world government? Discuss the Bahá'í view and other views.
25. What are the practical advantages of eliminating war as a means of resolving disagreements?
26. Discuss the practical implications of a world government as described by Shoghi Effendi.
27. What is meant by the Lesser Peace?

CHAPTER NINE—Administration

Order implies organization and a plan. The Bahá'í Administrative Order as envisioned by Bahá'u'lláh is moving humanity along its destined spiritual path. The mission of Bahá'u'lláh is part of the eternal Plan of God for mankind. Bahá'u'lláh explained that He was the latest in a long line of successive Manifestations of God, and that later Manifestations will appear at Their appointed times. Each Manifestation of God has His own special message to deliver as part of the continuing message of God. Bahá'u'lláh said that the next Manifestation of God will appear in not less than one thousand years.[261]

SYSTEM OF COVENANTS

The eternal Plan of God, called the **Great Covenant**, is, in the Bahá'í writings, a system of Covenants made between each Manifestation of God and mankind. In His Great Covenant, God promises a succession of Manifestations to guide mankind in return for mankind's acceptance of the Manifestation as the true Messenger of God, and obedience to His message and teachings when He appears. One of the earliest mentions of the Great Covenant is in the Old Testament (Genesis 17:9) in which God said to Abraham, **"...you must keep my Covenant, you and your descendants after you for the generations to come."**

The Covenant of God is the result of the act of creation itself. God's part of this agreement is to bestow life on each individual, provide for physical needs through the earth's resources, and to nurture each soul through the Revelations brought by each Manifestation of God.[262]

Every Manifestation of God has renewed this covenant with God on behalf of all humanity, i.e., every human being—with no exceptions. Every human being is automatically a party to this agreement by virtue of his own creation. Anyone can decide to ignore or violate the provisions of the agreement, but no one has the option to repudiate this covenant on his own behalf. Like it or not, we are all part of one humanity.

The Covenant of Bahá'u'lláh defines its provisions clearly. It consists of two parts, the *Greater Covenant* and the *Lesser Covenant*. The first part (the same for all Manifestations) is to accept His own Station and Revelation, and to follow (when He comes), the next Manifestation, the reappearance of His own spiritual reality.

The second part, the Lesser Covenant, is Bahá'u'lláh's appointment of 'Abdu'l-Baha as His immediate successor. A major responsibility under this appointment was the establishment of the Bahá'í Administrative Order.

BASIS OF THE ADMINISTRATIVE ORDER

Following His Father's description of the way the unification of mankind would be achieved, 'Abdu'l-Baha designed and organized the Bahá'í Administrative Order. His Tablets of the Divine Plan, the series of letters 'Abdu'l-Baha wrote to the American Bahá'ís to spread the message of Bahá'u'lláh, was part of His strategy for creating the core of the embryonic institutions of the Administrative Order.

The growth of the Bahá'í Administrative Order followed a simultaneous two-fold procedure. One was the spiritual growth process of the individuals who were to make up the administrative bodies, and the other was the development of the administrative bodies themselves. Those individuals who voluntarily responded to 'Abdu'l-Baha's call and changed their lives in some way to follow God's guidance were, in effect, reflecting spiritual growth. They were preparing themselves spiritually for participation in the Bahá'í institutions of the Administrative Order that would be formed. The spiritual level of its members is a key factor in the operation and functioning of these institutions.

The spiritualizing process of American (and other) Bahá'í pioneers who responded to 'Abdu'l-Baha's Tablets of the Divine Plan began just a few years before 'Abdu'l-Baha died. Thus, it fell to Shoghi Effendi to guide, nurture and instruct the Bahá'í world community in the growth process of the Administrative Order, much like a gardener tends and watches over the development of a seedling. A seedling is most vulnerable to almost any peril at this stage of its growth. It needs constant protection and care.

The still unformed institutions of the Administrative Order, consisting of immature individual elements who had yet to learn how to function as a unified group, needed a knowledgeable guide and consistent guidelines. The Bahá'í line of succession, from Bahá'u'lláh to 'Abdu'l-Baha to Shoghi Effendi, allowed the most consistent and error-free transmission of guidance and teachings possible. Despite numerous problems and determined attacks on its unity by trusted followers who had turned away from the Covenant of Bahá'u'lláh, the integrity of the Bahá'í line of leadership held firm and its purity remained unstained.

Like other Bahá'í teachings and principles, the Bahá'í Administrative Order is designed to promote the fundamental *unity* principle. During the twentieth century, the formation of both the League of Nations, and later the United Nations, reflected agreement in principle with the concept of global unity.

By the end of World War I, *absolute monarchy* (not the concept of kingship), the ancient governing concept of unquestioned God-given right to rule through blood inheritance, had been rejected. Essentially every royal line of kingship was either overthrown, crushed, or left without governing power, as Bahá'u'lláh had declared years earlier, **"From two ranks amongst men power hath been seized: kings and ecclesiastics."**[263]

Among the existing government systems, democracy appeared to be the most successful and the most popular. The *autocratic systems such as dictatorships, power blocs and strong man rulers* are generally unpopular and short-lived. Communism, although claiming to be a non-government system that dispenses fair treatment and equal justice for everyone, rose to prominence and inevitably was discredited by its leaders' corrupt use of autocratic power. All of these systems have both positive and negative features.

The negative features are limiting factors in the life of each government system. For example, negative features of the highly successful and admired American democratic system include negative campaigning and vote-pandering, mud-slinging, indecisiveness and corruption of officials. When these negative features become widespread and pervasive, disunity becomes apparent, and the system breaks down and starts to decline.

The Bahá'í Administrative Order, following Bahá'u'lláh's concept of a world order, combines the constructive features of the major governing systems and eliminates their negative aspects. It also adds a key spiritual element, *consultation*, which is described later in this chapter.

Although the Bahá'í system follows many of the democratic features of election, administration and governance for a global state, it avoids the pitfalls of current democratic practices. It has built-in checks against corruption and provides for selection of leaders with integrity from the widest possible choice of candidates. The election process, for example, excludes any form of campaigning, electioneering or nominations.[264]

Even though the unity of mankind required a world outlook, Bahá'u'lláh cautioned His followers against any disrespect of any lawful national or local requirements. Even if a law is unfair, it must be obeyed if it is legal. **"In every country where any of this people** (the Bahá'ís) **reside,"** He said, **"they must behave towards the government of that country with loyalty, honesty and truthfulness."**[265]

THREE-TIERED GOVERNMENT

The essential make-up of the Bahá'í Administrative Order is less complicated than many of the world's existing governmental organizations. Its governing functions operate at three levels: local, national and international. At the local and national levels, the administration of the Bahá'í Faith is carried out by local and national *spiritual assemblies*. These are nine-member councils elected annually by secret ballot.

The **Local Spiritual Assembly** functions at the

grassroots level of the community, and reaches each member in the local area, usually a town, village, city or local district. At this time, the Local Spiritual Assemblies are involved in such activities as education of children, study classes, social events, observance of holy days, marriages, divorces and funeral services, and in some cases educational, economic and developmental projects.

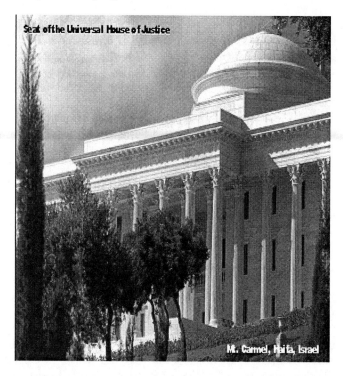
Seat of the Universal House of Justice
Mt. Carmel, Haifa, Israel

Delegates elected at district or unit conventions elect the **National Spiritual Assembly** at a national convention. The national assemblies oversee Bahá'í community affairs within a given country; they provide guidance for the local assemblies, and coordinate national activities throughout the national community. These may include large-scale projects, book publishing, relations with the national government, coordination with other religious groups and non-governmental organizations.

At the international level, the **Universal House of**

Justice serves as the supreme head of the Bahá'í administrative structure. The members of the national spiritual assemblies elect the Universal House of Justice every five years at an international convention. The World headquarters of the Bahá'í Faith is located in Haifa, Israel, at the Bahá'í World Center, on Mount Carmel.

The Universal House of Justice is the supreme body in both administrative and spiritual matters. Bahá'u'lláh, recognizing the changing needs of an evolving society, conferred upon the future Universal House of Justice the authority to rule on matters not clearly specified in the Bahá'í Writings.

This simple three-tiered system forms the framework of the Bahá'í Administrative Order. Within this three-level framework of elective bodies, other agencies and offices can be appointed to carry out the functions of each institution, much as the basic functional bodies of the American federal system, the Presidency, the Congress and the Supreme Court, can expand their capacities to carry out their specified duties.

An example of this expansion process was brought into being with the establishment of a new element of Bahá'í administration between the local and national levels. In 1997 the Universal House of Justice designated **Regional Bahá'í Councils** to serve selected national assemblies where community growth and complexity of issues reflected a new stage in the development of the Bahá'í community.

The functions and duties of the Regional Bahá'í Councils are part of the evolving nature of an administrative process that must keep pace with an evolving society. One function of these Regional Councils specified by the Universal House of Justice was to help maintain a proper balance of decentralization and centralization of the administrative bodies to the communities they serve. The Regional Council's functional authority is conferred by its National Spiritual Assembly. The first Regional Bahá'í Councils designated for the United States Bahá'í community were elected in November 1997.

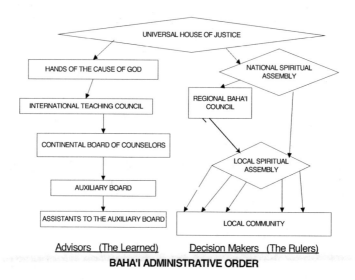

BAHA'I ADMINISTRATIVE ORDER

At first glance it would appear that the Bahá'í administrative order described here is too simple a plan. It does not seem so different from other governmental systems, especially systems for world government such as the League of Nations and the United Nations. Any such system would be vulnerable to the same weaknesses and shortcomings that encumbered all previous governments. The administrative framework as described would certainly be subject to the same negative forces. Among the distinguishing features of the Bahá'í administrative order are the spiritual procedures and qualifications for staffing its institutions, and the process for conducting its administrative affairs. It is such features that would resist these negative forces.

It should be clear by now that the Bahá'í Faith recognizes an inseparable spiritual linkage in all of its aspects. The basic Bahá'í institutions have been established by divine inspiration, a spiritual reality. It is this spiritual connection that is part of all Bahá'í concepts, ideas, plans and explanations. Every community elects its own Local Spiritual Assembly; each individual is encouraged to ask for divine guidance before voting. No elected Assembly members are directly responsible to their community for their actions on the Assembly—they are responsible to God.

Assembly membership does not confer special privileges on any individual member. It is the institution that has the power, not the individual. Anyone may communicate directly with any level of the Bahá'í Administrative Order.

Concerning membership qualifications for the Spiritual Assembly, Shoghi Effendi wrote, **"there is a distinction... between the Spiritual Assembly as an institution, and the persons who compose it. These (persons) are by no means supposed to be perfect, nor can they be considered as being inherently superior to the rest of their fellow-believers."** The elections permit the community to replace Assembly members whose actions have created problems.[266]

Voting in Bahá'í elections is a sacred duty for all declared believers twenty-one years and older. There are no nominations or campaigning for office. Shoghi Effendi cautioned against any reference to personalities in elections. Canvassing for and influencing others' opinions should be avoided, he wrote.[267] **"...the practice of nomination, so detrimental to the atmosphere of a silent and prayerful election, is viewed with mistrust... the elector... is called upon to vote for none but those whom prayer and reflection have inspired him to uphold."**[268]

INSTITUTION OF THE LEARNED

Prior to the first Universal House of Justice, in 1963, the affairs of the Faith were managed by the Guardian of the Faith, Shoghi Effendi, and after his death, by his appointed Hands of the Cause of God. The title, *Hands of the Cause of God*, was a mark of honor bestowed on selected believers who had demonstrated through service their devotion and dedication to the teachings of Bahá'u'lláh. Shoghi Effendi noted that **"the 'learned' are, on the one hand, the Hands of the Cause of God, and, on the other, the teachers and diffusers of His Teachings who do not rank as Hands, but who have attained an eminent position in the teaching work."**[269] After Shoghi Effendi's death it was determined that there was no one authorized in the Bahá'í writings to appoint any more Hands of the Cause.

In 1968, the Universal House of Justice created a new institution, **Continental Boards of Counselors**, to extend into the future the functions of protection and propagation previously conferred upon the Hands of the Cause. In 1973, the **International Teaching Center**, under the leadership of the remaining Hands of the Cause, was established to coordinate the activities of the Continental Boards of Counselors. The Continental Boards, assigned to each continent to serve as guides and advisors to the National Spiritual Assemblies, are assisted by members of the **Auxiliary Board** and their appointed **Assistants to the Auxiliary Board** in extending the same kind of guidance and advisory services to the Local Spiritual Assemblies. All of these appointive positions are strictly consultative and advisory. Only the elected bodies have decision-making authority within the Bahá'í community.

CONSULTATION

A distinctive feature of Bahá'í institutions is the Bahá'í process of **consultation**. Consultation as used by Bahá'ís is somewhat different from the meaning ordinarily associated with the term. As with all Bahá'í teachings, Bahá'í consultation proceeds from the underlying principle of *unity*, and an ever-present spiritual awareness. Bahá'u'lláh urges, **"Take ye counsel together in all matters, inasmuch as consultation is the lamp of guidance which leadeth the way, and is the bestower of understanding."**[270]

If we think of consultation as a meeting of minds to resolve an issue, or to settle a difference of opinion, then Bahá'í consultation may be considered a more advanced stage of group decision-making. The most primitive form of resolving differences is the *clash of strength*—the right of might, the struggle of opposing forces. Next would be a *clash of wills* between vested interests—such as the pro and con in political debate or economic competition, or legal disputes in court. In both instances there are opposing forces, a lack of unity. Every proposal offered as a solution stems from greed, self-interest and the desire to win. It is a contest of wills, and often the end is a compromise that is less than the best solution or it is the least of the evils. 'Abdu'l-Baha deplored the lack of maturity displayed at a session of the French senate, which he visited while in Paris:

In France I was present at a session of the senate, but the experience was not impressive. Parliamentary procedure should... not furnish a battleground for opposition and self-opinion. Antagonism and contradiction are... always destructive to truth. In the parliamentary meeting mentioned, altercation and useless quibbling were frequent... in one instance a physical encounter took place between two members. It was not consultation but comedy.[271]

Bahá'í consultation proposes a third kind of clash, *the clash of ideas*. All parties to the consultation contribute their ideas rather than their egos. Shoghi Effendi quoted 'Abdu'l-Baha in describing this process. He said that assemblies of consultation should be conducted so that 'no occasion for ill-feeling or discord may arise'. Each member must be allowed full freedom of expression. Truth must be allowed to emerge. **"The shining spark of truth cometh forth only after the clash of differing opinions."**[272]

'Abdu'l-Baha emphasized the spiritual elements that the participants must bring to their consultation process. A feeling of unity and closeness to God encourages individual humility and a sharing of ideas. Once an idea is shared, it belongs to the group, not to the one who proposed it. He said that *purity of motive* and *radiance of spirit* are prime requisites for the consultation process.

Two conditions are listed as evidence for attaining these prime requisites. The first is **'absolute love and harmony amongst the members of the assembly'. If all agree on the purpose of the meeting, i.e. to do what is right in the sight of God, then love and harmony is inevitable. Without this condition, it is unlikely that the consultation will prove fruitful.**

The second condition is to ask for divine help in

their deliberations, after which all views are expressed courteously. The aim of each participant is to discover the truth, and not to defend his own views. No one is allowed to belittle the thought of another. Finally, if differences cannot be resolved, 'a majority of voices must prevail'.[273]

Once the group makes a decision, all must support that decision, even if only in the interest of unity. If a decision turns out to be wrong, it will later become evident and the group can change it, but the unity and harmony of the group will be preserved.

CHAPTER REVIEW—Administrative Order

Summary
▶Each Manifestation of God continues the Great Covenant of God through His own Covenant with His followers.
▶The Bahá'í Administrative Order was conceived by Bahá'u'lláh, designed by 'Abdu'l-Baha and implemented by Shoghi Effendi.
▶The structure of the Bahá'í Administrative Order has both material and spiritual elements.
▶The Bahá'í consultation process promotes individual spiritual growth.
▶The Bahá'í Administrative Order operates at the local, national and international levels.
▶The Universal House of Justice is the supreme governing body of the Bahá'í Faith.

Discussion
1. How is the Great Covenant related to the Covenant of Bahá'u'lláh?
2. What roles do Bahá'u'lláh, 'Abdu'l-Baha and Shoghi Effendi have in the Administrative Order?
3. How were the early Bahá'í pioneers prepared to participate in the Bahá'í Administrative Order?
4. Identify some weaknesses of the American democratic process avoided by the Bahá'í Administrative Order.
5. Describe the three-tiered government of the Bahá'í Administrative Order.
6. Describe the role of the Regional Bahá'í Council.
7. Explain the roles of the four extensions of the Hands of the Cause of God which comprise the Institution of the Learned.
8. What is the relationship of the institutions of the Bahá'í Administrative Order and their members?
9. Describe the Bahá'í consultation process as related to the three types of consultation mentioned.
10. What is the role of humility in the consultation process? Courtesy? Harmony? Love? Truth?

CHAPTER TEN—Bahá'í Topics

As religions go, the Bahá'í Faith is very young. In its one hundred fifty-odd years (including the nineteen-year dispensation of the Bab), the Bahá'í Faith has experienced phenomenal growth, greater than any previous religion. In the course of its history, every religion accumulates a body of concepts, customs, traditions, stories and special events that make it distinctive and give it a cultural cohesion.

The drama and emotional intensity of the action-packed events of Babi and Bahá'í history recounted in this book reflect the significant meaning these events have for all Bahá'ís, and have thus taken their place in forming a *Bahá'í culture*. All Bahá'ís share, according to their spiritual commitment, the love, pain, anguish, joy and spiritual transcendence experienced by the early believers. This is becoming part of a distinctive cultural tradition. Other practices, concepts and customs, as they come into general use, are being gradually accumulated and assimilated into this developing Bahá'í culture.

This cultural tradition is related to, but may not necessarily be an essential part of, the Bahá'í fundamental teachings, but it does provide a more intimate sense of, and a more personal contact with, the social dimensions of the Bahá'í community.

BAHÁ'Í CALENDAR

A calendar is a way of measuring time according to the two biggest *lights in the sky*, the sun and the moon. All calendars are either lunar-based or solar-based, or a combination of the two, lunisolar. All of the earlier religions have established their own calendar to commemorate special events and holy days in their histories, e.g. the Jewish calendar dating from the creation of the world according to the Old Testament, the Muslim calendar commemorating the *hegira* of Muhammad from Mecca, or the Christian calendar dating from the birth of Jesus.

As the Christian calendar, called the Gregorian[274] calendar, is at this time most widely used internationally, the other religions use both the Gregorian and their own calendars. It is becoming more common to refer to the Christian abbreviations AD (Anno Domini, Latin for Year of Our Lord) and BC (Before Christ), as CE (Common Era) and BCE (Before the Common Era.) The calendars of Judaism and Islam are lunar, whereas the Christian and Bahá'í calendars are solar. The dates of Jewish and Muslim holidays and special events fall on different days of the Gregorian calendar each year. The months and days of the Gregorian calendar are taken from Roman and other mythological sources.

The Bahá'í calendar was inaugurated by the Bab. The year 1844 CE is 1 BE (Bahá'í Era). The Bahá'í year contains nineteen months of nineteen days each (a total of 361 days), plus four (five in leap years) intercalary days, called *Ayyam-i-Ha*, which come between the eighteenth and nineteenth months. The days of Ayyam-i-Ha are joyous celebrations commonly associated with feasting, hospitality, charity and gift giving.

Bahá'í months and days are named for a spiritual attribute. The Bahá'í year begins March 21, which is the vernal equinox, the first day of Spring. The Bahá'í day begins at sunset of the previous day, the same as the calendars of Islam and Judaism. Each of the nineteen days of each month has the same name as its corresponding month. For example, the day of Nur (5th day) in Rahmat (the 6th month) corresponds to June 28 of the Gregorian calendar.

BAHÁ'Í MONTHS

Month	Arabic	English	Beginning Date
1	Bahá	Splendor	21 March
2	Jalál	Glory	9 April
3	Jamál	Beauty	28 April
4	'Azamat	Grandeur	17 May
5	Nur	Light	5 June
6	Rahmat	Mercy	24 June
7	Kalimát	Words	13 July
8	Kamál	Perfection	1 August

9	Asmá'	Names	20 August
10	'Izzat	Might	8 September
11	Mashíyyat	Will	27 September
12	'Ilm	Knowledge	16 October
13	Qudrat	Power	4 November
14	Qawl	Speech	23 November
15	Masá'il	Questions	12 December
16	Sharaf	Honor	31 December
17	Sultán	Sovereignty	19 January
18	Mulk	Dominion	7 February
Ayyam i Ha		Intercalary Days	Feb 26- Mar 1
19	'Alá'	Loftiness	2 March

BAHÁ'Í DAYS

Day	Arabic	English	Translation
1st	Jalál	Saturday	Glory
2nd	Jamál	Sunday	Beauty
3rd	Kamál	Monday	Perfection
4th	Fidál	Tuesday	Grace
5th	'Idál	Wednesday	Justice
6th	Istijlál	Thursday	Majesty
7th	Istiqlál	Friday	Independence

BAHÁ'Í HOLY DAYS

There are nine Holy Days that commemorate significant events in Bahá'í history.

Naw-Ruz (Baha'i New Year)   21 March
Ridvan (Declaration of Bahá'u'lláh)   21 Apr - 2 May
Declaration of the Bab   23 May
Ascension of Bahá'u'lláh   29 May
Martyrdom of the Bab   9 July
Birth of the Bab   20 October
Birth of Bahá'u'lláh   12 November
Day of the Covenant   26 November
Ascension of 'Abdu'l-Baha   28 November

With some exceptions noted below, work is suspended, and students do not attend school on these days. There are no prescribed ceremonies for Bahá'í Holy Days, but it is common for Bahá'ís to combine a devotional program with fellowship or appropriate social activities.[275]

The twelve-day Ridvan Festival commemorates Bahá'u'lláh's declaration of His mission. It includes the days Bahá'u'lláh stayed in the Garden of Ridvan while departure preparations were being made for His second exile, to Istanbul. Only the first, ninth and twelfth days of this festival have the *'no work nor school'* restrictions.

The Holy Days commemorating 'Abdu'l-Baha (26 and 28 November) do not require suspension of work or school. At the request of the Bahá'í community, 'Abdu'l-Baha allowed the Day of the Covenant as a Holy Day replacement for His birthday (23 May), which He instructed should be celebrated as the Declaration of the Bab. The Day of the Covenant is the commemoration of Bahá'u'lláh's appointment of 'Abdu'l-Baha as the Center of His Covenant.

NINETEEN-DAY FEAST

The first day of each Bahá'í month (every nineteen days) is designated as Feast Day, a gathering of Bahá'ís in a local community for worship, consultation and fellowship. The main purpose of the Feast is to promote feelings of unity and closeness among the local community members. The program normally includes three parts: devotional, administrative and social. The devotional part usually consists of Bahá'í prayers and readings; the administrative portion may include reports, messages, and/or announcements from the local spiritual assembly, and consultation among community members. The fellowship portion may include a meal or light refreshments, and socializing or entertainment. The monthly Feast is important but not obligatory.

The monthly Feast is designed for Bahá'ís but may include non-Bahá'ís. If non-Bahá'ís attend, the administration part of the meeting is omitted from the activities.

CYCLES AND UNIVERSAL CYCLES

In the context of human evolution, the dispensation of each Manifestation of God is sometimes seen as a cycle or period of time in which God's educational program for mankind is moved forward another step, in line with humanity's spiritual growth. Each cycle is part of a series of cycles (dispensations of Manifestations), like grade levels in school, carrying mankind through a God-prescribed curriculum, to the time when humanity reaches a new stage of spiritual growth. The completion of the prescribed series of cycles, the *elementary curriculum*, prepares mankind for the next stage, a series of cycles, or *secondary curriculum*, and so on. As God's creation has no beginning and no ending, numerous cycles have passed prior to the one we now share.

Each of the Divine Manifestations has... a cycle, and during the cycle His laws and commandments prevail and are performed. When His cycle is completed by the appearance of a new Manifestation, a new cycle begins. In this way cycles begin, end and are renewed, until a universal cycle is completed in the world, when important events and great occurrences will take place which entirely efface every trace and every record of the past; then a new universal cycle begins in the world, for this universe has no beginning.[276]

Universal Cycles Without End

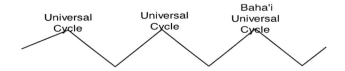

The Adamic Cycle is the term Bahá'ís use for the series of cycles (or dispensations) starting with Adam and ending with Muhammad. This is the series of dispensations encompassing the early stages (the infancy and adolescence) preceding the maturity stage of mankind's spiritual development. These cycles all promise a wonderful time (a Golden Age) of peace, beauty, and fulfillment. The process of establishing this Golden Age is, in the Bahá'í view, presently underway, despite the dire trials and obstacles we are experiencing in the early stages.

In the graphic below, the Adamic Cycle (Cycle of Prophecy) marks the beginning of the *Bahá'í Universal Cycle*. This is the infancy and adolescence stage, the early part of the Bahá'í Universal Cycle that began with Adam's Dispensation. Space precluded the listing of all of the prophets of the Adamic Cycle. The cycle of Baha[277] (Bahá'u'lláh) is the first of the next level (Cycle of Fulfillment), the maturity stage of spirituality for mankind. We are presently at the transitional peak of the Bahá'í Universal Cycle. The Prophetic Stage of cycles beginning with Adam and the Fulfillment Stage of cycles beginning with Bahá'u'lláh together compose the Bahá'í Universal Cycle. No trace remains of the Universal Cycles preceding Adam's Dispensation.

The Bab's Dispensation was a transitional period connecting the *early curriculum*, the Cycle of Prophecy ending with the Cycle of Muhammad to a *higher curriculum*, the Cycle of Fulfillment, starting with the Cycle of Baha inaugurated by Bahá'u'lláh. The Bahá'í

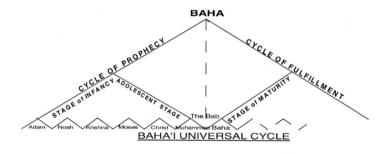

Dispensation, then, is the first cycle in the current stage of mankind's spiritual maturity. This is the beginning of the next stage of humanity's spiritual development, a time of momentous spiritual significance. Bahá'u'lláh's mission is the beginning of the fulfillment stage of the entire Bahá'í Universal Cycle of Dispensations. Thus Bahá'u'lláh fills a dual role in this dispensational graphic. He is the first Manifestation of the Cycle of Fulfillment and also the Supreme Manifestation of the entire Bahá'í Universal Cycle. The Supreme Manifestation appears at the peak of the Universal Cycle, not at its beginning.

Shoghi Effendi noted that we are too close to these events (the beginning of the culminating stage of a Universal Cycle) to realize their full importance. Bahá'u'lláh's Revelation exceeds the Revelations of the earlier Manifestations because His Revelation begins the realization of Their prophecies. The Revelation of Bahá'u'lláh is the beginning of the *new day of God*, the inauguration (not the completion) of the long-awaited *Kingdom of God on earth*.

Shoghi Effendi clearly pointed out that Bahá'u'lláh, because He brought a greater Revelation, is not God Himself nor is He greater than any other Manifestation of God. Of all the Manifestations of God, only Bahá'u'lláh has claimed to usher in the *Kingdom of God* which Moses, Jesus, Muhammad and the others promised. The spiritual preeminence of the Bahá'í Universal Cycle, because it encompasses and thus ranks above any single individual cycle, in no way alters the equality that Bahá'u'lláh shares with the other Manifestations of God (Chapter 8, Oneness of the Manifestations). Spiritually, all Manifestations are the same. **"Know thou assuredly that the essence of all the Prophets of God is one and the same. Their unity is absolute. God, the Creator, saith: There is no distinction whatsoever among the Bearers of My Message."**[278]

BAHÁ'Í WORLD CENTER

Halfway up the mountain, at the ninth level, stands the golden-domed Shrine of the Bab. Within are enshrined the tombs of the Bab and 'Abdu'l-Baha. The Shrine of the Bab offers visitors a panoramic view of the terraces leading down to the harbor and across the Bay of Haifa, to the city of Akka. The terraces extending above and below the Shrine of the Bab are

Night View
© *Bahá'í International Community*

part of a $250 million 10-year building project begun in 1990 and funded exclusively by Bahá'í contributions. The Shrine of the Bab, pictured on the cover of this book, stands at one end of an arc of buildings comprising the administrative complex of the Bahá'í World Center.

At the heart of this complex is an imposing marble structure, the seat of the Universal House of Justice, the highest governing body of the Bahá'í world community and the point of obedience for all Bahá'ís. Composed of nine elected members, the Universal House of Justice is the only Bahá'í institution considered to be infallible when acting as a unified body engaged in its official functions. The Universal House of Justice provides guidance and clarification to the world community in the light of the Bahá'í sacred writings; it does not have the authority to interpret the sacred writings. Nearby, and within the Arc complex, are other equally impressive administrative structures, including the Bahá'í Archives, the International Teaching Center, and the Center for the Study of the Texts.

The International Teaching Center guides the worldwide teaching efforts. It should be noted that Bahá'u'lláh prohibited teaching the Faith to non-Bahá'ís in Israel. Most Israelis know very little of the Bahá'í Faith. Bahá'ís work at the Bahá'í World Center, but there is no official Bahá'í community as there are in other countries.

The Center for the Study of the Texts researches questions and issues of Bahá'í concerns. Scholars and translators also work with Bahá'í documents, some of which have not yet been translated.

The Archives Building contains Bahá'í relics and artifacts such as original documents and personal items of Bahá'u'lláh, the Bab, 'Abdu'l-Baha, and other significant Bahá'í figures.

The Bahá'í World Center was built as a result of Bahá'u'lláh's instructions to 'Abdu'l-Baha. It serves as both a spiritual and administrative center for all Bahá'ís. It plays a key role in the growth of the Faith. For those who can manage it, the Bahá'í World Center and the Shrine of Bahá'u'lláh in the vicinity of nearby

Akka are points of Bahá'í pilgrimage.

BAHJI

Across the Bay of Haifa, in Akka, Israel, a short distance from the World Center, is the most holy spot in the Bahá'í world, the resting place of Bahá'u'lláh's earthly remains. The mansion of Bahjí (Arabic for "delight" or "joy") is visited by thousands of pilgrims every year. Surrounded by gardens, several paths lead to the small garden house to the right of the main mansion, the point of Bahá'í pilgrimage, where Bahá'u'lláh's physical remains are interred.

BAHÁ'Í TEMPLES

The Bahá'í Temple, or House of Worship, is a loose term for Mashriqu'l-Adhkar (the Dawning-place of the Praise of God), referring to a complex of buildings that serves as a center for devotion to God and service to man. Radiating out from its central building, the Temple itself, are the supporting institutions serving the people.

**Mother Temple of the West, 1953
Wilmette, Illinois, USA**
© *Bahá'í International Community*

**Mother Temple of the Antipodes, 1961
Sydney, Australia**
© *Bahá'í International Community*

**Mother Temple of Europe, 1964
Frankfurt, Germany**
© *Bahá'í International Community*

**Mother Temple of Latin America
Panama City, Panama, 1972**
© Bahá'í International Community

**Mother Temple of Africa, 1961
Kampala, Uganda**
© Bahá'í International Community

**Temple of the Pacific Ocean, 1984
Apia, Western Samoa**
© *Bahá'í International Community*

**Mother Temple of India, 1986
Bahapur, Delhi, India,**
© *Bahá'í International Community*

**Model, Mother Temple of South America, 2009
Santiago, Chile**
© Bahá'í International Community

**First Bahá'í Temple, 1902
Ishqabad Turkmenistan (Destroyed)**
© Bahá'í International Community

The central building is designated primarily for prayers and readings from the revealed Word of God; these may include the Holy Scriptures of any of the major religions. In connection with these devotions, however, no sermons, commentaries or interpretations of these readings are permitted. This practice precludes the likelihood of any disagreements arising from conflicting views of the Word of God.

'Abdu'l-Baha noted the design of the Temple to be a dome on top of a nine-sided building. The other parts of the complex would include a hospital and drug dispensary, a traveler's hospice, a school for orphans, and a university for advanced studies.

None of the seven existing Bahá'í Temples have yet built all parts of the Temple complex. The eighth Bahá'í Temple, in Santiago, Chile, is scheduled for completion in 2009.

BAHÁ'Í FIRESIDES

A fireside is the most popular technique used for teaching the Bahá'í Faith to interested individuals, although it does not require a fire or even a fireplace. Sharing the Bahá'í message with others is an important duty for all Bahá'ís.

Bahá'u'lláh prohibits the practice of *proselytism*, of pressuring for religious conversion. The message of God should be offered only to those who have indicated an interest.

The term *fireside* describes the setting for teaching the Faith, in which friendship, warmth and hospitality can be displayed. The Bab is considered the first to set the example of a fireside when he displayed great love and hospitality to the seeker, Mulla Husayn, at their first meeting. Shoghi Effendi spoke of the spirit of the fireside:

The most effective method of teaching is the fireside group, where new people can be shown Bahá'í hospitality, and ask all questions which bother them. They can feel there the true Bahá'í spirit—and it is the spirit that quickeneth.[279]

AGES OF THE BAHÁ'Í FAITH

The Bahá'í Era encompasses both the Dispensation of the Bab and the Dispensation of Bahá'u'lláh. It marks the end of the Adamic Cycle (the Prophetic Era) and the beginning of the final stage of the Bahá'í Universal Cycle (the Era of Fulfillment). The Bahá'í Era comprises the time periods, or ages separating the distinctive stages in the development and growth of the Bahá'í Faith. It includes the first two Dispensations in the series of cycles called the Maturity Stage of the Bahá'í Universal Cycle.

The stages of development of the Bahá'í Faith were identified by Shoghi Effendi as:

- *The Heroic Age* (also called the Apostolic Age, or Primitive Age), 1844 to 1921—this is the period starting with the declaration of the Bab and ending with the death of 'Abdu'l-Baha.
- *The Formative Age* (also called the Transitional Age, or Iron Age), 1921 to ?—the present age in which we currently live. Shoghi Effendi and later the Universal House of Justice further identified several *epochs* within the Formative Age according to the developing stages. The *first epoch* (1921-1946) marked the formation of local and national institutions on all five continents. The *second epoch* (1946-1963) saw the development of the Bahá'í World Center and expansion of a worldwide teaching effort. The establishment of the Universal House of Justice began the *third epoch* (1963-1986). The *fourth epoch* closed in 2000 with the completion of the Arc and Terraces at the World Center. The *fifth epoch* is the current stage, in which the Faith's continuing expansion and worldwide visibility is ever more evident.
- *The Golden Age* (the time of the Most Great Peace)—the future age promised by all religions will begin before the end of this Dispensation. Shoghi Effendi described this age as the time **"destined to witness the emergence of a world-embracing Order enshrining the ultimate fruit of God's latest Revelation to mankind... and the formal inauguration of the Kingdom of the Father upon earth as promised by Jesus Christ**

himself."[280]

SYMBOLS IN RELIGION

Symbols are commonly used in most religions for various purposes. Some may be used as an idea or ideal, an expression of social and moral values, the teachings of the religion itself, an icon to create a sense of solidarity among religious adherents, or even as a way to bring one to God.

The cross is probably the symbol now most commonly identified with Christianity. Although its roots as a religious symbol can be traced to pre-Christian times, a cross configured in the shape of a crucifixion device was not used as a Christian symbol until Christianity was adopted by the Emperor Constantine as the religion of the Roman Empire, three centuries after the time of Jesus.

The crescent moon and star is the internationally recognized symbol of Islam. This symbol appears on the flags of several Muslim countries, and is also featured as part of the official emblem for the International Federation of Red Cross and Red Crescent Societies.

✡ The Magen David (shield of David, or as it is more commonly known, the Star of David) is the symbol most commonly associated with Judaism today, but its use as a symbol of Jews and Judaism can be traced back no more than two hundred years. After the Jews in France were emancipated by the French Revolution, they selected the six-pointed Star of David as their symbol of identity. In 1897 Theodor Herzl, founder of the Zionist Movement, also adopted the Star of David. It now appears in the center of the flag of the Jewish State of Israel, established in 1948.

COMMON BAHÁ'Í SYMBOLS

NUMBER NINE   0 1 2 3 4 5 6 7 8 **9**
NINE-POINTED STAR

In the decimal system of progressive numbers, 9 is the largest single-digit number that can be written.

A number greater than nine requires a combination of digits from zero to nine. In a spiritual sense, the number nine, as the highest single-digit number, symbolizes completeness, the peak of all the other numbers. Bahá'ís regard their Faith as the fulfillment of the prophecies foretold in the Scriptures of all the prior religions, and the number nine serves as the Bahá'í symbol of spiritual completion. The emphasis placed on the number nine is seen in the nine-sided design of all the continental Bahá'í temples of worship.

In many Bahá'í homes the number nine is displayed as a star in various configurations, such as shown here, but its use as an identifying icon is most common in its simplest configuration.

GREATEST NAME

In past ages the followers of the earlier religions were given a name by which they could call upon the infinite powers of God. This name usually expressed the attributes of God, and served as the epitome of the mysterious power which the Manifestation of God brought to the earth. The power contained within the Greatest Name can be released when the believer calls upon it, in prayer, or times of stress.

Jews consider the name **"Jehovah"** as the sacred name of God, a word never to be pronounced. When reading this word aloud in Hebrew (YHVH) it is replaced with the less precise word **"Adonai"** (Lord). In times of mortal danger, Jews often recite the **"Shema Yisroel"** (Hear O Israel), a six-word incantation of spiritual reinforcement.

For Buddhists, the vibration and energy contained in the mantra, **"Om,"** may sometimes be invoked prior to embarking on a new activity in order to forestall obstacles to success.

Christians often call upon the name of **Jesus** for protection from danger, e.g. "Jesus help me." "Stop in the name of Jesus." "For Jesus' sake"...

Bahá'ís identify **"Baha"** (Arabic for Glory) as the Greatest Name for this Dispensation. Baha is the root word of Bahá'u'lláh (Glory of God) and other related derivative names and titles. Bahá'ís call upon the power of God in prayer by saying **"Allah'u'Abha"** (God the All-Glorious).

"Ya Baha'u'l-Abha" (O Glory of the All-Glorious) is an invocation, often used by pioneers and teachers of the Faith.

"Ya Baha'u'l-Abha," a derivative of the Greatest Name drawn here in Arabic calligraphy is sometimes surprising at first glance to English-reading Bahá'ís who forget that Arabic is read from right to left.

SYMBOL OF THE GREATEST NAME

The Symbol of the Greatest Name is also called the Ringstone Symbol because it is worn on rings by many believers. This symbol is said to have been designed by 'Abdu'l-Baha to explain the meaning of the Greatest Name.

The three horizontal lines represent the world of God, the world of Revelation (the Manifestations), and the world of Creation (humanity). The vertical line represents the connection of these worlds, a recapitulation of the spiritual bonds uniting everything in one Divine Unity. The stars on either side represent the Báb and Bahá'u'lláh, the founder/Prophets of the Bahá'í Faith, and also the connecting link between the world of God and the world of Creation.

INVESTIGATING THE BAHÁ'Í FAITH

In addition to the growing number of books available about the Bahá'í Faith, all large cities and many communities maintain a local telephone listing for any inquiries about the Faith. The United States National Bahá'í Center is located in Evanston, Illinois. Telephone: 1-847-733-3500.

On the Internet there are numerous bulletin boards, websites, and discussion and study groups, in many languages, devoted to Bahá'í topics. At the Bahá'í World Center in Haifa, Israel, the Office of Public Information of the Bahá'í International Community maintains a site on the World Wide Web. Additional references can be found by doing a search on the web or at any public library.

Bahá'í firesides offer a friendly small-group atmosphere for anyone interested in learning more about Bahá'í teachings. Many schools, colleges and universities maintain informal Bahá'í groups for discussion of Bahá'í principles and concepts.

While Bahá'u'lláh encourages all Bahá'ís to share the message He brought to the world with all sincere seekers of truth, He also cautions against any kind of proselytism. **"Teach ye the Cause of God, O people of Baha, for God hath prescribed unto every one the duty of proclaiming His Message..."**[281] **We should never insist on teaching those who are not really ready for the Cause. If a man is not hungry you cannot make him eat.**[282]

In addition to the writings of Bahá'u'lláh, 'Abdu'l-Baha and Shoghi Effendi, the following books from the Bibliography are a few of the author's personal favorites for further exploration of the Bahá'í teachings:

Esslemont, J.E., *Bahá'u'lláh and the New Era*. Dr. Esslemont wrote this while a guest of 'Abdu'l-Baha during His last days. A popular introductory book for more than seventy years.

Mathews, Gary, *The Challenge of Bahá'u'lláh*. Easy to read. Bahá'u'lláh's proofs based on numerous prophecies.

Sears, William, *Release the Sun*. The story of the Bab. Reads like a dramatic thriller.

Loehle, Craig, *On the Shoulders of Giants*. Religious teachings harmonize with natural laws.

Holley, Horace, *Religion for Mankind*. Scholarly presentation of Baha'i principles needed for a changing world.

Conow, B. Hoff, *The Bahá'í Teachings: A Resurgent Model of the Universe*. A philosophical approach to the Bahá'í view of the universe.

Khursheed, Anjam, *Science and Religion*. A research scientist clarifies the harmony of science and religion.

BECOMING A BAHÁ'Í

Becoming a Bahá'í is a voluntary act. Those who so choose may declare their acceptance of the Bahá'í teachings. Often they will sign a card stating their desire to enroll in the Baha'i community. The card is then submitted to the Local Spiritual Assembly for its acceptance. The purpose of the card is an administrative procedure designed to keep track of Bahá'í membership.

Although it is not a universal practice, signing the card symbolizes a declaration of faith and denotes the declarant's acceptance of Bahá'u'lláh as the Manifestation of God for this day, of the Bab as the Herald of Bahá'u'lláh, and of 'Abdu'l-Baha as the center of Bahá'u'lláh's Covenant. It also denotes acceptance of Their teachings.

Maintaining membership in another Faith after becoming a Bahá'í is not an option for a sincere and thoughtful believer. How can a person say, "I believe Bahá'u'lláh is the current Manifestation of God as a Bahá'í, but I deny it as a member of another Faith?" The Bahá'í can also say, "I believe Bahá'u'lláh is the current Manifestation of God, and Jesus, Muhammad and Moses are earlier Manifestations of God." A member of the other Faith must deny this. We can't have it both ways without being hypocritical.

Once he recognizes the station of Bahá'u'lláh, the new believer is urged to energize and act upon his spiritual discovery. Newly declared Bahá'ís are expected to make their new faith a part of their lives. They are expected to **"become basically informed about the Central Figures of the Faith, as well as the existence of laws they must follow and an administration they must obey."**[283]

O ye beloved of God! Repose not yourselves on your couches, nay bestir yourselves as soon as ye

recognize your Lord, the Creator, and hear of the things which have befallen Him, and hasten to His assistance. Unloose your tongues, and proclaim unceasingly His Cause. This shall be better for you than all the treasures of the past and of the future, if ye be of them that comprehend this truth.[284]

BAHÁ'Í FUNDS

The act of giving carries a significant spiritual commitment. Any amount offered with love and sincerity is acceptable. A small contribution that is given from the heart brings greater spiritual benefit than a large contribution that is made grudgingly.

Financial support for the Faith is a privilege reserved for Bahá'ís; donations are not accepted from non-Bahá'ís. Solicitations for support may be made to the entire community, but never to individuals. Individual contributions are made anonymously and are strictly voluntary. Donations from non-Bahá'ís may be accepted only for non-Bahá'í charitable projects.

CHAPTER REVIEW—Bahá'í Topics

Summary
▶The Bahá'í Faith uses a nineteen-month solar calendar consisting of nineteen-day months plus some intercalary days.
▶Bahá'í Holy Days commemorate significant events in Bahá'í history.
▶A monthly Feast day is designed to help maintain the unity of the Bahá'í community.
▶The dispensation of each Manifestation of God is one of a series of cycles in a great universal cycle.
▶There are presently seven Bahá'í temples in different parts of the world; an eighth temple is under way.
▶A fireside is the most popular technique used for teaching the Bahá'í Faith.
▶We live in the Formative Age, the second of three developmental stages in the growth of the Bahá'í Faith.
▶It is very easy to learn more about the Bahá'í Faith.

Complete the following sentences
1. The Bahá'í calendar is based on the motion of the _____.
2. The Islamic calendar is based on the motion of the _____.
3. The Gregorian calendar is based on the motion of the _____.
4. World War I began in the year 1914 CE, or (year) BE.
5. The Bahá'í (day) in (Month) corresponds to 18 January.
6. The three parts of the Bahá'í Nineteen-Day Feast are: _____, _____ and _____.
7. In the Bahá'í view, the dispensation, or cycle, of Adam (began, ended) a universal cycle.
8. In the Bahá'í view, the dispensation, or cycle, of Jesus (ended, continued) the Cycle of Prophecy.
9. In the Bahá'í view, the dispensation, or cycle, of Muhammad (began, ended) the Cycle of Prophecy.
10. In the Bahá'í view, the dispensation, or cycle, of Bahá'u'lláh (began, ended) the Cycle of

Fulfillment.
11. In the Bahá'í view, the dispensation, or cycle, of Bahá'u'lláh (began, ended) the Bahá'í Universal Cycle.
12. Bahá'í temple complexes have been (completed, not yet completed) on every continent.

Indicate all correct choices
13. Bahá'í firesides:
    A. must be conducted with at least five people.
    B. are held primarily for the purpose of teaching the Bahá'í Faith.
    C. are a duty required of all Bahá'ís.
    D. must be attended by all people who plan to become Bahá'ís.
14. Bahá'í temples:
    A. open only to Bahá'ís at all times.
    B. may include prayers of other religions.
    C. open to members of all religions at all times.
    D. must have a nine-sided dome on top.
15. The Bahá'í Dispensation:
    A. the same as the Bahá'í Universal Cycle.
    B. the same as the Bahá'í Cycle.
    C. the same as the Cycle of Prophecy.
    D. continues after the death of Bahá'u'lláh.
16. A Bahá'í Feast:
    A. held each Gregorian month.
    B. held each Bahá'í month.
    C. held mainly for Bahá'ís.
    D. consists of three parts.
17. The Bahá'í World Center is:
    A. situated on Mount Sinai.
    B. where `Abdu'l-Bahá is buried.
    C. where the Universal House of Justice meets.
    D. based in Haifa, Israel.
18. The Shrine of the Bab:
    A. overlooks Haifa harbor.
    B. is situated on a slope of Mount Carmel.
    C. is a popular tourist attraction.
    D. is surrounded by the Bahá'í garden terraces.

CHAPTER ELEVEN—General Topics

The general topics discussed from a Bahá'í perspective in this chapter are of concern to individuals of all faiths and societies.

MAN AND THE ENVIRONMENT

Our environment and the world we live in are part of God's creation. Man, the highest life form, has powers that make him superior to nature, and to the natural laws that govern all lower life forms. With his spiritual powers (of reason and intelligence) man can discover the secrets of nature and overcome many of the restrictions and limitations which nature imposes on all material forms of life. This special ability to gain mastery over the environment also places a moral responsibility on man to use his God-given powers positively. The Universal House of Justice said, **"the proper exercise of this responsibility is the key to whether his inventive genius produces beneficial results, or creates havoc in the material world."**[285]

In the past, efforts to understand God led to a belief that God and Nature are the same. Earlier primitive cultures taught a reverence for nature based on a feeling of kinship with nature spirits, e.g. the wind, or the waters. While appropriate for an earlier day, man's present spiritual level precludes a retreat to belief in such personalized spirits. Rather than the belief that God is in the trees and rocks, Bahá'u'lláh explains that nature is the expression of God's Will in the material world.[286]

Shoghi Effendi pointed out how man's rejection of Bahá'u'lláh's message had resulted in crises with both social and spiritual dimensions, a process that is now defacing the earth's beauty and poisoning the atmosphere. He listed several examples: the spread of tyranny; the decline of ecclesiastical institutions; the increase of anarchy and chaos; growing racial strife; the burning of cities, and the contamination of the atmosphere of the earth.

The *unity* theme of Bahá'u'lláh's message extends not only to man and his social institutions, but also to the ecological balance between man and nature, and beyond—to the interconnectedness of everything in the universe. As the highest life form, man has the greatest powers, including an awareness of the ecological balance that God has created for us. It becomes our implied responsibility to use these powers to help maintain (instead of despoil and destroy) God's perfectly balanced creation.

'Abdu'l-Baha spoke of the interrelatedness of all created things. He cited the example of the vegetable and animal kingdoms in ecological balance; each provides the elements that benefit the other. **"Co-operation and reciprocity," He said, "are essential properties... without which the entire creation would be reduced to nothingness."**[287] **Until such time as the nations of the world... work together in looking after the best interests of all humankind, and unite in the search for ways and means to meet the many environmental problems besetting our planet... little progress will be made towards their solution...**[288]

Environmental protection and conservation are mankind's responsibility through humanity's recognition of Bahá'u'lláh's message. Whether or not we recognize this as a divine command—we must assume an appropriate role in its survival.

HEALTH AND HEALING

The Bab called the human body the throne of the inner temple, and taught that it should be protected and treated with respect. Individuals are encouraged to seek the best medical advice and treatment available. The Bab pointed out that it is really the inner temple (the soul) and not the body that takes delight in joy or is saddened by pain. **"Since this physical body is the throne whereon the inner temple is established, God hath ordained that the body be preserved to the extent possible..."**[289]

Psychosomatic factors can promote or retard our health. Laughter and happiness are conducive to good health. 'Abdu'l-Baha said that laughter is the visible effect of an invisible cause. Happiness, He said, is healthy, **"while depression of spirit begets**

disease..."[290]

'Abdu'l-Baha describes disease in terms of Oriental medicine—an imbalance of the body's constituent elements. The medical treatments of the future, He declared, will focus more on the use of natural selected foods and herbs rather than medicines and drugs to restore the natural equilibrium of the body's essential substances.

Medical treatment should be sought, but only when necessary. When the science of medicine is further developed, 'Abdu'l-Baha noted, cures will often be effected by natural means, by foods such as fruits and vegetables. Foods containing elements needed for restoring bodily equilibrium will be commonly used to maintain good health. **"Treat disease through diet, by preference, refraining from the use of drugs; and if you find what is required in a single herb, do not resort to a compounded medicament. Abstain from drugs when the health is good, but administer them when necessary.**[291]

Psychiatric treatment is also recommended, but only when necessary. Shoghi Effendi wrote, **"As Bahá'u'lláh has urged us to avail ourselves of the help of good physicians Bahá'ís are certainly not only free to turn to psychiatry for assistance but should, when available, do so. This does not mean psychiatrists are always wise or always right; it means we are free to avail ourselves of the best medicine has to offer us."**[292]

DRUGS, ALCOHOL AND TOBACCO

All mood-altering and habit-forming drugs such as marijuana, opium, hashish, heroin, hallucinogens, psychedelic substances and their like are forbidden except when medically prescribed for beneficial purposes. Stimulation of the spirit may be achieved spiritually—through prayer and meditation.

'Abdu'l-Baha considered opium *'foul and accursed'*. Hashish, He said, is the worst of all intoxicants. It **"extinguishes the mind, freezes the spirit, petrifies the soul, wastes the body and leaves man frustrated and lost."**[293]

The drinking of wine and other alcoholic beverages is

forbidden except when prescribed by a doctor as medical treatment. The reason is that liquor **"leads the mind astray and is the cause of weakening the body. If alcohol were beneficial it would have been brought into the world by the divine creation, not by the effort of man. Whatever is beneficial for man exists in creation..."**[294]

The use of cigarettes, cigars and tobacco is not forbidden, but it is considered dirty, unpleasant and injurious to the health. Its use is strongly discouraged. In addition to its obvious injurious effects, 'Abdu'l-Baha said, it is a cause of expense and loss of time. Eliminating this nasty habit will permit one **"to have stainless hands and a clean mouth, and hair which is not pervaded by a bad odor."**[295]

NUTRITION

Man is not required to deprive himself of the good things around us, so long as it does not interfere with his main purpose in life—to develop his spiritual qualities. We can enjoy the physical pleasures of the earth, but it is necessary that we maintain control over them and not misuse them; we must not become attached to them and put them before spiritual things.

'Abdu'l-Baha foreshadowed a growing awareness of the dietary concerns about the eating of meat. When asked, "What will be the food of the future?" He replied, **"Fruit and grains."** **"Meat,"** He said, **"will no longer be eaten." Eventually people will recognize that natural food is that which grows out of the ground.** [296]

Bodily characteristics are used by 'Abdu'l-Baha as an illustration for determining natural foods. The teeth and stomach formation of the lion require that he obtain his nourishment through meat. The eagle's beak is designed for tearing meat. The domestic animals—cows, sheep, horses, etc., are required by their bodies to subsist on grasses. For man, his incisors are for fruits—and his molars are formed to mash grain. **"When mankind is more fully developed the eating of meat will gradually cease."**[297]

SELF DEFENSE

Although violence is prohibited in the Bahá'í writings, a person is allowed to defend himself when his life is in danger. 'Abdu'l-Baha advised that if a Bahá'í is attacked, he should, if circumstances permit, defend himself and later lodge a complaint with the authorities. Generally, Bahá'ís are not encouraged to own weapons for protection, but under certain extreme conditions, it would be permissible to keep weapons, if the law permits.[298]

EUTHANASIA (MERCY KILLING)

...on the removal or withholding of life support in medical cases where intervention prolongs life in disabling illnesses, nothing has been found in the Sacred Text specifically on this matter. In such cases decision must be left to those responsible, including the patient.

Until such time as the Universal House of Justice considers legislation on euthanasia, decisions in [these matters] ... must be left to the consciences of those responsible.[299]

CREMATION

Bahá'í law requires burial of the dead body and forbids cremation. 'Abdu'l-Baha explained that decomposition of the body slowly is according to natural law. The elements of all bodies are continually being used in the formation of other beings, and this requires the gradual process of decomposition. **"If it had been better for it** (the body) **to be burned after death, in its very creation it would have been so planned that the body would automatically become ignited after death, be consumed and turned into ashes..."**[300]

PARTY POLITICS

Bahá'ís do not engage in party politics. They vote in elections if required or if they so wish, and they carry out all the obligations expected of law-abiding citizens. Unlike the growing political militancy of conservative religious groups as seen in the United States, political party affiliations by Bahá'ís are avoided because it would lead to disunity.

Recognizing that Bahá'ís are engaged in building a new world order that is divine in origin, Shoghi Effendi asked, **"How can we do this if every Bahá'í is a member of a different political party—some of them diametrically opposed to each other?"**[301]

The avoidance of partisan politics among Bahá'ís extends to any elective political office. Bahá'ís, Shoghi Effendi explained, must **"refrain from entering into the tangled affairs of political parties and to have neither concern for, nor involvement in, the controversies of politicians, the wranglings of theologians or any of the ailing social theories current amongst men."**[302]

MUSIC AND ART

Both music and art are recognized in the Bahá'í writings for their spiritual value. Art is a form of worship, according to Bahá'u'lláh. Bahá'í temples, shrines and gardens have won many architectural awards for their construction and physical beauty and are attracting visitors in increasing numbers yearly.[303]

Bahá'u'lláh called music a ladder for our souls, that can raise our spirits,[304] and 'Abdu'l-Baha described music as **"the food of the soul and spirit. Through the power and charm of music the spirit of man is uplifted."**[305]

Although music is *'a material affair'*, Shoghi Effendi wrote, it has a great effect on the human spirit. It is one of the important arts.[306]

REINCARNATION

Supposed memories of a previous life are not supported by scientific proof. The mind has almost infinite capacity for believing what it imagines. It is easily within the power of the mind to believe firmly that something had happened without it having really happened. Shoghi Effendi declared, **"It is not necessary for us to come back and be born into another body in order to advance spiritually and grow closer to God."**[307]

None of the founders of any of the major religions

taught the concept of reincarnation. If any major religion or its practitioner makes such a claim, it is based upon a misinterpretation or a corruption of the original teachings.

Laura Clifford Barney, an early believer visiting 'Abdu'l-Baha in the Holy Land asked, **"What is the truth of the question of reincarnation, which is believed by some people?"** His reply became part of her book, *Some Answered Questions*:

"The object of what we are about to say is to explain the reality—not to deride the beliefs of other people; it is only to explain the facts; that is all. We do not oppose anyone's ideas, nor do we approve of criticism.

Know, then, that those who believe in reincarnation are of two classes: one class does not believe in the spiritual punishments and rewards of the other world, and they suppose that man by reincarnation and return to this world gains rewards and recompenses; they consider heaven and hell to be restricted to this world and do not speak of the existence of the other world. Among these there are two further divisions. One division thinks that man sometimes returns to this world in the form of an animal in order to undergo severe punishment and that, after enduring this painful torment, he will be released from the animal world and will come again into the human world; this is called transmigration. The other division thinks that from the human world one again returns to the human world, and that by this return rewards and punishments for a former life are obtained; this is called reincarnation. Neither of these classes speak of any other world besides this one.

The second sort of believers in reincarnation affirm the existence of the other world, and they consider reincarnation the means of becoming perfect—that is, they think that man, by going from and coming again to this world, will gradually acquire perfections, until he reaches the inmost perfection. In other words, that men are composed of matter and force: matter in the beginning... is imperfect, but on coming repeatedly to this world

it progresses and acquires refinement and delicacy, until it becomes like a polished mirror; and force, which is no other than spirit, is realized in it with all the perfections.

This is the presentation of the subject by those who believe in reincarnation and transmigration ... No logical arguments and proofs of this question are brought forward; they are only suppositions and inferences from conjectures, and not conclusive arguments. Proofs must be asked for from the believers in reincarnation, and not conjectures, suppositions and imaginations."[308]

'Abdu'l-Baha noted that reincarnation, which is the repeated appearance of the same spirit, with its former essence and conditions, is impossible in the material world. If all the granaries of the world were full of grain, you would not find two grains absolutely alike, the same and identical without any distinction.

HOMOSEXUALITY

Scientific opinions related to homosexuality have been expressed about human behaviors which are *"innate"*– the result of genetic development, and those which are *"learned"*– the result of environmental influences. In this respect, 'Abdu'l-Baha indicated **"that the Bahá'í Writings do not uphold the materialistic view that nature is perfect... if one considers that "nature" sometimes provides examples that are unworthy of emulation by human beings. For example, the fact that some species eat their young does not mean that it is acceptable for human beings to do so. The Bahá'í concept of human nature is teleological; that is, there are certain qualities intended by God for "human nature", and qualities which do not accord with these are described as "unnatural." This does not mean that such aberrations may not be caused by the operations of "nature." Alcoholism is a good example... evidence indicates that it may possibly be induced by a genetic flaw. In that sense it is due to "natural" causes, but this does not necessarily mean that it is."**[309]

God judges each soul on its own merits. Though

Bahá'u'lláh has categorically forbidden the practice of homosexuality, Shoghi Effendi noted that we do not know what God's attitude would be towards a person who lives a good life in most ways, but not in this way. Overemphasis on sex is just one of the many evils afflicting human society which is presently skirting a spiritual low water mark in history. [310]

"No matter how devoted and fine the love may be between people of the same sex, to let it find expression in sexual acts is wrong. To say that it is ideal is no excuse... It is not the condition of being attracted to someone of the same sex which Bahá'u'lláh condemns, but the action of engaging in sexual relations with someone of the same sex. This distinction places homosexuality in the category of one of many problems, from which an individual may suffer, both physical and psychological. Some are the result of the individual's own behaviour, some are caused by the circumstances in which he grew up, some are congenital. Some human beings are born blind, some suffer from incapacitating accidents or diseases. Such conditions present the individual affected, and those around him, with serious problems, and it is one of the challenges of the human condition that all those concerned should strive to overcome such problems and have understanding and sympathy for the individual so afflicted."[311]

"To regard homosexuals with prejudice and disdain would be entirely against the spirit of Bahá'í Teachings. The doors are open for all of humanity to enter the Cause of God, irrespective of their present circumstances; this invitation applies to homosexuals as well as to any others who are engaged in practices contrary to the Bahá'í Teachings. Associated with this invitation is the expectation that all believers will make a sincere and persistent effort to eradicate those aspects of their conduct which are not in conformity with Divine Law."[312]

CHAPTER REVIEW—General Topics

Summary

▶Man's power to understand the importance of ecological balance in the environment automatically confers upon him the responsibility to help maintain that balance.

▶Medical treatment in the future will focus more on natural foods than it will on drugs and medicines.

▶The Bahá'í Faith specifically prohibits the use of all mood-altering and habit-forming drugs, and strongly discourages the use of tobacco.

▶Physiologically, man is better suited to the consumption of natural foods that grow out of the ground.

▶Although violence is prohibited in the Bahá'í writings, a person is allowed to defend himself when his life is in danger.

▶The question of shortening life because of a disabling illness is left to the conscience of those responsible.

▶The Bahá'í Faith forbids cremation and rejects the idea of reincarnation.

▶Bahá'ís must not engage in party politics.

▶Both music and art have spiritual value.

Discussion

1. Discuss, in terms of the Bahá'í unity concept, the ecological imbalance that is disrupting the environment.
2. Identify some of the social and spiritual dimensions of the crises mentioned earlier in this chapter.
3. What is the significance of the term 'throne of the inner temple'?
4. What is the Bahá'í view of the ways medical treatment will change in the future?
5. What kinds of medical treatments are Bahá'ís urged to seek?
6. What nutritional advice did 'Abdu'l-Baha offer about the foods of the future?
7. Bahá'ís are forbidden to use violence against another person, or to take someone's life. Are there any circumstances under which these prohibitions may be disregarded?
8. What is the Bahá'í view of reincarnation, or the 'return in another life on earth'?
9. How can running for public office lead to disunity within the Bahá'í community?

CHAPTER TWELVE—Plan Of God

PERSPECTIVES ON UNITY

Humanity is sometimes viewed as a traveler on a timeline or path leading to what may vaguely be called his destiny. The adventures humanity encounters along that path are part of its history. These adventures often include notable disasters and catastrophes both natural and self-inflicted. Natural disasters such as earthquakes, tsunamis, volcanic eruptions and major floods do not pose for humanity the same degree of danger and risk as the self-inflicted disasters.

Some of the current disasters and catastrophes which humanity has brought upon itself include:
- **world hunger**
- **depletion of fossil fuel reserves**
- **reduction of rain forests**
- **pollution of the atmosphere and the oceans**
- **urban sprawl**

Some of our technological 'fixes' for such problems have been generally less than adequate and only temporary at best:
- **emission control devices**
- **energy efficient cars**
- **new miracle food strains**
- **better contraceptives**
- **urban renewal projects**

We seem to be our own worst enemy because we can't reverse the problems we have already created for ourselves, and we can't stop creating more problems. We are just beginning to recognize that local and national efforts cannot solve global problems. And even more to the point, we do not recognize these problems as symptoms of other problems. **"They are outward manifestations of inner causes: the symptoms of malfunctions, not the malfunctions themselves."**[313]

The blame for these problems (more correctly symptoms of humanity's malfunctions) has been unfairly placed on our planet's limitations rather than on improper overuse and exploitation of planetary resources by humanity. The capacity to influence changes of planetary dimensions has been termed man's *'outer limits.'* The individual and collective mismanagement, irresponsibility and shortsightedness connected with humanity's treatment of its planetary home can be traced to religious strife, social discrimination, racism, sexism, chauvinism, economic injustice, political repression and totalitarianism, torture and terrorism, the proliferation of nuclear arms, and illiteracy and ignorance. These are some of the psychological, cultural and political problems plaguing individuals and societies, which may be described as the *'inner limits of mankind.'*

"Many world problems involve outer limits, but most of them are due fundamentally to inner limits. There are hardly any world problems that cannot be traced to human agency... We suffer from a serious case of 'culture lag'... we squabble among ourselves to acquire or retain the privileges of bygone times. We cast about for innovative ways to satisfy obsolete values."[314]

EVERYTHING IS RELATED

The Bahá'í Faith presents a perspective of reality that in a number of ways is different from the views of the mass of humanity and its major world leaders. One perceived difference that is opposed to the Bahá'í view of reality is the current perspective that all events are unrelated and occur randomly—purely by chance. This fragmented view of reality creates a challenge to identify which fragment (event) is the cause of the other fragments that make up our lives. We then seek to change that *causing fragment* and thus promote our own benefit.

The Bahá'í view sees a unified reality, an interlocking of events, in which God is the underlying cause of all. But more than providing the underlying cause of everything (through creation), God continues to direct the course of world events, primarily through the periodic appearances of His Manifestations.

The notion that *everything affects everything else* is

part of the philosophy of the so-called *New Age Movement*, a bold view of reality embodying the *New Physics*, the *New Biology*, and other new basic branches of study. The Bahá'í Faith, although clearly an independent world religion without any ties to the New Age Movement, is in agreement with this view of reality.

The renowned physicist, Fritjof Capra, wrote: **"the world-view implied by modern physics is inconsistent with our present society, which does not reflect the harmonious interrelatedness we observe in nature."**[315] From the *New Mathematics*, *Chaos Theory* has identified the *Butterfly Effect*, which one mathematician describes as *the notion that a butterfly stirring the air today in Peking can transform storm systems next month in New York*. A social researcher illustrated this concept of universal interrelationships with a generic newspaper story of a common tragedy:

What caused this apparent needless loss of life? Well in this case it's easy to see what happened—the person in the other car had been drinking and came around the corner on the wrong side of the road. Poor John hadn't a chance. But wait—is it as simple as that?

What if John hadn't been impeded in his journey by that slow-moving lorry[316] **that took him almost ten minutes to pass? Surely the lorry driver contributed in some way to his death? After all, if he hadn't been on the road at that time, then John wouldn't have arrived at that fatal corner at the exact moment when some fool decided to change lanes. What about the lorry driver's wife? Did she have a hand in it, too? Didn't she talk him into returning home early that evening? Normally he wouldn't have been on that road at that particular time. In fact, he had just put off another delivery so that he could get home in time for his daughter's birthday party. What if his daughter hadn't been born on that particular date? Yes, that might have saved John. What about all the events leading up to the birth of the lorry driver's daughter? His marriage. The marriages of his and**

his wife's parents. His very existence and all the factors leading up to that existence. These were all, in some way, instrumental in John's death.

But of course this is getting a bit silly now. We can't really point the finger at an innocent lorry driver and his family. It was the other driver who caused it... and maybe the other driver's workmates, who bought all those drinks for him at lunch time. They did tell him that those last three gins were small ones, even though they were really doubles. Well, he deserved a celebration; after all, he'd been waiting almost seven years for that promotion. Does that mean that his bosses had some part in the accident? Or perhaps it was Mr. Brown's early retirement, which made the promotion and consequent celebration possible? In fact, if Mr. Brown hadn't sustained that back injury last year, he would never have retired so soon. And it was such a stupid incident that led to the injury. It isn't wise to make a wild swipe at a passing fly while precariously balanced on a stepladder. However, such is life, and it's no use crying over it now. It would appear, then, that the fly in Mr. Brown's living room has a lot to answer for.

And all the time John's wife is mourning the loss of a loving husband and father, and suffering from terrible feelings of guilt. If she hadn't asked John to drive over to her sister's house... she even told him to hurry back. It was obviously her fault that John was now dead, and would not be around to help shape the lives of his two sons and only daughter. His death would alter the future of the whole family. If only...

Clearly, John's death can be attributed to the actions of a lot of people and to a lot of chance occurrences. But what really killed John? The answer is—everything. Everything worked together in a certain way to produce a particular set of consequences. And so it is with everything in life.[317]

The search for causes is futile in an interconnected world. In the old traditional view of reality, we keep looking haphazardly for causes that we can blame for misfortune, and for those causes we can change to make things better—truly a futile quest. Looking, for example, for the one or more cause(s) that will prevent war, is a hopeless task. Even if one war is prevented, the elemental causes leading to later wars are always around the corner.

SYSTEM THEORY

Unless we can recognize the interrelatedness of the factors that shape our lives, our efforts to better our condition will be no more effective than a person without a compass looking for a way out of a trackless waste. One model for picturing an interconnected universe has been advanced by *system theory*.

Everything in our universe can be called a system in its own right as well as a sub-system of a larger system containing smaller, lesser systems, each hierarchically organized. From ecosystems to family systems, from planetary systems to individual biological systems—all can be envisaged in this way.[318]

A human being may be considered a system of interconnected systems (e.g., digestive, skeletal, nervous, muscular, etc.), each working together for the benefit of the whole. Each smaller system (the circulatory system, for example) is composed of its own set of still smaller systems (heart, veins, blood, arteries) composed of yet smaller systems (the four-chambered heart with its own component systems of walls, muscles, valves), and so on.

Regard ye the world as a man's body, which is afflicted with divers ailments, and the recovery of which dependeth upon the harmonizing of all of its component elements.[319]

In a macrocosmic direction, each human being may be viewed as part of a larger family, or social system, extending hierarchically outward to ever-larger societies, and ultimately to a planetary social system, ecologically and environmentally balanced. If any component at any level is not working properly in its contribution to the health of the larger systems, the defective component can, according to the severity of the defect, affect the health of all the other systems.

THE PLAN OF GOD

The unification of the world, instead of being an afterthought, or of needing an improvised miracle for its completion, is the normal conclusion of a process that has been going on since the race began. Each of the world religions has its own set place within this vast economy. Each is radiated through a Master Prophet from God by one and the same principle and bears witness to some phase of one indivisible truth. No religion has been exhaustive or final.[320]

The suffering that humanity has experienced is not God's vengeance for our wrongdoing. We are suffering the consequences of our own actions. Man has freedom to choose how he will live within the natural laws all must obey. **"Where people act and live in unity, the result is peace and harmony. Where they disregard this basic principle and groups of people rise up in enmity against each other the result is destruction and suffering." It is not God's Will that millions should die as victims of war, disease or famine. All these calamitous happenings are the product of man disobeying the laws and teachings of God, which have been revealed in this age.**[321]

Bahá'u'lláh has renewed for humanity the true guidelines of the earlier religions in a format that is appropriate for today, in terms that are more explicit and detailed than those of the past. The earlier promises of the Kingdom of God on earth are now spelled out as never before.

In one of His tablets, Bahá'u'lláh outlines a philosophy of life that mirrors and expands on the teachings of earlier faiths. It also carries a hint of urgency that now is the time to reflect these values through matching words and deeds. Man's brief lifespan on this plane of existence requires immediate efforts to maximize spiritual growth here and ensure greater spiritual powers upon rebirth in the next world.

Strive to be shining examples unto all mankind, and true reminders of the virtues of God amidst men. He that riseth to serve My Cause should manifest My wisdom, and bend every effort to banish ignorance from the earth. Be united in

counsel, be one in thought. Let each morn be better than its eve and each morrow richer than its yesterday. Man's merit lieth in service and virtue and not in the pageantry of wealth and riches. Take heed that your words be purged from idle fancies and worldly desires and your deeds be cleansed from craftiness and suspicion. Dissipate not the wealth of your precious lives in the pursuit of evil and corrupt affection, nor let your endeavours be spent in promoting your personal interest. Be generous in your days of plenty, and be patient in the hour of loss. Adversity is followed by success and rejoicings follow woe. Guard against idleness and sloth, and cling unto that which profiteth mankind, whether young or old, whether high or low.[322]

The Bahá'í view of reality recognizes that there is an organization, a plan that is guiding our destiny, and which will lead us to a world of peace and spiritual growth, i.e. the Kingdom of God on earth, as promised in all the religions. All we need do to create that world is to choose to follow the guidelines (of the plan) set down for us by God through His Messengers. Till now we have exercised our *freedom to choose* to reject those guidelines (and create the causes of war and other misfortunes) by following our own fragmented (egotistical, self-indulgent, and shortsighted) choices. Until we recognize that our freedom to choose can (and ultimately must) lead to the acceptance of God's guidelines, as His Messengers offer, the promised Kingdom will elude us.

These guidelines (the Message, or the Plan) have come to us through every Manifestation of God in a format that was most appropriate for that historical period. Each Revelation offers mankind not only the same message of hope, but also the promise that it will be renewed by the next Revelation. When the new religion appears, it displays a spiritual vitality that once existed in the earlier religion but which has for a long time been in a decline.

In the Qur'an it is stated: **'Unto every nation there is a preordained term; therefore, when their term is expired, they shall not** [be renewed]...' **Like those** nations that have reached their peak and have begun their decline, the influence of the earlier religions on modern society has been steadily decreasing. Their teachings have become less clear as new interpretations are added to the numerous conflicting earlier interpretations. **No wonder the numbers of agnostics and atheists are growing.** [323]

The emergence of science as a potent force in the acquisition of knowledge demands that religious truth may not be in conflict with scientific truth. But instead of closing the gap with science, religious leaders have done just the opposite. Religious teachings now are tolerated rather than respected. More and more intelligent people look upon anything religious with suspicion. Some people have made a mockery of religion by **"creating sects which have proved to be nothing short of nests of corruption and profiteering." Others have used religion as a front for political or commercial activities.** [324]

OLD ORDER/NEW ORDER

Bahá'u'lláh affirmed that humanity is now spiritually ready to implement the guidelines and attain that which has been promised by all of the earlier religions. If this is so, why, then, one might ask, are we not moving in that direction? The answer is—we are moving in that direction, but in a more circuitous path of our own choosing. Certainly the warnings of approaching calamities can no longer be regarded as the ravings of wild-eyed fanatics—the breakdown of many established social institutions are already underway. However, the destruction of these bulwarks of the Old is accompanied by the less visible emergence of the New. Replacing an old bumpy road with a smooth highway is a mess until the job is completed. The focus must be on the processes at work rather than the conditions of the moment.

"Soon," Bahá'u'lláh's own words proclaim it, "will the present-day Order be rolled up, and a new one spread out in its stead. Verily, thy Lord speaketh the truth and is the Knower of things unseen." "By Myself," He solemnly asserts, "the day is approaching when We will have rolled up the world

and all that is therein, and spread out a new Order in its stead. He, verily, is powerful over all things." "The world's equilibrium," He explains, "hath been upset through the vibrating influence of this Most Great, this new World Order. Mankind's ordered life hath been revolutionized through the agency of this unique, this wondrous System, the like of which mortal eyes have never witnessed." "The signs of impending convulsions and chaos," He warns the peoples of the world, "can now be discerned, inasmuch as the prevailing Order appeareth to be lamentably defective."[325]

Bahá'u'lláh described the transition of human society from the **Old Order** to the **New Order** as the birth process from the womb world to this world. The transition is a process of blood, sweat, and tears, in which the **Old-Order womb-world** is devastated, shattered and destroyed as the **New-Order this-world** is born. Humanity is at the same time the Old Order and the New Order. The duration of this birthing process depends upon the willingness of the Old Order to cast its burden and allow the New Order to come forth. The world is presently in the labor stage of this analogy. The longer the crumbling but still powerful Old Order resists God's call for a maturing humanity to emerge as the infant New Order, the longer its painful and difficult labor will persist.

Such simultaneous processes of rise and of fall, of integration and of disintegration, of order and chaos,... are but aspects of a greater Plan, one and indivisible, whose Source is God, whose author is Bahá'u'lláh, the theater of whose operations is the entire planet, and whose ultimate objectives are the unity of the human race and the peace of all mankind.[326]

We are indeed living in an age which... is witnessing a dual phenomenon. The first signalizes the death pangs of... [a dying] Order... The second proclaims the birth pangs of an Order... that will inevitably supplant the former, and within whose administrative structure an embryonic civilization, incomparable and world-embracing, is imperceptibly maturing. The one is being rolled

up, and is crashing in oppression, bloodshed, and ruin. The other opens up vistas of a justice, a unity, a peace, a culture, such as no age has ever seen. The former has spent its force, demonstrated its falsity and barrenness, lost irretrievably its opportunity, and is hurrying to its doom. The latter, virile and unconquerable, is plucking asunder its chains, and is vindicating its title to be the one refuge within which a sore-tried humanity, purged from its dross, can attain its destiny.[327]

In terms of social history, Alvin Toffler recognized the momentous changes that are taking place:

Indeed, a growing body of reputable opinion asserts that the present movement represents nothing less than the second great divide in human history, comparable in magnitude only with that first great break in historic continuity, the shift from barbarism to civilization.[328]

Arnold Toynbee pictured in a dramatic theatrical setting the simultaneous balance of the **two orders**, the destruction of the old and the emergence of the new:

During the disintegration of a civilization, two separate plays with different plots are being performed simultaneously side by side. While an unchanging dominant majority is perpetually rehearsing its own defeat, fresh challenges are perpetually evoking fresh creative responses from newly recruited minorities, which proclaim their own creative power by rising, each time, to the occasion. The drama of challenge-and-response continues to be performed, but in new circumstances and with new actors.[329]

The destruction of the Old Order has been most evident in the political changes that occurred after World War I; the collapse of the most powerful European monarchies, in Germany, Austria-Hungary, and Russia, and the fall of Persia and the Turkish Empire. This destructive process has continued in a less obvious but equally relentless manner through the gradual breakdown of long-cherished traditions and social institutions. It has demoralized family relationships, religious beliefs, the educational system, and economic and interpersonal relationships. Like mice in a maze, mankind has tenaciously clung to familiar but now ineffectual standards that worked well in the past; we sentimentally follow the tried and true old ways and traditions that no longer work. Shoghi Effendi argued eloquently:

If long-cherished ideals and time-honored institutions, if certain social assumptions and religious formulae have ceased to promote the welfare of the generality of mankind, if they no longer minister to the needs of a continually evolving humanity, let them be swept away and relegated to the limbo of obsolescent and forgotten doctrines. Why should these, in a world subject to the immutable law of change and decay, be exempt from the deterioration that must needs overtake every human institution? For legal standards, political and economic theories are solely designed to safeguard the interests of humanity as a whole, and not humanity to be crucified for the preservation of the integrity of any particular law or doctrine.[330]

NEW ORDER—NEW DAY

This, then, is the present stage of the Plan of God for mankind that Bahá'u'lláh described. Once they hear it, many people will believe it because it is a reasonable explanation for present world conditions. Bahá'ís not only believe it—they are actively working to make it a reality. The growing Bahá'í world community and its Administrative Order is the seed of the New Order that is germinating and developing in the womb of the Old Order, waiting to come forth to build humanity's promised Kingdom of God on earth. The world is on the verge of major social changes. The violence and the crumbling of the Old Order institutions that are accompanying these social changes reflect the resistance of these still-powerful institutions to the irresistible power of the Plan of God—to proceed to the next stage of mankind's glorious destiny.

...the main purpose of the Revelation of Bahá'u'lláh is to instill into the hearts of men a measure of God's love and endow their souls with

the spirit of faith. Only when this happens on a universal scale will man-made sufferings and calamities be replaced by the Most Great Peace. When humanity attains to this exalted state and the causes of disunity are thus eliminated, then trials and tribulations will be limited to those which God ordains for each individual. The sufferings which come from God are essential for the spiritual development of the soul. Whereas man-made sufferings today are intolerable, God-sent ordeals and difficulties are never imposed upon a soul beyond its capacity.[331]

As God's Representative today, Bahá'u'lláh's clarion call to humanity promises untold blessings to the spiritually sensitive individuals who can recognize the truth of His message and will rise to heed His summons. This call is couched in mighty metaphoric terms hinting of the rich rewards awaiting the alert seeker—and the incalculable loss to be suffered by underestimating the significance of a call from God:

O My servants! My holy, My divinely ordained Revelation may be likened unto an ocean in whose depths are concealed innumerable pearls of great price, of surpassing luster. It is the duty of every seeker to bestir himself and strive to attain the shores of this ocean, so that he may, in proportion to the eagerness of his search and the efforts he hath exerted, partake of such benefits as have been pre-ordained in God's irrevocable and hidden Tablets. If no one be willing to direct his steps towards its shores, if every one should fail to arise and find Him, can such a failure be said to have robbed this ocean of its power or to have lessened, to any degree, its treasures? How vain, how contemptible, are the imaginations which your hearts have devised, and are still devising! O My servants! The one true God is My witness! This most great, this fathomless and surging Ocean is near, astonishingly near, unto you. Behold it is closer to you than your life-vein! Swift as the twinkling of an eye ye can, if ye but wish it, reach and partake of this imperishable favor, this God-given grace, this incorruptible gift, this most potent and unspeakably glorious bounty.

O My servants! Could ye apprehend with what wonders of My munificence and bounty I have willed to entrust your souls, ye would, of a truth, rid yourselves of attachment to all created things, and would gain a true knowledge of your own selves—a knowledge which is the same as the comprehension of Mine own Being. Ye would find yourselves independent of all else but Me, and would perceive, with your inner and outer eye, and as manifest as the revelation of My effulgent Name, the seas of My loving-kindness and bounty moving within you. Suffer not your idle fancies, your evil passions, your insincerity and blindness of heart to dim the luster, or stain the sanctity, of so lofty a station. Ye are even as the bird which soareth, with the full force of its mighty wings and with complete and joyous confidence, through the immensity of the heavens, until, impelled to satisfy its hunger, it turneth longingly to the water and clay of the earth below it, and, having been entrapped in the mesh of its desire, findeth itself impotent to resume its flight to the realms whence it came. Powerless to shake off the burden weighing on its sullied wings, that bird, hitherto an inmate of the heavens, is now forced to seek a dwelling-place upon the dust. Wherefore, O My servants, defile not your wings with the clay of waywardness and vain desires, and suffer them not to be stained with the dust of envy and hate, that ye may not be hindered from soaring in the heavens of My divine knowledge.

O My servants! Through the might of God and His power, and out of the treasury of His knowledge and wisdom, I have brought forth and revealed unto you the pearls that lay concealed in the depths of His everlasting ocean. I have summoned the Maids of Heaven to emerge from behind the veil of concealment, and have clothed them with these words of Mine—words of consummate power and wisdom. I have, moreover, with the hand of divine power, unsealed the choice wine of My Revelation, and have wafted its holy, its hidden, and musk-laden fragrance upon all created things. Who else but yourselves is to be blamed if ye choose to remain unendowed with so great an outpouring of God's transcendent and all-encompassing grace, with so bright a revelation of His resplendent mercy?...[332]

O Offspring of dust! Be not content with the ease of a passing day, and deprive not thyself of everlasting rest. Barter not the garden of eternal delight for the dust-heap of a mortal world. Up from thy prison ascend unto the glorious meads above, and from thy mortal cage wing thy flight unto the paradise of the Placeless.[333]

Whoso followeth this counsel will break his chains asunder, will taste the abandonment of enraptured love, will attain unto his heart's desire, and will surrender his soul into the hands of his Beloved. Bursting through his cage, he will, even as the bird of the spirit, wing his flight to his holy and everlasting nest.[334]

CHAPTER REVIEW—THE PLAN OF GOD
Summary
▶Rather than a view of the universe as discrete, independent causes and events, there is a growing recognition of an interdependent relatedness of everything to everything else.
▶Humanity is slowly moving toward a destiny that is part of God's plan for mankind.
▶The difficulties humanity is experiencing are self-inflicted, not a punishment from God.
▶A new civilization, the New Order, is growing within the Old Order, which is dying.
▶The New Order is part of God's Plan for the next step toward mankind's glorious destiny.
▶Every individual is offered a priceless opportunity to embrace this vision and join the army of God in establishing His promised kingdom on earth.

Discussion
1. Describe the 'inner' and 'outer' limits of mankind in terms of the problems we face.
2. How does the theory that 'everything affects everything else' relate to the common practice of seeking to resolve a problem by changing its root cause?
3. How does system theory explain a heart attack in terms of a person's health?
4. Are the sufferings mankind is experiencing a retribution from God or are they self-inflicted? How can this situation be remedied?
5. How can the teachings of the earlier religions be reconciled with the Plan of God described in this book?
6. Why are there so many problems in the transition from the 'Old Order' to the 'New Order'?
7. Cite some examples of the inadequacy of the 'Old Order' to meet the needs of present-day society.
8. How do Bahá'ís view the Bahá'í community and the Bahá'í Administrative Order in relation to the promised Kingdom of God on earth?
9. How does Bahá'u'lláh describe the bounties God offers those who respond to His call?

ENDNOTES

1 Bahá'í International Community, booklet, *Turning Point for All Nations*, p.1.
2 Bahá'í International Community, booklet, *Turning Point for All Nations*, p 2.
3 Conow, B. Hoff, The Bahá'í Teachings: A Resurgent Model of the Universe, p. 145.

Chapter 1

4 Bahá'u'lláh, *Gleanings from the Writings of Bahá'u'lláh*, p. 78.
5 Bahá'u'lláh, *Gleanings*, pp. 54-55.
6 Bahá'u'lláh, *Prayers and Meditations*, p. 108.
7 Sears, William, *The Wine of Astonishment*, p. 69.
8 Townshend, George, *The Promise of All Ages*, p. 38.
9 Townshend, George, *The Promise of All Ages*, p. 50.
10 Bahá'u'lláh, *Gleanings*, pp. 66-67.
11 Bahá'u'lláh, *Gleanings*, pp. 65-66.
12 Bahá'u'lláh, *Epistle to the Son of the Wolf*, p. 13.
13 `Abdu'l-Bahá, *Paris Talks*, pp. 142.
14 `Abdu'l-Bahá, *Paris Talks*, pp. 142.
15 Momen, Wendi, gen. ed., *A Basic Bahá'í Dictionary*, p. 72.
16 Townshend, George, *The Promise of All Ages*, p. 54.
17 Sears, William, *The Wine of Astonishment*, p. 68.
18 Shoghi Effendi, *World Order of Bahá'u'lláh*, p. 60.
19 Bahá'u'lláh, *The Kitab-i-Iqan*, pp. 12-13.
20 Bahá'u'lláh, *Gleanings*, p. 213.
21 Udo Schaefer, *The Imperishable Dominion*, p. 121.
22 F. Max Müller, letter to the Rev. M.K. Schermerhorn in 1883, quoted in *The Portable World Bible*, p.xix.
23 Shoghi Effendi, *World Order of Bahá'u'lláh*, p. 58.
24 The 'gate' to the new revelation brought by Bahá'u'lláh.

Chapter 2

25 Compilations, The Compilation of Compilations, Vol. I, p. 19
26 Johnson, Paul, *History of the Jews*, p. 17.
27 Discovered in 1933 at the Syrian excavations of Tel Hariri, near the Euphrates River.
28 Kaplan, Rabbi Aryeh, *The Handbook of Jewish Thought*, p. 121.
29 Townshend, George, *Christ and Bahá'u'lláh*, p. 32.
30 The early Jewish kings were anointed with 'holy oil', symbolizing their spiritual appointment by God.
31 Townshend, George, *Christ and Bahá'u'lláh*, p. 21.
32 Shoghi Effendi, *The Promised Day is Come*, p. 107.
33 Dimont, Max I., *The Indestructible Jews*, p. 217.
34 Rops, Daniel, *Jesus and His Times*, pp. 158-162.
35 Townshend, George, *Christ and Bahá'u'lláh*, p. 28.
36 Sometimes called the '*Zend-Avesta*', which includes commentaries on the original writings.
37 Parrinder, Geoffrey, ed., *World Religions*, p. 191.
38 Arabians are an ethnic group of people who trace their roots to Abraham, the same ancestor claimed by Jews and Christians. The term 'Arab' refers to an ethnic group of people and should not be confused with the term 'Muslim', which is a follower of Islam.

[39] Shiah Islam, also known as Shiite Islam, began in Arabia and reached its greatest influence in Persia. Even today, Iran (formerly Persia) is more than 90% Shiah.
[40] The Imam, by Shiah tradition, is a divinely inspired, infallible, spiritual leader.
[41] The Sunni sect, comprising about 85% of all Muslims, reject the Shiah claims, saying that the "sunna"—the 'way' or mode of conduct prescribed by Muhammad, was sufficient to guide the faithful.
[42] The title of Caliph was given to the person chosen as leader of the Muslim community. According to the Qur'an, the leader was supposed to be elected; in fact, he never was.
[43] Lippman, Thomas W., *Understanding Islam*, p. 141.
[44] Qur'an is used in preference to the more common Western spelling of 'Koran', as it is closer to the Arabic pronunciation.
[45] Lippman, Thomas W., *Understanding Islam*, p. 6.
[46] The Awaited One.
[47] The Mahdi (The Guided One) and the Qa'im (He Who Will Arise) are a Shiah tradition leading to one of the claims by the Bab, the Herald of the Bahá'í Faith.
[48] The Bab (Arabic for 'gate') was the title taken by Ali-Muhammad of Shiraz, Persia, who announced in 1844 that he was the returned Mahdi of the Shiahs, and the Herald of Another much greater than Himself.
[49] Motlagh, H., *I Will Come Again*, p. 289.
[50] Mustafa, M., *Bahá'u'lláh, the Great Announcement of the Qur'an*, p. 108.

Chapter 3
[51] Followers of William Miller in Pennsylvania, whose Bible study led him to expect Christ's return in 1844. Similar predictions of Christ's imminent return were made by Bible scholars in other parts of the world, e.g. Edward Irving in England, Archibald Mason in Scotland, Leonard Kelber in Germany, and Josef Wolff in Palestine. The Millerites, whose numbers approached two hundred thousand prior to Miller's 'greatest Day in human history', later gave rise to the Seventh-day Adventist Church and a few other denominations.
[52] Designers created special robes for those who wished to be in fashion on that Day. In a letter written August 21, 1921, to Clara E. Sears, Ida Wing wrote: "I have heard my mother tell that when she was a girl she remembers that her mother made a white robe, put her house in order, put lamps in the windows and sat up all night waiting for the end of the world to come."
[53] Motlagh, H., *I Shall Come Again*, p. 191.
[54] Muslims believed Islam was the next Revelation in line with Christianity. Even if the Christians did not conduct themselves according to their own holy writings, Christ's return as promised in the Gospels was true.
[55] J.E. Esslemont, *Bahá'u'lláh and the New Era*, pp. 11-12.
[56] The Turkish Empire in the 1800's was already in a steep decline from its period of glory four centuries earlier when it conquered the Byzantine Empire and took over as the ruling power of the Islamic Empire.
[57] The Shaykhis were a devout Shiah sect led by Shaykh Ahmad-i-Asa'i and Siyyid Kazim-i-Rashti.

⁵⁸ A Siyyid is one who is descended from the family of the Prophet Muhammad.
⁵⁹ Nabil-i-Azam, *The Dawn Breakers*, translation by Shoghi Effendi, p. 40. (British edition-see Bibliography)
⁶⁰ Nabil-i-Azam, *The Dawn Breakers*, translation by Shoghi Effendi, pp.43-44.
⁶¹ Nabil-i-Azam, *The Dawn Breakers*, translation by Shoghi Effendi, p. 65.
⁶² Nabil-i-Azam, *The Dawn Breakers*, translation by Shoghi Effendi, p. 65.
⁶³ Balyuzi, H.M., *The Bab*, p 71.
⁶⁴ Equivalent of king.
⁶⁵ Nabil-i-Azam, *The Dawn Breakers*, translation by Shoghi Effendi, p. 126.
⁶⁶ Nabil-i-Azam, *The Dawn Breakers*, translation by Shoghi Effendi p. 229.
⁶⁷ Sears, William, *Release the Sun*, p. 78.
⁶⁸ Caning on the soles of the feet as punishment or torture.
⁶⁹ Browne, W.G., quoted in Balyuzi, H., *The Bab*, p. 147.
⁷⁰ Sears, William, *Release the Sun*, p. 80.
⁷¹ This was a severe test for some of the more conservative members. It led one man to cut his own throat.
⁷² Nabil-i-Azam, *The Dawn Breakers*, translation by Shoghi Effendi Chaps. XIX-XX.
⁷³ Sears, William, *Release the Sun*, p. 87.
⁷⁴ Shoghi Effendi, *God Passes By*, p. 64.
⁷⁵ Shoghi Effendi, *God Passes By*, pp. 65-66.
⁷⁶ Hatcher, W.S. and Martin, D.W., *The Bahá'í Faith: The Emerging Global Religion*, pp 99.
⁷⁷ Sears, William, *Release the Sun*, p. 103.
⁷⁸ Sears, William, *Release the Sun*, p. 118.
⁷⁹ Sears, William, *Release the Sun*, p. 119.
⁸⁰ The prime minister's brother, responsible for the execution proceedings.
⁸¹ Hatcher, W.S. and Martin, D.W., *The Bahá'í Faith: The Emerging Global Religion*, pp. 18-19.
⁸² Shoghi Effendi, *God Passes By*, p. 55.
⁸³ Sears, William, *Release the Sun*, p. 184-5.
⁸⁴ Such as Isaiah, Jeremiah, Elijah, Hosea, Amos.

Chapter 4
⁸⁵ Bahá'u'lláh, *Epistle to the Son of the Wolf*, p. 71.
⁸⁶ Nabil-'i'-Azam, *The Dawn Breakers*, translation by Shoghi Effendi, p. 461.
⁸⁷ Bahá'u'lláh, *Epistle to the Son of the Wolf*, p. 11.
⁸⁸ Bahá'u'lláh, *Epistle to the Son of the Wolf*, p. 21-22.
⁸⁹ For details of this event, see Taherzadeh, *Revelation of Bahá'u'lláh*, Vol. 1, pp. 53-54.
⁹⁰ Bahá'u'lláh in Arabic means Glory of God (Allah). His spiritual name was Baha (Glory); a Bahá'í is a follower of Baha.
⁹¹ A member of a Muslim mystical order.
⁹² Bahá'u'lláh, *Seven Valleys and Four Valleys*, p. 5.
⁹³ Yahya was designated by the Bab as 'Subh-i-Azal' (Morn of Eternity).

94 Bahá'u'lláh, *Kitab-i-Aqdas*, p. 48-49.
95 Bahá'u'lláh, *Gleanings*, p. 249.
96 Bahá'u'lláh, *Proclamation of Bahá'u'lláh*, p. 83.
97 Bahá'u'lláh, *Proclamation of Bahá'u'lláh*, p. 87.
98 Bahá'u'lláh, *Gleanings*, p. 117-118.
99 Bahá'u'lláh, *Kitab-i-Aqdas*, p. 16
100 Bahá'u'lláh, *Proclamation of Bahá'u'lláh*, pp. 20-21.
101 Taherzadeh, Adib, *The Revelation of Bahá'u'lláh*, Vol. III, pp. 416-417.
102 Taherzadeh, Adib, *The Revelation of Bahá'u'lláh*, Vol. III, pp. 248-249.
103 Browne, E.G., *A Traveller's Narrative*, pp. 39-40.
104 Mathews, Gary L., *The Challenge of Bahá'u'lláh*, p. 14.
105 Literally "Servant of Baha" or "Servant of Glory."

Chapter 5

106 The grandson of `Abdu'l-Bahá and his appointed successor as 'Guardian of the Bahá'í Faith'.
107 Shoghi Effendi compared the growth of the Bahá'í Faith to the growth of the individual. The Heroic Age corresponds to the birth stage in the life of the individual. The Formative Age can be compared to his early development years.
108 Universal House of Justice, Research Department, *The Covenant*, Introduction.
109 Universal House of Justice, letter, quoted in Tanyi, E.N., comp., *The Covenant: Daily Readings from the Bahá'í Teachings*, intro.
110 Taherzadeh, Adib, *The Covenant of Bahá'u'lláh*, p. 105.
111 Browne, E.G., *A Traveller's Narrative*, p. xxxvi.
112 Shoghi Effendi, The World Order of Bahá'u'lláh, p. 139.
113 Balyuzi, H.M., `Abdu'l-Bahá, p. 288.
114 `Abdu'l-Bahá, *Promulgation of Universal Peace*, p. xii.
115 `Abdu'l-Bahá, *Promulgation of Universal Peace*, p. xvi.
116 Balyuzi, H.M., `Abdu'l-Bahá, pp. 405-406.
117 Shoghi Effendi, *The World Order of Bahá'u'lláh*, p. 53.
118 Shoghi Effendi, *The Advent of Divine Justice*, p. 86.
119 Lady Blomfield, *The Chosen Highway*, p. 220.
120 Esslemont, J.E., *Bahá'u'lláh and the New Era*, pp. 64-65.
121 Shoghi Effendi, *God Passes By*, p. 310.
122 Balyuzi, H.M., `Abdu'l-Bahá, p. 464.

Chapter 6

123 Also known by the title *Greatest Holy Leaf*, which her father, Bahá'u'lláh, had given her.
124 Martin, J. Douglas, *The Bahá'í Faith in its Second Century*, p. 62.
125 Shoghi Effendi, *The World Order of Bahá'u'lláh*, pp. 18-19.
126 Shoghi Effendi, *The World Order of Bahá'u'lláh*, pp. 20-22.
127 Shoghi Effendi, *The Promised Day is Come*, pp. 3-5.
128 Shoghi Effendi, *The Advent of Divine Justice*, pp. 46-47.
129 As of this revision, one Hand of the Cause was still living.

Chapter 7

130 Danesh, H.B., *Unity, the Creative Foundation of Peace*, p. 31.
131 Sheppherd, Joseph, *The Elements of the Baha'i Faith*, p. 57.
132 Bahá'u'lláh, cited in Shoghi Effendi, *World Order of Bahá'u'lláh*, p. 113.
133 Bahá'u'lláh, *The Kitab-i-Iqan*, pp. 103-4.

134 Bahá'u'lláh, *Gleanings from the Writings of Bahá'u'lláh*, p. 65.
135 Shoghi Effendi, *The World Order of Bahá'u'lláh*, pp. 42-43.
136 Shoghi Effendi, *The World Order of Bahá'u'lláh*, p. 163.
137 `Abdu'l-Bahá, *Promulgation of Universal Peace*, p. 197.
138 `Abdu'l-Bahá, *Promulgation of Universal Peace*, p. 201.
139 Bahá'u'lláh, *Epistle to the Son of the Wolf*, p. 13.
140 Bahá'u'lláh, *Epistle to the Son of the Wolf*, p. 62.
142 Loehle, Craig, *On The Shoulders of Giants*, p. 50.
142 Holley, Horace, *Religion for Mankind*, p. 121.
143 Bahá'u'lláh, *Gleanings*, p. 87.
144 Bahá'u'lláh, cited in Shoghi Effendi, *The World Order of Bahá'u'lláh*, p. 115.
145 The Manifestation of God.
146 Shoghi Effendi, *The World Order of Bahá'u'lláh*, p. 58-59.
147 Sabet, Huschmand, *The Heavens are Cleft Asunder*, pp. 103-105.
148 Conow, B. Hoff, *The Bahá'í Teachings: A Resurgent Model of the Universe*, pp. 50-51.
149 `Abdu'l-Bahá, *Paris Talks*, pp. 90-91.
150 `Abdu'l-Bahá, *Some Answered Questions*, pp. 233-234.
151 `Abdu'l-Bahá, *Some Answered Questions*, p. 163.
152 Bahá'u'lláh, *The Kitab-i-Iqan*, p. 120.
153 `Abdu'l-Bahá, *Paris Talks*, p. 60.
154 Esslemont, J.E., *Bahá'u'lláh and the New Era*, p. 206.
155 `Abdu'l-Bahá, *Promulgation of Universal Peace*, p. 295.
156 `Abdu'l-Bahá, *Paris Talks*, p. 85.
157 Taherzadeh, Adib, *The Covenant of Bahá'u'lláh*, p. 9-10.
158 Bahá'u'lláh, *Gleanings*, pp. 169-71.
159 Shoghi Effendi, *Directives from the Guardian*, p. 86.
160 Bahá'u'lláh,, *Persian Hidden Words*, No. 5.
161 Bahá'u'lláh, *Gleanings*, pp. 157.
162 `Abdu'l-Bahá, *Promulgation of Universal Peace*, pp. 47-48.
163 `Abdu'l-Bahá, *Promulgation of Universal Peace*, pp. 225-226.
164 Bahá'u'lláh, *Gleanings*, pp. 151-153.
165 `Abdu'l-Bahá, *`Abdu'l-Bahá in London*, p. 95.
166 `Abdu'l-Bahá, *Some Answered Questions*, p. 241.
167 New Testament, *Matthew* 6:10.
168 Blomfield, Lady, *The Chosen Highway*, p. 172.
169 *The Significance of Bahá'u'lláh's Revelation*, p. 74.

Chapter 8

170 Udo Schaefer, *The Imperishable Dominion*, p. 133.
171 `Abdu'l-Bahá, *The Promulgation of Universal Peace, p. 313*.
172 Bahá'u'lláh, quoted in *The Promised Day Is Come*, p. 20.
173 Shoghi Effendi, *The Promised Day Is Come*, pp. 89-90.
174 ibid., p. 100.
175 ibid., pp. 103-4.
176 ibid., p. 108.
177 ibid., p. 110.
178 `Abdu'l-Bahá, *The Promulgation of Universal Peace, p. 445*.
179 `Abdu'l-Bahá: *Paris Talks*, p. 137.
180 `Abdu'l-Bahá, *Paris Talks*, pp. 135-37.
181 Hatcher, William S., *The Concept of Spirituality*, p. 12.
182 Bahá'u'lláh, *Gleanings from the Writings of Bahá'u'lláh*, p. 78.
183 Bahá'u'lláh, *Kitab-I-Iqan*, p. 151.

184 Bahá'u'lláh, Gleanings from the Writings of Bahá'u'lláh, p. 49
185 Compare this quotation with: I and the Father are One. (*John 10:30*)
186 Bahá'u'lláh, *Kitab-i-Iqan*, p. 143.
187 Fazel, S. & Fananapazir, K., *A Bahá'í Approach to the Claim of Exclusivity and Uniqueness in Christianity*.
188 Sours, Michael, *Understanding Christian Beliefs*, p. 114.
189 Bahá'u'lláh, *Gleanings*, p. 159.
190 Bahá'u'lláh, *Kitab-i-Aqdas*, p. 19.
191 Bahá'u'lláh, *Bahá'í Prayers*, p. 4.
192 Shoghi Effendi, *Messages to the Antipodes*, p. 256.
193 Letters from the Universal House of Justice, 1987 Sept 14, Resurrection of Christ
194 Fozdar, Shirin, *I Found God*, p. 21
195 Whitehead, Alfred North, quoted in Sabet, Huschmand, *The Heavens Are Cleft Asunder*, p. 129.
196 Zukav, Gary, *The Dancing Wu Li Masters*, quoted in Khursheed, Anjam, *Science and Religion*, p.119.
197 Because of His recent appearance, the known facts of Bahá'u'lláh's life are more easily provable and testable than that of the other Manifestations. As the Bahá'í Faith is the contemporary form of religion, it should not be surprising that it is so accessible to the scientific methods of contemporary science.
198 Wm. S. Hatcher, *The Science of Religion*, p. 11.
199 Mathews, Gary L., *The Challenge of Bahá'u'lláh*, p. 34.
200 Bahá'u'lláh, *Tablets of Bahá'u'lláh*, p. 69.
201 Blomfield, Lady, *The Chosen Highway*, p. 184.
202 `Abdu'l-Bahá, *Japan Will Turn Ablaze*, p. 38.
203 `Abdu'l-Bahá, *Paris Talks*, p. 143.
204 `Abdu'l-Bahá, *Paris Talks*, p. 146.
205 `Abdu'l-Bahá, *Some Answered Questions*, p. 123.
206 Popper, K.R., *Objective Knowledge*, quoted in A. Khursheed, *Science and Religion*, p. 68.
207 Medawar, P., *The Limits of Science*, quoted in A. Khursheed, *Science and Religion*, p. 68.
208 Anjam Khursheed, *Science and Religion*, pp. 68-9.
209 Khursheed, Anjam, *Science and Religion*, p. 73.
210 Martha L. Schweitz, *Kitab-i-Aqdas: Bahá'í Law, Legitimacy, and World Order*, article in Journal of Bahá'í Studies, Vol. 6, No. 1, p. 47.
211 Ibid., quoted from The Universal House of Justice, letter dated Oct. 1985.
212 `Abdu'l-Bahá, *Women*, p. 369.
213 Bahá'í International Community, *Turning Point for all Nations*, p. 18.
214 Loehle, Craig, *On the Shoulders of Giants*, p. 35.
215 Shoghi Effendi, *Lights of Guidance*, p. 534.
216 `Abdu'l-Bahá, *Promulgation of Universal Peace*, p. 113
217 Bahá'u'lláh, Arabic *Hidden Words*, p. 68.
218 Bahá'u'lláh, quoted in Shoghi Effendi, *The Advent of Divine Justice*, p. 37.
219 Bahá'u'lláh, *The Kitab-i-Aqdas*, p. 88.
220 `Abdu'l-Bahá, *Paris Talks*, pp. 155-156.
221 `Abdu'l-Bahá, *Paris Talks*, p. 178.
222 `Abdu'l-Bahá, *Some Answered Questions*, pp. 8-11.

[223] Esslemont, J.E., *Bahá'u'lláh and the New Era*, pp. 197-198.
[224] `Abdu'l-Bahá, *Promulgation of Universal Peace*, pp. 411-414.
[225] Tunick, Mark, *Punishment*, p. 68.
[226] Tomlinson, Gerald, comp. ed., *Treasury of Religious Quotations*, p. 300.
[227] Taherzadeh, A., *The Revelation of Bahá'u'lláh*, Vol. III, p. 295.
[228] Taherzadeh, A., *The Revelation of Bahá'u'lláh*, Vol. III, p. 295.
[229] `Abdu'l-Bahá, *Bahá'í World Faith*, pp. 412-13.
[230] Bahá'u'lláh, *Arabic Hidden Words*, p. 2.
[231] Taherzadeh, A., *The Revelation of Bahá'u'lláh*, Vol. III, p. 295.
[232] `Abdu'l-Bahá, *Some Answered Questions*, pp. 305-306.
[233] Taherzadeh, A., *The Revelation of Bahá'u'lláh*, Vol. III, pp. 296.
[234] Hatcher, John S., *The Purpose of Physical Reality*, p. 79.
[235] Hatcher, John S., *The Purpose of Physical Reality*, pp. 80-81.
[236] `Abdu'l-Bahá, *Some Answered Questions*, pp. 83-86.
[237] Sears, William, *The Wine of Astonishment*, pp. 137-38.
[238] Bahá'u'lláh, *Gleanings*, p. 295.
[239] Bahá'u'lláh, *Gleanings*, p. 278.
[240] Shoghi Effendi, *Guidelines for Teaching*, p. 314.
[241] Bahá'u'lláh, *Tablets of Bahá'u'lláh*, p. 165.
[242] Holley, Horace, *Religion for Mankind*, pp. 135-6.
[243] Bahá'u'lláh, *Tablets of Bahá'u'lláh*, p. 167.
[244] Shoghi Effendi, *World Order of Bahá'u'lláh*, p. 202.
[245] `Abdu'l-Bahá, *Paris Talks*, p. 153.
[246] Bahá'u'lláh, *Tablets of Bahá'u'lláh*, p. 26.
[247] Universal House of Justice, *The Promise of World Peace*, p. 1.
[248] Holley, Horace, *Religion for Mankind*, pp. 141-42.
[249] Shoghi Effendi, *The Promised Day is Come*, pp. 119-120.
[250] Described in Chapter Nine -- The Bahá'í Administrative Order.
[251] Shoghi Effendi, *World Order of Bahá'u'lláh*, pp. 203-204.
[252] Shoghi Effendi, *World Order of Bahá'u'lláh*, p. 204.
[253] Norman Myers, ed., *Gaia Atlas of Planet Management*, p. 244, quoted in Tyson, p. 25.
[254] Norman Myers, ed., *Gaia Atlas of Planet Management*, p. 246-47, quoted in Tyson, p. 26.
[255] Tyson, J., *World Peace and World Government*, pp. 27-28.
[256] Bahá'u'lláh, *Proclamation of Bahá'u'lláh*, p. 122.
[257] Bahá'u'lláh, *Proclamation of Bahá'u'lláh*, pp. 12-13.
[258] Bahá'í International Community, *Turning Point for all Nations*, p.7
[259] Bahá'u'lláh, *Tablets of Bahá'u'lláh*, p. 89.
[260] Lee, Kathy, *Prelude to the Lesser Peace*, p. 91.

Chapter 9
[261] Bahá'u'lláh, *Kitab-I-Aqdas*, par. 37
[262] Taherzadeh, A., *The Covenant of Bahá'u'lláh*, p. 2.
[263] Bahá'u'lláh, quoted in Shoghi Effendi, *The Promised Day is Come*, p. 20.
[264] *The Bahá'ís*, 1992, Bahá'í Publishing Trust of the United Kingdom, p. 41.
[265] Bahá'u'lláh: Tablets of Bahá'u'lláh, p. 23.
[266] Shoghi Effendi, *The Local Spiritual Assembly*, pp. 42-43.
[267] Shoghi Effendi, *Directives of the Guardian*, p. 23.
[268] Shoghi Effendi, *Bahá'í Administration*, p. 136.
[269] Bahá'u'lláh, *Kitab-i-Aqdas: Notes*, p. 245.

270 Bahá'u'lláh, *Tablets of Bahá'u'lláh*, p. 168.
271 'Abdu'l-Bahá, *Promulgation of Universal Peace*, p. 72
272 Shoghi Effendi, *Bahá'í Administration*, p. 21.
273 Shoghi Effendi, *Bahá'í Administration*, p. 22.

Chapter 10

274 Reformed in 1582 by Pope Gregory XIII to correct the miscalculations of the earlier Christian calendar, the Julian calendar, introduced by Julius Caesar in 46 BC. The Eastern Orthodox (Christian) Church still uses the Julian calendar.
275 Momen, Wendi, gen. ed., *A Basic Bahá'í Dictionary*, pp. 103-104.
276 Abdu'l-Baha, *Some Answered Questions*, p. 160.
277 Bahá'u'lláh (Glory of God) was named Baha (Glory), a spiritual attribute, by the Bab
278 Bahá'u'lláh, *Gleanings from the Writings of Bahá'u'lláh*, p. 78.
279 Shoghi Effendi, *Guidelines for Teaching*, p. 323.
280 Shoghi Effendi, *God Passes By*, p. 324.
281 Bahá'u'lláh, *Gleanings*, p. 278.
282 Shoghi Effendi, *Guidelines for Teaching*, p. 314.
283 Shoghi Effendi, *Lights of Guidance*, #185, p. 5.
284 Bahá'u'lláh, *Gleanings*, p. 330.

Chapter 11

285 Universal House of Justice, *letter to an individual believer*, May, 1971.
286 Bahá'u'lláh, *Tablets of Bahá'u'lláh*, p. 142.
287 'Abdu'l-Bahá, *Huququ'lláh*, p. 509.
288 Universal House of Justice, *letter to an individual believer*, Oct. 1981.
289 The Bab, *Selections from the Writings of the Bab*, p. 95.
290 'Abdu'l-Bahá, *239 Days in Akka*, p. 1, quoted in Zohoori, E., comp. *The Throne of the Inner Temple*, p.23.
291 Bahá'u'lláh, *Health and Healing*, p. 460.
292 Shoghi Effendi, *Directives of the Guardian*, p. 62.
293 Universal House of Justice, *National Bahá'í Review*, No. 3, Mar. 1968.
294 'Abdu'l-Bahá, quoted in Letters from the Universal House of Justice
295 'Abdu'l-Bahá, *Bahá'í World Faith*, p. 335.
296 'Abdu'l-Bahá, *Health and Healing*, p. 475.
297 'Abdu'l-Bahá, *Star of the West*, Vol. III, No. 10, p. 29.
298 Universal House of Justice, quoted in Zohoori, E., *The Throne of the Inner Temple*, p. 12.
299 Shoghi Effendi, *Lights of Guidance*, p. 522.
300 'Abdu'l-Bahá, quoted in Zohoori, E., *The Throne of the Inner Temple*, p. 14.
301 Shoghi Effendi, *Light of Divine Guidance*, Vol.1, p. 123.
302 Shoghi Effendi, *Trustworthiness*, p. 348.
303 Hatcher/Martin, *The Bahá'í Faith: The Emerging Global Religion*, p. 183.
304 Bahá'u'lláh, *Kitab-i-Aqdas*, p. 38.
305 'Abdu'l-Bahá, *Promulgation of Universal Peace*, p. 52.
306 'Abdu'l-Bahá, *Music*, pp. 76-77.
307 Shoghi Effendi, *Lights of Guidance*, p. 415.
308 'Abdu'l-Bahá, *Some Answered Questions*, p. 282-3

309 Universal House of Justice, *Homosexuality*, p. 1-2.
310 Shoghi Effendi, *Lights of Guidance*, p. 365-366.
311 Universal House of Justice, *Homosexuality*, p. 3.
312 National Spiritual Assembly, USA, *Compilations, The Bahá'í Faith and Homosexuality*.

Chapter 12

313 Laszlo, Ervin, *The Inner Limits of Mankind*, pp. 25.
314 Laszlo, Ervin, *The Inner Limits of Mankind*, pp. 26.
315 Capra, Fritjof, quoted in Danesh, H.B., *Unity: The Creative Foundation of Peace*, p. 112.
316 British term for a truck.
317 Barry, Robert, *A Theory of Almost Everything*, pp. 16-18.
318 Conow, B. Hoff, *The Bahá'í Teachings: A Resurgent Model of the Universe*, p. 146.
319 Bahá'u'lláh, *Epistle to the Son of the Wolf*, p. 55.
320 Townshend, George, *The Promise of All Ages*, p. 28.
321 Taherzadeh, Adib, *The Revelation of Bahá'u'lláh*, Vol. IV, p. 157.
322 Bahá'u'lláh, *Tablets of Bahá'u'lláh*, p. 136.
323 Taherzadeh, Adib, *The Revelation of Bahá'u'lláh*, Vol. IV, p. 155-6
324 Taherzadeh, Adib, *The Revelation of Bahá'u'lláh*, Vol. IV, p. 156.
325 Shoghi Effendi, *World Order of Bahá'u'lláh*, pp. 161-62.
326 Shoghi Effendi, *Advent of Divine Justice*, pp. 72-73.
327 Shoghi Effendi, *The Promised Day is Come*, p. 17.
328 Toffler, Alvin, quoted in Danesh, H.B., *Unity: The Creative Foundation of Peace*, p. 113.
329 Toynbee, A., quoted in Danesh, H.B., *Unity, The Creative Foundation of Peace*, p. 18.
330 Shoghi Effendi, *The World Order of Bahá'u'lláh*, p. 42.
331 Taherzadeh, Adib, *The Revelation of Bahá'u'lláh*, Vol. IV, p. 158.
332 Bahá'u'lláh, *Gleanings*, pp 326-328.
333 Bahá'u'lláh, Persian *Hidden Words*, p. 39.
334 Bahá'u'lláh, *Gleanings*, p. 321.

BIBLIOGRAPHY

'Abdu'l-Baha, 239 Days in Akka, p. 1, quotation from software, Ocean Research Library.
---- Bahá'í World Faith, quotation from Software, Ocean Research Library.
---- Foundations of World Unity, comp., Wilmette, Ill.: Bahá'í Publishing Trust, 1971.
---- Guidelines for Teaching, quotation from Software, Ocean Research Library.
---- Health and Healing , quotation from Software, Ocean Research Library.
---- Huququ'llah, quotation from Software, Ocean Research Library.
---- Japan Will Turn Ablaze, quotation from Software, Ocean Research Library.
---- Music, quotation from Software, Ocean Research Library.
---- Paris Talks: Addresses given by 'Abdu'l-Baha in Paris in 1911, London: Bahá'í Publishing Trust, 1979.
---- Proclamation of Bahá'u'lláh, quotation from Software, Ocean Research Library.
---- Promulgation of Universal Peace, quotation from software, Ocean Research Library.
---- Selections from the Writings of 'Abdu'l-Baha, quotation from software, Ocean Research Library.
---- Some Answered Questions, quotation from Software, Ocean Research Library.
---- Star of the West, Vol. III, No. 10, quotation from software, Ocean Research Library.
---- Star of the West, Vol. XIII, No. 5, quotation from software, Ocean Research Library.
---- Star of the West, Vol. XIX, quotation from Software, Ocean Research Library.
---- Women, quotation from Software, Ocean Research Library.
American Bahá'í, The, periodical publication of the National Spiritual Assembly of the Bahá'ís of the United States, Vol. 28, No. 5.
Bab, The, Selections from the Writings of the Bab, quotation from software, Ocean Research Library.
Bahá'í International Community, Turning Point for all Nations, United Nations Office, 1995.

Bahá'í World Faith—Selected Writings of Bahá'u'lláh and 'Abdu'l-Baha, Wilmette, Illinois: Bahá'í Publishing Committee, 1943.
Bahá'ís, The, A Profile of the Bahá'í Faith and its Worldwide Community, Oakham, Leicestershire: Bahá'í Publishing Trust of the United Kingdom, 1992.
Bahá'u'lláh, Bahá'í Prayers, Wilmette, Illinois: Bahá'í Publishing Trust, 1985.
---- Epistle to the Son of the Wolf, quotation from Software, Ocean Research Library.
---- Gleanings from the Writings of Bahá'u'lláh, quotation from software, Ocean Research Library.
---- Health and Healing, quotation from Software, Ocean Research Library.
---- Hidden Words, Arabic, quotation from Software, Ocean Research Library.
---- Hidden Words, Persian, quotation from Software, Ocean Research Library.
---- Kitab-i- Iqan, The Book of Certitude, quotation from software, Ocean Research Library.
---- Kitab-i-Aqdas, The Most Holy Book, quotation from software, Ocean Research Library.
---- Proclamation of Bahá'u'lláh, quotation from Software, Ocean Research Library.
---- Seven Valleys and Four Valleys, quotation from software, Ocean Research Library.
---- Tablets of Bahá'u'lláh, quotation from Software, Ocean Research Library.
Balyuzi, H.M., 'Abdu'l-Baha, the Centre of the Covenant of Bahá'u'lláh, Oxford: George Ronald, 1972.
---- The Bab, The Herald of the Day of Days, Oxford: George Ronald, 1973.
Barry, Robert, A Theory of Almost Everything, Oxford: Oneworld Publications, 1993.
Bible, The Holy, Revised Standard Version, containing the Old and New Testaments, New York: Thomas Nelson & Sons, 1953.
Bible, The Portable World, Robert O. Ballou, ed., New York: The Viking Press, 1958.
Blomfield, Lady, The Chosen Highway, London, Bahá'í Publishing Trust, undated.
Browne, Edward Granville, A Traveller's Narrative, Cambridge: Cambridge University Press, 1891.
Conow, B. Hoff, The Bahá'í Teachings: A Resurgent Model of the Universe, Oxford: George Ronald, 1990.
Danesh, H.B., Unity: The Creative Foundation of Peace, Ottawa, Canada: Bahá'í Studies Publications, 1986.

Dimont, Max, The Indestructible Jews, New York: New American Library, 1973.
Esslemont, J.E., Bahá'u'lláh and the New Era, Wilmette, Ill.: Bahá'í Publishing Trust, 1980.
Fazel, S. & Fananapazir, K., A Bahá'í Approach to the Claim of Exclusivity and Uniqueness in Christianity, article in The Journal of Bahá'í Studies, 1990, Vol. 3, No. 2, p. 15.
Fozdar, Shirin, I Found God, pamphlet, Calcutta, India: Daw Sen & Co. undated.
Hatcher, John S., The Purpose of Physical Reality, the Kingdom of Names, Wilmette, Ill: Bahá'í Publishing Trust, 1987.
Hatcher, Wm. S., The Science of Religion, Canadian Association for Studies of the Bahá'í Faith, 1980.
---- The Concept of Spirituality, Association for Bahá'í Studies, 1982.
Hatcher, Wm. S. and Martin, J. Douglas, The Bahá'í Faith: The Emerging Global Religion, San Francisco: Harper and Row, 1989.
Holley, Horace, Religion for Mankind, London: George Ronald, 1966.
Johnson, Paul, History of the Jews, Harper & Row, 1987.
Kaplan, Rabbi Aryeh, The Handbook of Jewish Thought, New York: Maznaim Publishing Co., 1979.
Khursheed, Anjam, Science and Religion, Towards the Restoration of an Ancient Harmony, London: Oneworld Publications, 1987.
Laszlo, Ervin, The Inner Limits of Mankind, London: Oneworld Publications, 1989.
Lee, Kathy, Prelude to the Lesser Peace, New Delhi: Bahá'í Publishing Trust, 1989.
Lippman, Thomas W., Understanding Islam, New York: Penguin Books, 1990.
Loehle, Craig, On the Shoulders of Giants, Oxford: George Ronald, 1994.
Martin, J. Douglas, The Bahá'í Faith in its Second Century, presentation at a symposium on The Bahá'í Faith and Islam, ed., Heshmat Moayyad, Ottawa: Bahá'í Studies Publications, 1990.
Mathews, Gary L., The Challenge of Bahá'u'lláh, Oxford: George Ronald, 1993.
Momen, Wendi, gen. ed., A Basic Bahá'í Dictionary, Oxford: George Ronald, 1989.
Motlagh, Hushidar, I Will Come Again, Mt. Pleasant, Michigan: Global Perspective, 1992.
---- Unto Him Shall We Return, Wilmette, Ill: Bahá'í Publishing Trust, 1985.

Mustafa, Muhammad, Bahá'u'lláh, the Great Announcement of the Qur'an, Dhaka, Bangladesh: Bahá'í Publishing Trust, undated.
Nabil-i-Azam, The Dawn Breakers, Nabil's Narrative, trans. by Shoghi Effendi, London: Bahá'í Publishing Trust, 1975.
National Spiritual Assembly, USA, Compilations, The Bahá'í Faith and Homosexuality.
Ocean Research Library Software Compilations, The Compilation of Compilations, Vol. I
Parrinder, Geoffrey, ed., World Religions, New York: Facts on File Publications, 1983.
Rops, Daniel, translation, by R. Millar, Jesus and His Times, New York: Dutton & Co., Inc., 1954.
Sabet, Huschmand, The Heavens are Cleft Asunder, translation from German, London: George Ronald, 1975.
Schaefer, Udo, The Imperishable Dominion, Oxford: George Ronald, 1986.
Schweitz, Martha L., Kitab-i-Aqdas: Bahá'í Law, Legitimacy, and World Order, article in Journal of Bahá'í Studies, Vol. 6, No. 1
Sears, William, Release the Sun, Wilmette: Bahá'í Publishing Trust, 1964.
---- The Wine of Astonishment, London: George Ronald, 1963.
Sheppherd, Joseph, The Elements of the Baha'i Faith, Rockport, MA: Element Books, Inc., 1992.
Shoghi Effendi, The Advent of Divine Justice, quotation from software, Ocean Research Library.
---- Bahá'í Administration, quotation from Software, Ocean Research Library.
---- A Chaste and Holy Life, quotation from Software, Ocean Research Library.
---- Directives of the Guardian, quotation from Software, Ocean Research Library.
---- Shoghi Effendi, God Passes By, quotation from MARS software program, Crimson Publications, 1995.
---- Guidelines for Teaching, quotation from Software, Ocean Research Library.
---- Light of Divine Guidance, Vol. 1, quotation from software, Ocean Research Library.
---- Lights of Guidance, quotation from Software, Ocean Research Library.
---- The Local Spiritual Assembly, quotation from software, Ocean Research Library.
---- Messages to the Bahá'í World, quotation from software, Ocean Research Library.
---- The Promised Day is Come, quotation from Software, Ocean Research Library.

---- Trustworthiness, quotation from Software, Ocean Research Library.
---- World Order of Bahá'u'lláh, quotation from Software, Ocean Research Library.
Significance of Bahá'u'lláh's Revelation, booklet, Wilmette: Bahá'í Publishing Trust, 1989.
Sours, Michael, Understanding Christian Beliefs, Vol. 2 , Oxford: Oneworld Publications, 1991.
Taherzadeh, Adib, The Covenant of Bahá'u'lláh, Oxford: George Ronald Press, 1992.
----The Revelation of Bahá'u'lláh, Vol. III, Oxford: George Ronald Press, 1983.
----The Revelation of Bahá'u'lláh, Vol. IV, Oxford: George Ronald Press, 1987.
Tanyi, Enoch N., comp., The Covenant: Daily Readings from the Bahá'í Teachings, Oxford: Geo. Ronald, 1989.
Tomlinson, Gerald, comp. ed., Treasury of Religious Quotations, Englewood Cliffs, NJ: Prentice Hall, 1991.
Townshend, George, Christ and Bahá'u'lláh, Oxford: George Ronald Press, 1985.
---- The Promise of All Ages, Oxford: George Ronald Press, 1972.
Tunick, Mark, Punishment, Berkeley: University of California Press, 1992.
Tyson, J., World Peace and World Government, from Vision to Reality, Oxford: George Ronald Press, 1986.
Universal House of Justice, Canadian Bahá'í News, Special Section, Mar. 1973.
   ---- National Bahá'í Review, No. 3, Mar. 1968.
   ---- Research Department, The Covenant, London: Bahá'í Publishing Trust, 1988.
   ---- The Promise of World Peace, London: Oneworld Publications, 1986.
   ---- Homosexuality, Letters to an individual, Jun 05 1993.
Zohoori, Elias, comp, The Throne of the Inner Temple, Kingston, Jamaica: University of the West Indies, 1985.

ISBN 142510134-8